# Different Paths, Different Summits

# Different Paths, Different Summits

## *A Model for Religious Pluralism*

Stephen Kaplan

ROWMAN & LITTLEFIELD PUBLISHERS, INC.
*Lanham • Boulder • New York • Oxford*

ROWMAN & LITTLEFIELD PUBLISHERS, INC.

Published in the United States of America
by Rowman & Littlefield Publishers, Inc.
4720 Boston Way, Lanham, Maryland 20706
www.rowmanlittlefield.com

12 Hid's Copse Road, Cumnor Hill, Oxford OX2 9JJ, England



British Library Cataloguing in Publication Information Available

**Library of Congress Cataloging-in-Publication Data**

Kaplan, Stephen.
Different paths, different summits : a model for religious pluralism
Stephen Kaplan
p. cm.
Includes bibliographical references and index.
ISBN 0-7425-1331-9 (alk. paper) — ISBN 0-7425-1332-7 (pbk. : alk. paper)
1. Religious pluralism. 2. Philosophical theology. 3. Salvation. I. Title.

BL85 .K29 2001
291.1'72—dc21 2001048268

Printed in the United States of America

™ The paper used in this publication meets the minimum requirements of American National Standard for Information Sciences—Permanence of Paper for Printed Library Materials, ANSI/NISO Z39.48-1992.

*In memory of*
*my esteemed teacher*
*and*
*dear friend*
*Dr. Bibhuti S. Yadav,*
*whose incomparable flair*
*is sorely missed*

*and*

*In gratitude to*
*my wife,*
*Suzanne,*
*and my children,*
*Seth & Hannah,*
*who teach me*
*what is important*

# Contents

# Preface

As a new millennium dawns, we find ourselves looking back on a century unrivaled for its religious hatred and persecution. From Nazi Germany to South Asia, from Bosnia to the Middle East, religious beliefs have been invoked to justify slaughter. The seeds for this hatred among religious groups are terribly complex and cannot be explained by one theological factor any more than they can be explained by one economic or social factor. While it is not within my purview to discuss the multitude of issues that have led to religious hatred and wars, I will look at one of the theological and philosophical issues that divide religions and peoples—namely, the question of truth: Who has it and who does not have it?

Throughout history, different religious traditions have claimed that they have the truth. Each of these traditions has contended that it alone knows the way to salvation or liberation. In its eyes, other traditions are, at best, lesser vehicles. At worst, the other traditions are nothing but misguided efforts leading one astray. Essentially, both of these attitudes tell us that the vast majority of the religious people in the world are wrong; they do not know the truth because the truth is contained in one religious tradition. Since there is no one religious tradition that has contained a majority of the world's population, the majority of people must be wrong.

Such is the harsh assessment of religious truth by the traditional religions of the world. As we will see, the modern attempt to develop a system in which all (or some) religious traditions are heading up different paths to a single summit does not change this blunt assessment. The one summit tends to look like only one of the religious traditions; and thus, we are again faced with the notion that the rest are wrong.

This book is an attempt to envision how more than one religious tradition can be ultimately true, not penultimately true. It is an attempt to conceptualize the logical framework in which ultimate reality, in an ontological sense not an epistemological sense, may be conceived of as plural, not singular. It is an attempt to imagine different paths to different summits.

Some may find any such attempt arrogant and bordering on the absurd. Others may presume any such attempt will be stuck in a logical quagmire and therefore futile. On the other hand, my hope is that this presentation coherently illuminates a distinctive form of religious pluralism, specifically one that does not demand that so many are wrong and so few are right. I began contemplating this idea almost two decades ago when thinking about the unsuccessfulness of so many religious traditions according to the judgment of each of the other traditions. Maybe all religious truths are wrong; maybe only one religious truth is right; or maybe several religious truths are simultaneously and equally right? As academicians, all options should be considered and the implications of each position should be brought to light. It is from this perspective that I offer the following proposal.

I wish to acknowledge those whose assistance has been invaluable to me, but who certainly cannot be held responsible for any of my mistakes or mistaken ideas. First, I would like to thank Manhattan College for its continued support over the years, specifically for my sabbatical leave (1997–1998) when I finally began to write this book. I also owe a good deal of gratitude to a number of colleagues at Manhattan College who have read and commented upon various parts of this work. In this regard, I would like to thank Judith Plaskow, Claudia Setzer, Lois Harr and John Keber. A very special note of appreciation must be offered to my friend, John Keber, who has unselfishly listened to me moan about this project for years, but who has never failed to help me with particular problems. There should be a blessing for academics that reads "may you be so lucky as to have a John Keber for a colleague."

I would also like to thank David Ray Griffin who reviewed and offered extensive editorial comments on an earlier draft of this manuscript. Peter Cooper, formerly of Rowman & Littlefield, whose editorial comments helped me reshape the introduction to this book is likewise owed a note of thanks. In this book, there are four individuals whose work is extensively reviewed—namely, Professors David Bohm, John Hick, Steven Katz and Raimundo Panikkar. My analysis of their work may appear critical insofar as my proposal is different from each of theirs. However, I must say that all such comments are said with great respect for their work and with the recognition that without their thoughts, this project would have been impossible. An additional note of thanks needs to be offered to Professor Panikkar, whose personal correspondence on a draft of this manuscript has led me to reshape some of my earlier comments about Reality.

Two final acknowledgments reveal how fortunate I have been. I am truly fortunate to have been a student and friend of Professor Bibhuti S. Yadav. No one could challenge students like him. His relentless critiques and his outbursts of commentary transformed a great deal of my thoughts and writings. His review of this manuscript was our last serious conversation and it will not be forgotten. His untimely passing will leave him greatly missed by so many friends, students and colleagues.

Finally, I would be completely remiss if I did not acknowledge the significance of my wife, Suzanne Doran, and my children, Seth and Hannah, without whom I would be even more prone to overestimate the importance of my work and fail to see what is truly important.

## *Chapter One*

# An Overview of the Problem and the Proposal

### REFLECTING UPON THE TITLE

The title of this book, *Different Paths, Different Summits,* is an obvious twist on the often invoked metaphor "different paths up the one mountain." The image of a single mountain with different paths is used to explain the relationship between the religions of the world. It expresses a form of religious pluralism.[1] As the image implies, at least some of the world's religious traditions lead to the same place—to the same summit, to the same ultimate goal. This image tells us that we no longer need to envision that there is only one way to salvation, only one religious tradition capable of leading its followers, and possibly others, to the mountaintop. This metaphor also tells us there is only one summit. From this perspective, the goal or ultimate reality to which these diverse religions are leading their followers is the same, whether they know it or not, whether they like it or not. Diversity is ultimately transcended when one reaches the one summit.[2]

Religious pluralism is a modern position born not out of an openness of one religious tradition to another; but rather, out of a philosophical attempt to confront the confluence of cultural boundaries and the growth of relativism.[3] The major world religions were not traditionally pluralistic; they were either exclusivistic or inclusivistic. Exclusivism tells us that there is no salvation outside of one particular religious tradition. Inclusivism extends the possibility of salvation to those outside its fold, but the means of salvation and the form of salvation are restricted to that which is found within the inclusivist's tradition.

Critics of pluralism find the metaphor "different paths, one summit" deceptive. They see it as expressive of either crypto-exclusivism or crypto-inclusivism since both exclusivism and inclusivism envision a single and universal final end, like the one mountaintop of the pluralist's metaphor.[4]

But what, one may ask, is the alternative? Should religious pluralism be abandoned? Should exclusivism or inclusivism be touted? Should exclusivism and inclusivism be rejected because asserting such religious-truth claims seems so politically incorrect in a pluralistic world? Should all religious truths be declared relative and without any universal value? Should religion itself be rejected if its truth claims are all relative? While each of these questions yields different options and each of these options is the choice of many, there is at least one more possibility.

In this book, I propose a different form of religious pluralism—namely, an ontological and soteriological pluralism. In this form of religious pluralism different individuals with different beliefs and with different religious practices reach different ultimate conclusions to human existence—different soteriological conclusions.[5] This model proposes that within one, and only one, metaphysical universe there can be different ontological natures. In this model, each of these equal and simultaneous ontological natures provide different individuals with the opportunity to achieve different soteriological ends—different forms of liberation or salvation.[6] In this form of religious pluralism there are different paths and different summits.

Specifically, this model for religious pluralism allows us to envision, as simultaneously existing, three distinct soteriological conclusions to human existence—a theistic salvation, a monistic nondualistic liberation and a process nondualistic liberation. We will see how it is possible to imagine that salvation for some people can be discovered in an I–Thou relationship with the Divine Other, while others achieve liberation when they realize that there is no other and no Other, just the one Self. In addition, we will see how it is possible to imagine not only those two forms of ultimate truth, but also to imagine that still others realize ultimate truth by realizing that there is no self, nor Self, only no-self.

In this proposal for religious pluralism, the truth of a religion is distinctly defined in terms of its soteriological effectiveness.[7] Can the religious tradition deliver salvation? More specifically, can it deliver the form of salvation that it promises and in which its adherents have put their faith?[8] While religious traditions make lots of proclamations on a variety of subjects from ethics to social structure, from hagiographies to history, I am confining this discussion of the truth of a religion to this one topic—namely, to soteriology and the concomitant ontological structure or ultimate reality that supports such a soteriological possibility. This focus may not be acceptable to all, but we will see that its significance within the history of the different religious traditions cannot be underestimated.

This form of religious pluralism does not demand that one religious tradition tell another tradition that it is wrong with regard to its particular view of ultimate truth. It simply refuses to tell a specific religious tradition that it is the only one that is right. In this model, with regard to the issue of ultimate truth, being right does not necessitate that someone else is wrong. One need not demand that the other abandon or denigrate her claim to truth in order to ensure one's own claim to truth. This form of religious pluralism does not require that individuals relinquish their claim to truth in the hope of better relations with others in different religious traditions. Such demands are not only counterproductive; they are, I believe, also antithetical to the vast majority of the religious individuals outside the academy for whom these truth claims are an essential component of their faith.

Immediately, a series of questions and problems comes to mind. How can the ultimate truth that is realized by the theist, the monistic nondualist and the process nondualist be different and yet still be ultimate? Are not each of these positions, as ultimate, contradictory and mutually exclusive?[9] This is certainly the claim of many. Others declare that the notion of more than one ultimate reality is nonsensical.[10] And still others ask, how can one develop a model for religious pluralism when the model would itself become more ultimate than the ultimate realities it presents? Needless to say, these questions and declarations, as well as others, must be answered. I am raising them here to indicate to the reader that I am aware of these issues and to indicate that I will answer each of these questions in the course of this work. Before addressing these issues, I offer the following vignettes in an attempt to highlight the difference between this proposal for religious pluralism and the other form of religious pluralism in which there is only one summit. I begin with an exclusivist position in order to set the stage for the two pluralist positions.

## THREE VIGNETTES: EXCLUSIVISM AND TWO FORMS OF PLURALISM

### Vignette 1: "One Path, One Summit"

*The Scene:* On a dusty road, somewhere along the famed Silk Road, three elderly men meet. Each is on the way home, hoping to get there before he dies. Each knows within his heart that his time is short. Sharing a meal, they begin to converse, telling their individual stories about travel, adventure and their religious longing. More than anything, each has committed himself to a religious path. One is a Christian mystic seeking communion in the afterlife with the Holy Trinity. The second is a member of an Advaita Vedānta (Hindu) *āśrama*. He believes that he is on the brink of liberation about to realize that the one and only True Self (*ātman*) is the universal Being of all (Brahman). The third person is a Buddhist monk—a Yogācārin adept. He is looking to realize the enlightenment of the renown Śākyamuni Buddha—an enlightenment revealing the emptiness of the Self and the emptiness of all else.

*The Encounter:* Dinner conversation was intense. Each recognized within the others a bond of purpose—the search for spiritual perfection. But their knowledge and experience, arising out of their specific religious traditions, made each one certain that his two fellow travelers were barking up the wrong trees. "Nice fellows," each thought, but each intimated that the others were spiritually naive. Each one implored his two new friends to follow the one and only true path—his path—before it was too late. Anything less would certainly not only fail to lead the others to ultimate reality, but would be unfortunately detrimental. And thus, they parted, wishing that the others would find it within their hearts to convert, but saddened by the improbability.

**Vignette 2: "Different Paths, One Summit"**

*The Scene:* Same as above.
*The Encounter:* Dinner conversation was intense. Each recognized within the others a bond of purpose—the search for spiritual perfection. Each had heard less-than-flattering things about the other two traditions. However, their conversations were not only slowly eroding this negativity, but were producing a genuine respect for the other individuals and the insights that each had to offer. Each became convinced that they were all heading to the same state of spiritual perfection. What exactly that state would be, they agreed, was beyond their present wisdom. And so they parted. The Christian theist, acknowledging to himself the uncertainty about the nature of spiritual salvation, was nonetheless confident that he would "someday" stand in a spiritual relation with his two new friends. His two nondualist companions smiled, assured that no matter what liberation is, all three would overcome the bondage of particularity and relationship. [Note: this vignette could be told in such a way that each not only acknowledges that ultimate reality is beyond his comprehension, but also does

not try to infuse his alleged agnosticism with the categories of his own position. As we will see, the former attitude seems to be more prevalent in this position.]

**Vignette 3: "Different Paths, Different Summits"**

*The Scene:* Same as above.
*The Encounter:* Dinner conversation was intense. Each recognized within the others a bond of purpose—the search for spiritual perfection. Each had heard less-than-flattering things about the other two traditions. However, their conversation was not only eroding this negativity, but producing a genuine respect for the other individuals. Each became convinced that the "spiritual" experiences that his fellow companions described were genuine. The Advaitin's description of *saccidānanda* (Being, Consciousness and Bliss) struck his two companions as overwhelming yet different from the fantastic realization of emptiness that their Yogācārin companion elucidated. Their theistic friend astonished them with his personal encounters with the Holy Thou. Listening to each other, looking into the eyes of the others, each became convinced that his own experience was no better, nor worse than his companions'. But they were different experiences. Each was also convinced that his own experience was ultimate. Each felt assured that his own salvation or liberation was at the door. Each became equally convinced that his new friends were also at the verge of their ultimate goal and that these ultimate goals were not the same as his own. All of a sudden, each man scratched his head, developed a thoughtful twinkle in his eyes and momentarily pondered how all three experiences could be simultaneously ultimate, not penultimate, liberating and yet radically different. Recognizing the twinkle in each other's eyes, they began to laugh, knowing that such pondering could be left to the philosophers. And so they parted; each confident that his two new friends would realize the ultimate solution that each was seeking, but also knowing that their solutions would lead them to different ultimate realities.

***Vignette 3—Absurd or Intriguing?***

How can that be? How can some individuals achieve salvation in an I–Thou relation while others overcome all such relations—all such duality? How can there be two different ways of overcoming duality—a nonduality of Being and a nonduality of becoming? How can ultimate reality be both Being—undivided and unchanging—and becoming—constantly changing—at the "same time" and in the "same place"? And furthermore, how can ultimate reality be both nondualistic (nonrelational) and dualistic (relational) at the "same time" and in the "same place"? How can there be three different ultimate realities supporting or underlying three different soteriological possibilities? How can three different visions of salvation/liberation with their three concomitant and allegedly mutually exclusive views of ultimate reality be simultaneously possible and equally ultimate?

This book explains how all this is conceivable. I offer a model based upon holography, the process by which three-dimensional optical artifacts are produced from a film that has no images. In this form of religious pluralism there can be different paths and different summits. However, I must note that the metaphor of "different paths, different summits" is inadequate. *Different summits* gives us the image of separate spatial domains distant from each other and unrelated to each other.[11] The holographic model that is offered in this book overcomes this very serious limitation.

Before proceeding any further, I must make the following declarations. First, it must be clear that the different ultimate realities that are discussed in this book arise from the religious traditions of the world. Nowhere in this book do I invent a single ultimate reality. Second, I cannot verify nor do I pretend to know that any of the following is true. I do not know whether any particular form of salvation discussed in this book is true and I certainly do not know if more than one form of salvation is true. I do not know whether any of this actually happens. However, different religious traditions have made different truth claims with regard to the issues of soteriology and ultimate reality. Therefore, this book presents a model by which we can conceptualize how more than one of these truth claims can be simultaneously possible and equal, but yet not the same. This model is offered in spite of all the exhortations, made by both pluralists and their critics, that pluralists cannot have models. Since many have asserted that such a project is conceptually impossible and since no one, to the best of my knowledge, has offered a concrete model, I believe that this proposal is worthy of review. I leave the truth of these positions to others—to the mystics, prophets and others who claim to have the revelations.

## AN OVERVIEW OF HOLOGRAPHY AND THIS HOLOGRAPHIC MODEL

Before navigating through the next three chapters that deal with the quandaries that this form of religious pluralism encounters, a brief introduction to holography and this holographic model for religious pluralism will provide a useful overview of my thesis and an indication of the direction of this work. (The details of holography and the holographic model are presented in chapters 4 and 5.)

## Holography

As indicated, holography is the technique by which one can reproduce three-dimensional optical images from an imageless film. Holography is very different from other forms of optical-imaging reproductions. Photography, for example, uses lenses to capture an image on a piece of film. In photography, a point-by-point correspondence exists between the object and the image captured. The lens focuses the light onto the film in a manner that corresponds to the object being photographed. The patterns produced on the film resemble the object. As we all know, one can look at the photographic negative to see what object was photographed. The photographic image can be printed on paper, flashed on a wall, or called up on a computer screen. In each of these cases, the photographic image is flat—it has only two dimensions. We have only one perspective from which to view the recorded object. One does not have the ability to change one's angle of viewing and see a different side or face of the recorded object.

Holograms are different. They record information about the whole object—the object as three-dimensional. Holography means to write the whole. Holography is a lensless process of optical recording and reproduction. The hologram refers to the medium on which the information necessary to reproduce a three-dimensional image is recorded. Generally speaking, holograms are made with silver halide film similar to regular black-and-white photographic film, except with a much higher resolution.[12] This higher-resolution film is used to record the interference patterns that form the basis of the hologram. The interference patterns do not resemble in any way, shape or form the object that is being filmed.

The holographic interference patterns are produced with a laser. A laser is a single-frequency light source that is in phase—in other words, the light waves are in step with each other. (Light from an ordinary lightbulb is neither in phase nor single frequency.) The hologram records not only the varying intensities of the light as it reflects off the object, as does a photograph, but it also records the phase relations of the light reflecting off the object.[13]

In order to produce a hologram, the laser is aimed at a device that splits the beam into two separate light waves. One of the waves is directed toward the film; the other is directed toward the object and then, reflecting off the object, toward the film. The former is called the reference beam and the latter is the scene or object beam. At the film, the two beams of light converge. Their convergence creates the interference patterns, which spread across the film. These interference patterns are like waves created in a pool of water into which two stones are thrown. No image of the object is recorded on the film, just the confluence of the waves from the reference beam and the scene beam are recorded on the film.

In order to reconstruct an image of the original object, a laser beam of the same frequency as that which was used to construct the hologram is directed at the holographic film.[14] This procedure of passing a reference beam back through the film causes that which was originally coded onto the hologram in the form of interference patterns to be decoded from the hologram. This decoding process presents us with the optical conditions that allow us to perceive the image as a three-dimensional object. As a three-dimensional image, a holographic image cannot be displayed on a wall, on a piece of paper or on a computer screen. Any such attempt would yield only a two-dimensional reproduction. The holographic image appears suspended in space. You can look at this three-dimensional image from different perspectives. Holograms have the visual characteristics of our everyday visual world. These images have height, width and depth.

A description of my favorite hologram may help illuminate a bit of the distinctiveness of holography. Consider a holographic image of a computer panel replete with silicon chips.[15] Six inches in front of the middle of the computer panel is a holographic image of a magnifying glass. Thus, there are two images—one anterior and one posterior. Look horizontally through the holographic image of the magnifying glass and the corresponding section of the holographic image of the computer panel is magnified. Shift the perspective from which you look through the holographic image of the magnifying glass and you magnify a different section of the holographic image of the computer panel. Look around the holographic image of the magnifying glass, rather than through it, and nothing appears magnified. If this all seems natural, try to touch the holographic image of the magnifying glass. There is no object there; only an image appears. Step to the side of the holographic images so that you are now parallel to the images, and all the images disappear. Move farther back and you will see the holographic film which contains no images of the computer panel or the magnifying glass; it has only interference patterns. Step back again to look at the holographic image of the computer panel and the magnifying glass and you realize that you have looked through one holographic image that definitely seems to be there but is not there at another image that definitely seems to be there but is not there, and the first image can magnify the second image. All this is produced from a film with no images. Maybe within all this lies a model by which we can envision a plurality of ultimate realities and soteriological possibilities.

In order to begin utilizing holography as a model for religious pluralism, three highly unusual characteristics of the film must be noted. First, since the film is without any images, it does not exhibit the subject–object dichotomies found in our spatial-temporal world. For example, a photographic negative of my two children would exhibit two discreet individuals that stand in subject–object relationship to each other. On the negative, one can also observe these individuals and the various parts that constitute them—legs, arms, heads. However, the holographic film does not exhibit any such subject–object relations corresponding to the object filmed—no son, no daughter, no arms, no legs. Here, the information about the individuals is enfolded throughout the interference patterns that are spread over the film. When the holographic images are projected from the film, the subject–object dichotomies are represented.

Second, the film exhibits redundancy whereby each piece of the hologram can reproduce the entire holographic image, yet the whole film only produces one holographic image. Concretely illustrated, one can tear a hologram into four parts, for example, and each part will reproduce the entire holographic image. Recall, the film has no images; rather, only interference patterns are recorded on the film and they are spread throughout the film. As we see in chapter 4, the spreading of the interference patterns across the film allows any part of the film to produce a complete holographic image of the original object. Thus, while the sum of the parts of a hologram equal the whole of the hologram, each part also equals the whole.

Finally, one holographic film is able to record multiple scenes. In distinction to photography, in which double exposure of the negative blurs both images, one may record on one holographic film different scenes by changing either the angle at which the laser hits the film or the frequency of the laser used to create the hologram. In fact, color holograms are produced by recording the same scene on the same holographic film with lasers of different frequencies.

This holographic situation presents us with two domains called the explicate domain and the implicate domain.[16] The *explicate domain* refers to the object or objects filmed and to the holographic images that are reproduced. The *implicate domain* refers to the film with its unusual characteristics.

The explicate domain is that order with which we are most familiar. It is our normal spatial-temporal world in which objects are made up of parts and in which objects and parts of objects stand in relation to other objects and parts. Distinctness, difference, duality and relationship are the chief characteristics of the explicate domain.

The second domain—the implicate domain—refers to the film with its unusual characteristics. In this domain in which each part is enfolded into all other parts, one does not talk about subjects or objects, discreet parts, or the relations between parts. The nonduality of subject and object, and of part and whole, is the appropriate language for the implicate domain.

## Three Presuppositions of This Holographic Model

In order to utilize holography as a model for religious pluralism three presuppositions concerning the relationship between the implicate and explicate domains must be proposed. These presuppositions structure my use of holography as a model for metaphysics. In chapter 4, the multivalent nature of an artifact, such as holography, to develop a variety of models is discussed. At that time, I show that other models can be developed from holography and those models operate with different presuppositions. For example, David Bohm, the renowned physicist, developed a different holographic model. His model is a scientific model and it is also a model for the ultimacy of undivided wholeness. In spite of the significant debt that this project owes to Professor Bohm, my project aims at resolving problems in religious thought, not physics, and my project imagines a plurality of ultimate answers, not just one.

Insofar as there is no assumption on my part that this model proves the truth of religious pluralism, but rather only provides us with a way to envision religious pluralism, I do not need to prove the truth of these presuppositions. It must also be clear that since I am not trying to offer a scientific model for the structure of the cosmos, this model and these presuppositions in no way need to correspond to the current state of physics. (This point is discussed further in the following chapters.)

The first presupposition in the development of this model is that the implicate and explicate domains logically demand each other. In this model, there would be no implicate domain without something explicate to implicate, and there would be no explicate domain without the implicate domain from which it unfolded. Therefore, this model presupposes that neither domain is ontologically prior or more important, in any way, than the other. Second, this model assumes that the implicate and the explicate domains are simultaneously existing. Consistent with the first presupposition, neither domain temporally precedes the other, nor exists independently from the other. As indicated, the film represents the implicate domain; the objects that the film records as well as the holographic images it produces comprise the explicate domain. Both sets exist simultaneously. Just as in holography, an explicate holographic image is simultaneously enfolded in the implicate domain of the film as interference patterns, so also this model presupposes that all objects in our spatial-temporal world are somehow simultaneously enfolded in the implicate domain of this metaphysical model. In other words, in this model what manifests as explicate entities in our spatial-temporal world is simultaneously enfolded in the implicate world.

Finally, these two domains are mutually interpenetrating.[17] In this model, there is no spatial separation between the implicate and explicate domains. The assumption here is that the implicate domain is coextensive with the totality of existence—whether that be Being, Emptiness or both Being and Emptiness. Therefore, the explicate domains could not be unfolded someplace separate from the implicate domain since there is no place separate from the implicate domain.

In presenting this model with three distinct ultimate realities, the implicate domain is utilized as the focus for understanding the two nondualistic positions. The nature of the explicate domains and their relationship to the implicate domain allows us to envision the theistic position described in the following sections.

## The Monistic Nondualistic Position

A monistic nondualist, such as an Advaita Vedāntin, maintains that all is one—one Being which is universal, without beginning or end, without measure or end to measure. It is everywhere and everything—all that has been, is and will be. This one Being (Brahman) is the true nature of each individual—the true self, *ātman*. There is only one *ātman* and it is Brahman—thou art that (*tat tvam asi*).

For the Advaitin, the distinctions between self and other—subject and object—that normally bind our attention are only an illusion (*māyā*). These distinctions conceal the reality of Brahman. Until one realizes that reality is one, undivided and unborn, one is trapped by the demands of individuality; one is deluded by the appearance of difference, multiplicity and relationship. However, when one realizes that the one true self is Brahman, then one realizes that one's being is the one Being. This is liberation from all duality; it is freedom (*mokṣa*).

The implicate domain of holography can help us imagine such a state of existence—a oneness of Being in which there is no self that stands in opposition to an other, to a world of other beings and things. In the explicate world there is an "I," the typist, and an it, the keyboard; however, in the implicate domain the duality of "I" and the "keyboard" do not exist. In this domain, both are folded into a oneness of being—into an implicate domain that lacks such distinctions. In this proposal for religious pluralism, the implicate domain is a model for that which is coextensive with all that exists and it is without subject and object—without duality. In this model, as in the Advaita view of ultimate reality, the implicate domain is everywhere and everywhere equal—where each part can reproduce the whole.

This model can also help us picture the Advaita claim that knowledge of the true self is knowledge of Brahman. By analogy, the knowledge of any part of the implicate domain would be the knowledge of all since each part can reproduce the whole and since the implicate domain is coextensive with the being of all. Furthermore, a realization of the implicate domain of this metaphysical model could not entail a subject knowing an object since the implicate domain does not contain these characteristics. Such a realization would be different from viewing a piece of holographic film and noting its lack of subject–object dichotomies. As a model for metaphysics, we are not talking about one object, the viewer, looking at a second object, the film. In the metaphysical situation, the implicate domain like Brahman is everywhere—it is coextensive with all that exists. Therefore, if a realization of the implicate domain of this model were to occur, the alleged realizer would not be separate from the "object" of this realization, namely, the being of this domain. There are no subjects and objects in this domain.

With this in mind, we can also see why the Advaitins tell us that *cit* (consciousness) is *sat* (being). For the Advaitins, consciousness and being cannot be dual, nor could they be dual in this model. The consciousness that knows the nonduality of the implicate domain cannot be other than the implicate domain since the subject–object dichotomies have been eliminated. Therefore, the consciousness that knows the nonduality of the implicate domain cannot be other than the Being of the implicate domain (Brahman). (The epistemological problems of achieving such a state of consciousness are discussed extensively in chapter 3.) As the Advaitins tell us, in this realization there is no knower apart from the known. For the Advaitin, this knowledge, coextensive with the Being of all, would be liberation—it would allow one to overcome the confines of the duality of subject and object. Freedom from duality—from individuality—would be achieved in the realization of the implicate domain understood as coextensive with all that exists.

## The Process Nondualistic Position

On another hand, in this model, the implicate domain can be viewed as a dynamic web of interrelationships that exhibit neither subject nor object. The emphasis, from this perspective, is on the dynamic nature of the implicate domain because it is nothing but a series of interference patterns—a convergence of patterns of energy. Rather than reifying the interference patterns into a static filmlike nature, as the monistic nondualist does, this second perspective perceives the convergence of energy patterns as a dynamic process.[18] It is an ongoing process in which explicate entities are unfolding and enfolding. David Bohm states this as follows:

> The implicate order is particularly suitable for the understanding of such unbroken wholeness in flowing movement, for in the implicate order the totality of existence is enfolded within each region of space (and time). So, whatever part, element, or aspect we may abstract in thought, this still enfolds the whole and is therefore intrinsically related to the totality from which it has been abstracted.[19]

In this model, this dynamic process would be pervasive—coextensive with all; and therefore, if experienced, it would be experienced as ultimate.

From this second perspective, the implicate domain, as pervasive, is viewed as the conditions from which and in which all particulars arise, yet itself is without particularity. Although it is the conditions from which the explicate entities appear, the implicate domain is itself not how things appear. They manifest as subjects and objects. In addition, one can say that the implicate domain is neither nothing nor some thing. In spite of the fact that the implicate domain lacks explicit things, we cannot call it nothing. It is the dynamic flow of interference patterns. However, since it lacks the nature of discreet objects, we cannot call it "some thing." We can say that the implicate domain is empty of things. It is without particularity, without subject and object. It is empty of anything that looks like a self nature. (In this sense, we can say it is emptiness.)

This second perspective on the implicate domain corresponds to the view of a process nondualist such as the Yogācāra Buddhist. Like other Buddhists, they believe that reality is dynamic; it is constantly changing. As such, each thing is without a fixed nature—without a self (*anātma*). All things are likewise without a fixed nature—without unchanging Being (Brahman). Reality is best described according to the Yogācārin as a dynamic web of interrelationships that lack the duality of subject and object—that lack particularity. Reality is empty of such duality—empty of particulars that stand in opposition to other particulars. Emptiness—*śūnyatā*—is the term used by Yogācārins to describe ultimate reality.

*Śūnyatā* does not mean nothingness any more than the implicate domain is a nothingness. Rather, it is the dynamic conditions from which and in which the duality of subjects and objects appear to arise. As we will see, *śūnyatā* is the relative nature of all things (*paratantra*). Yogācāra tells us that this *paratantra* nature is the causes and conditions of all things, but it is itself without duality, like the implicate domain of this model. *Paratantra* is what appears, but it is not how things appear. They appear as subjects and objects; they appear with the characteristics of the explicate world.[20] The similarities between the Yogācāra view of *śūnyatā* and the preceding understanding of the implicate domain seem so obvious as to not need further elucidation at this point. One need only say that if *śūnyatā* is understood in terms of the implicate domain as dynamic, then the realization of the implicate domain at any point and time would allow one to see the emptiness of all (implicate) reality and to realize the emptiness of the self. Such a realization is, for the Yogācārin, liberation—nirvana.

## The Theistic Positions

While the first two views focus on the implicate domain, the third view of ultimate reality—the theistic view—focuses on incorporating the relationship between the implicate domain and the explicate domains.[21] It must be recalled that in this model just as the implicate domain is ultimate, so also is, at least, one explicate domain. Remember also, that there may be more than one explicate scene recorded on a single holographic film and these different explicate scenes can each be unfolded. Likewise, in this model it may be assumed that there can be more than one explicate domain enfolded into the implicate domain. The simultaneous existence of the implicate and explicate domains as well as the ability of the implicate domain to enfold multiple explicate domains is crucial in the understanding of theism.

Theists find no solace in the transcendence of the subject–object dichotomy that so intrigues the nondualists; rather they maintain that one's identity is defined in relationship to that which is other. Human identity is defined and fulfilled in relationship to the Other, to the Numinous, to God. For the theist, individual selves are real, not *māyā*. However, for the theist, the reality of the individual cannot be understood apart from God. God may be understood as that particular power, that ultimate power, that calls forth individuality. In this sense, God is that power that can guarantee individuality and that can ensure that individuality is not limited to the ephemerality of the passing moment. God as that power that calls forth individuality and that ensures that individuality is not a passing fancy can be understood as both creator and sustainer of existence.

This God who guarantees the individual's existence and with whom one's relation is a defining mark of one's existence would be worthy of adoration and devotion. This God, the guarantor of individuality, would also be individual. As individual, this God must be explicate and as such can stand in relation to the individual. Particularity, individuality and relationship are the essential characteristics of the theistic view. They are also essential characteristics of the explicate domain.

Returning to the holographic model, we can reflect upon one of the great puzzles of the theistic worldview—namely, what is the relationship between God and the world and how is this relationship actualized? For purposes of this discussion, two views of God's relation to the world can be highlighted. The first view can be associated with the classical Western theistic view that stresses God's transcendence from the world. In this view, God is understood to dwell elsewhere, not in the world, nor the world in God. These statements are made in spite of the fact that God is said to be everywhere. God is seen as separate from the world, yet able to interact with the world. Where this separate domain would be—how far beyond the farthest galaxy—and how this interaction would take place has certainly been a puzzle for contemporary theologians.[22]

Panentheism is the second theistic view. This view stresses both the transcendence and the immanence of God. From this perspective, all things are part of God, but God transcends all things as well. Here, one must ponder in what sense God is all things, yet itself not limited to the sum total of those things? Again, it can be asked, how and where is God transcendent to the world?

This holographic model can shed some light on these quandaries. Insofar as this holographic model has assumed that there can be more than one explicate domain enfolded within the implicate domain, the locus of God's explicateness—God's individualness—need not be the locus of our spatial temporal, explicate domain. Like different holographic images produced from the same film by different lasers or by tilting the hologram at different angles, so also can we envision that God and the world unfold in different ways. God as particular and this world as particular may be presumed to be the presentation of different explicate domains. The locus of God's explicateness would not be situated within this spatial-temporal explicate domain, but in a different explicate domain; nonetheless both would be enfolded in the same implicate domain.

In this model, the relationship between our world as explicate and the world of God as explicate would be secured by the fact that both are enfolded within the same implicate order. The image of a common implicate domain shared by God and this world allows us to envision how there can be interaction between these two worlds. These explicate domains would be completely distinct, just as two completely separate images recorded on one hologram are completely distinct. However, these explicate domains would not be separate since both are enfolded into one implicate order. In this model, God as explicate would be very different than the world as explicate, but they would not be separate. Thus, God's explicate nature would not be beyond the farthest reaches of the galaxy. It would only be a different explicate order not readily accessible (perceivable) to us who perceive from a "particular angle" or with a "particular frequency," which is different from the "angle" or "frequency" from which God's explicateness is perceived. (I must reiterate that I am not offering a scientific model for an understanding of the universe. Rather, I am offering a model within the field of comparative religion for overcoming the apparent contradictoriness of different views of ultimate reality.)

This notion of an implicate domain containing and manifesting different explicate domains allows us to envision both the position of the classical theist and the panentheist. The former focuses more strongly upon the explicateness of the God and the world. It is through their explicate natures that individuals and God have a relationship. This relationship is key to the classical theist's soteriological hope; and therefore, the distinctness of their explicate natures is paramount. Thus, this type of theist is only minimally concerned with the fact that God is everywhere; or by analogy, is only minimally concerned with the all pervading implicate domain. On the other hand, the panentheist believes that the world is part of the being or body of God, but God transcends the world. Here, one can imagine that the panentheist sees the implicate domain as the body of God that is everywhere yet also understands that the explicate domain of God is different from the explicate domain of the world.

It must be noted that neither the classical theist nor the panentheist would find soteriological comfort in the nonduality of the implicate domain. They find salvation in a personal relation with God—in an I–Thou relation in which all parties are explicate. In light of this and for simplicity's sake, I will treat these two views of theism as offering one soteriological position. I am certainly not wedded to that notion.

## The Epistemological Foundation of Religious Pluralism

While this model presents three views of ultimate reality as true, it must be acknowledged that I cannot accept as true that which each of these religious traditions declares to be soteriologically ineffective, inadequate or essentially false. One religious tradition might declare that A is true but that B and C are false. A second tradition may declare that B is true and that A and C are false. Accepting what each tradition says is true will provide the material from which one can develop a model for religious pluralism. However, accepting the falsity of that which each tradition says is false would eliminate the material that can be used to develop a model for religious pluralism. Since individual religious traditions have not historically been pluralistic, accepting that which one tradition says is true as well as accepting the falsity of that which that tradition says is false leads us to eliminate all the religious views that that tradition rejects. Thus, in order to carry forth this type of pluralistic project, one must proceed by accepting that which at least some religious traditions declare to be true; but one cannot accept that which those same traditions declare to be false.

This procedure may appear completely arbitrary and seem to be merely a ruse through which to carry this project forward. It is not. This procedure is based upon my epistemological analysis of mysticism (chapter 3). The constructivist approach that I take illuminates the fact that mystics who claim to have experienced ultimate reality are each rooted in their particular religious tradition. As such, they engage in particular religious practices, have particular religious beliefs, expect to have particular experiences and employ particular theological concepts to convey these experiences to other individuals. They are not trained to have other kinds of ultimate experiences, even though they may be trained to have other kinds of nonultimate religious experiences.[23] Their religious experiences are interpreted in light of the theological and philosophical concepts of their own tradition. Therefore, if we take epistemological constructivism seriously and recognize that religious traditions have traditionally not been pluralistic, we must expect that experiences other than those sanctified by one's own tradition as ultimate will be understood as not ultimate. While one tradition might reject an experience because it does not fit its mould, we see that another tradition may declare this experience to be ultimate because it seems to be soteriologically effective for its adherents. Given this, I accept as a possible form of salvation that which a religious tradition declares to be true, but I do not accept as false that which a religious tradition did not find soteriologically effective for its members. (Needless to say, those who break out of their own tradition break out of their old epistemological confines as well.)

## This Model as Metaphysical Democracy

This holographic model allows us to envision in very concrete terms how different religious traditions may reach different summits and each of these summits can be equally as soteriologically effective. In this model, no form of salvation would be superior to the next; nor would any other form of salvation or liberation be superior to these. The notion that there could be additional forms of salvation or liberation is acceptable to this type of project. If other religious traditions claim to experience other forms of salvation, then one would have to see if this holographic model could accommodate those positions.

Otherwise, one would need to devise a new model for a more comprehensive view of religious pluralism.

In this form of religious pluralism, there are different paths and different summits. To reach one of these ultimate realities, one must choose a particular path and diligently engage that path. There are real commitments to be made and these real commitments can have real consequences, ultimate consequences. There are some who want to be sugar, some who want to taste sugar, and some who want to dissolve sugar.[24] In this model, individuals can strive for that which they want and they can achieve that which they seek. There is more than one ontological option. One's ultimate "state of existence" is not metaphysically dictated; it is not ontologically limited. One's ultimate "state of existence" is a matter of choice. This form of religious pluralism is metaphysical democracy.

## AN OVERVIEW OF THE CHAPTERS

In order to present this model for religious pluralism, I examine why other pluralists have rejected this notion. Specifically, chapter 2 turns to the work of John Hick, one of the most respected pluralists, who has been strongly opposed to the notion that there can be more than one ultimate reality. For Hick, there is only one Real *an sich* which is beyond the grasp of all traditions. Hick's rejection of a plurality of ultimate realities is consistent with his contention that such a pluralism would present us with a mutually exclusive and contradictory situation. I show that his position is based upon assumptions which fit a nonpluralistic paradigm, not a pluralistic paradigm.

Chapter 2 must also face the fact that both pluralists and their critics agree that pluralism cannot be rooted in a model. Both sides contend that if one uses a model to develop a notion of pluralism, then that model would usurp the supremacy of the various religious positions that are supposed to be equal and equally "true." The alleged problem with a model for pluralism is that the model becomes more ultimate than the individual religious positions; and therefore, it becomes either the inclusive or exclusive measure of all other religious positions. In addition to reviewing some of the critics of religious pluralism who find a model lurking behind all alleged pluralists, this chapter also focuses on Raimundo Panikkar's treatment of this subject. Panikkar, clearly one of the most eloquent spokespersons for religious pluralism, provides us with a detailed explanation of the dangers of using a model. My response to Panikkar illuminates that it is not models that destroy pluralism, but rather a type of model. Any model that uses only one type of logic—one theory of negation—is shown to be incapable of handling a pluralistic proposal.

The mystic is often the one who claims to have experienced ultimate reality and to have uncovered the soteriological conclusion to human existence. The third chapter turns to the philosophy of mysticism to examine some of the issues that challenge such claims. My focus in this endeavor is the work of Steven Katz, whose three edited volumes have dominated the discussion for the past two decades. Katz's basic position is a call for the recognition that there are no unmediated experiences. Holding that all mystical experiences are contextual, he makes a plea for the recognition of the diversity of mystical experiences. Katz's position strikes at the heart of those who contend that there is an underlying core experience to mysticism. It also strikes at those proposals, like mine, that contend that there is an underlying typology to mystical experience.

With regard to the notion of an underlying core experience to mysticism, my analysis reveals that Katz and his opponents who affirm an underlying pure consciousness event each make ontological assumptions that limit the viability of their epistemological positions. Their epistemological analyses only confirm their prior ontological assumptions. Specifically, Katz conflates mind and consciousness while his opponents disassociate consciousness from both mind and the brain.

With regard to the development of a typology, my analysis agrees with Katz about the necessity for seeing mystical experiences in their contexts, but it also reveals the dangers of overcontextualizing mystical experience. We see that Katz actually recognizes that particular traditions embody specific types of mystical experience(s). However, he does not think that these types are applicable across traditions because he finds too much diversity across traditions and cultures. In response, I show that Katz has forgotten his basic premise—namely, that all mystical experiences are contextual. If each experience is contextual, then we must expect that any typology will contain a diversity of descriptions consistent with the cultural and philosophical diversity it encompasses.

The goal of the fourth chapter is to present David Bohm's holographic model and to distinguish his model from mine. As indicated, his is a scientific model; mine is a model for comparative religions. His is nondualistic; mine is pluralistic. Before presenting an overview of holography and Bohm's model, the nature of models must be discussed. It is shown that a single object or metaphor can be used to develop several different models of the same subject. For example, the wheel can be a model for a metaphysics of Being, a metaphysics of becoming or a theistic metaphysics. Holography can also be used to develop a variety of different metaphysical models.

Chapter 5 presents the major thesis of this work—a holographic model in which there is a plurality of ultimate realities and a concomitant diversity of soteriological views. Specifically, I review (1) a theistic ultimate reality in which salvation is rooted in a personal relation of self to Other, (2) a nondualistic ultimate reality of Being in which one realizes that all is the one Self, and (3) an ultimate reality that envisions all as interrelated flux in which there is no Self or self. The relationship between each of these views of ultimate reality and the holographic model is carefully delineated. While the discussion of each of these positions grows out of a number of sources, the presentation of each of these positions is rooted in a particular religious thinker. This methodology allows us to avoid unsubstantiated generalities. We turn to Gauḍapāda, an Advaita Vedāntin, for a nondualistic view of Being and to Vasubandhu, a Buddhist of the Yogācāra school, for the second nondualistic position.[25] For a theistic position, we refer to Richard of St. Victor, a Christian mystic.

The final chapter must not only articulate the uniqueness of this proposal but it must also face the problems that such a proposal creates. This proposal, which tells us that there can be different forms of salvation, must face the fact that each of the individual views of salvation is part of larger religious systems. These larger systems are often in conflict with each other on many issues. While we must be careful not to overcontextualize religious experience, we must be equally cautious about overlooking the context of these different views. Therefore, we must address the implications for this proposal of such questions as (1) does God or *karma* oversee morality? (2) would God permit some individuals to find a form of soteriology that did not include a personal relationship with God? and (3) can some "souls" overcome their individual immortality by realizing a different ultimate reality? Finally, I must face the fact that the simultaneity and mutually interpenetrating natures of the different domains not only allow us to envision a plurality of ultimate realities and soteriological experiences, but also allow us to ponder whether an "individual" can realize more than one ultimate reality as ultimate. I look at whether such a notion is conceivable within this schema and reflect upon the uniqueness of this proposal. The merits of this proposal may lie as much in the questions it raises as the ideas it puts forth.

## NOTES

1. *Religious pluralism* is a term encompassing a wide variety of proponents. At this juncture I am only trying to contrast this metaphor with the metaphor that forms the title of this book. In chapter 2, a few authors are reviewed in detail as their work bears most closely on the proposal being put forth here. However, one should be aware of the variety of positions that get labeled religious pluralism. Anselm Kyongsuk Min provides a useful overview that is worth quoting in its entirety. For the references that Min cites, one is referred to his bibliography or mine.

> To apply a tentative typology, there are the phenomenalist pluralism of John Hick and Paul Knitter that takes religions as diverse phenomenal responses to what is ultimately the same ineffable transcendent reality, and the universalist pluralism of Leonard Swidler, Wilfred Cantwell Smith, Ninian Smart, Keith Ward, and David Krieger that stresses the possibility and necessity of a universal theology based on insights from the history of religions. Rosemary Ruether, Marjorie Suchocki, Tom Driver, and Paul Knitter propose an ethical or soteriocentric pluralism that insists on justice as a measure of all religions (Hick and Knitter), while Raimundo Panikkar advocates an ontological pluralism that asserts the pluralism not only of knowledge of being but of being itself (Swidler 1987; Hick and Knitter). There is, finally, the confessionalist pluralism of Hans Kung (Swidler 1987), John Cobb (Swidler 1987; D'Costa), Jurgen Moltmann, J. A. DiNoia, John Milbank, Kenneth Surin (D'Costa), and Mark Heim that insists on the legitimacy and necessity of each religion to confess itself precisely in its particularity including the claim to finality. (Anslem Min, "Dialectical Pluralism and Solidarity of Others: Toward a New Paradigm," *Journal of the American Academy of Religion* 65 [1998]: 587–588).

Min offers a position that he calls dialectical pluralism:

> It is confessionalist in that it understands religion to be a matter of existential commitment, discipleship, and transformation that includes but also transcends objective rationality and thus more a (salvific) way of existing to be confessed in faith and praxis than a theory to be understood in detached reflection (Swidler 1987, 245–246). As such, this pluralism encourages each religion to confess its distinctive beliefs and claims including the claim to finality. (Ibid., 588)

To this list, one could add a number of other names such as Masao Abe (1995), with his dynamic emptiness pluralism, and Michael LaFargue (1992), with his epistemological pluralism rooted in a comparison with mathematics. It also becomes apparent in the next chapter that Panikkar's ontological pluralism as described by Min is different from the ontological pluralism of this proposal. One might also see William H. Austin's "explanatory pluralism"—"the view that (sometimes at least) the best account of a phenomenon will include several partial explanations" ("Explanatory Pluralism," *Journal of the American Academy of Religion* 66 [1998]: 14).

2. While the general meaning of the metaphor "different paths, one summit" is fairly straightforward, different nuances lead to different interpretations of the relationship between the religious traditions. For example, one may say that some paths up the mountain are easier but slower; whereas other paths are harder and faster. Others may claim that there are different paths because there are different types of individuals. Some people are more inclined to actions, some to emotions and some to concentration. In this, we find a case of different yogic paths for individuals of different natures, but all the paths reach the same goal. Still others may invoke this metaphor to claim that there are different paths for different historical periods. Periods of moral and intellectual decline among human beings need a path that can be easily invoked. An example of the latter position can be found in East Asian Buddhism.

3. It must not be forgotten that religious pluralism is a modern phenomenon and not part of the landscape of traditional religious beliefs. Richard Hayes articulates this point as follows:

> Most of the historical religions are based in some way either on an explicit rejection or denigration of another religious tradition or traditions or on aristocratic claims of ethnic or racial supremacy. Examples of religions based on the denigration of other religions are original Buddhism, Mahāyāna Buddhism, Christianity, and Islam; examples of essentially racist or ethnocentric religions are the religion of ancient Israel and the Brahmanism of Vedic India. That all these religions are traditionally triumphalist and not pluralistic is simply something that must be acknowledged; it would be ideologically anachronistic and intellectually dishonest to try to find anticipations of a now fashionable way of thinking in traditions that evolved in a social and political setting entirely different from that of the present world." (Richard P. Hayes, "Gotama Buddha and Religious Pluralism," *Journal of Religious Pluralism* 1 [1991]: 94–95)

One need not look too far to see the nonpluralistic attitude of even contemporary religious thinkers. For example, Pope John Paul II is clear that Buddhism presents only a "negative soteriology" and that it should not be confused with the fullness of salvation that is attained through union with God (John Paul II, *Crossing the Threshold of Hope*, Vittorio Messori ed. [New York: Alfred A. Knopf, 1994], 81 ff). We find Tenzin Gyatso, the XIVth Dalai Lama, stating:

> Liberation in which "a mind that understands the sphere of reality annihilates all defilements in the sphere of reality" is a state that only Buddhists can accomplish. This kind of *moksha* or *nirvana* is only explained in the Buddhist scriptures, and is achieved only through Buddhist practice. According to certain religions, however, salvation is a place, a beautiful paradise, like a peaceful valley. To attain such a state as this, to achieve such a state of *moksha*, does not require the practice of emptiness, the understanding of reality. (H. H. the

> XIVth Dalai Lama, " 'Religious Harmony' and Extracts from the Bodhgaya Interviews," in *Christianity through Non-Christian Eyes*, Paul J. Griffiths ed. [Maryknoll, N.Y.: Orbis Books, 1990], 169)

It must be noted that in a more recent publication, the XIVth Dalai Lama says:

> From the perspective of human society at large, we must accept the concept of "many truths, many religions." . . . The contradictory understanding of creation and beginninglessness articulated by Buddhism, Christianity, and Hinduism, for example, means that in the end we have to part company when it comes to metaphysical claims, in spite of the many practical similarities that undoubtedly exist. These contradictions may not be very important in the beginning stages of practice. But as we advance along the path of one tradition or another, we are compelled at some point to acknowledge fundamental differences. (Dalai Lama, *Ethics for the New Millennium* [New York: Riverhead Books, 1999], 226–227)

4. Chapter 2 examines some of the critiques of religious pluralism.

5. The term *soteriology*, literally the study or doctrine of being saved, is used in a generic sense to apply to any doctrine of salvation or liberation that a religious tradition espouses. It is not being used in the specifically Christian context in which it was developed. I am also not confining its use to theistic systems in which one is saved by God. This term is being used as a general category to apply to a wide variety of ultimate conclusions to the problems of human existence found in the different religious traditions of the world.

6. In order to present a model for ontological and soteriological pluralism, I must allude to the way that these words shift meaning in this pluralistic context. (The details of this position are developed in chapter 2.) I am going to distinguish ultimate reality and metaphysics. When a religious tradition tells us that it has discovered ultimate reality, I understand that declaration in the context of its soteriological position. An ultimate reality is that ontological nature that provides individuals with a soteriological conclusion to existence—with a form of salvation or liberation. In this context, ultimate reality is not synonymous with metaphysics. Metaphysics is the more comprehensive term; it is the most comprehensive term. It refers to the theory about all reality—all forms of being (and nonbeing) and any relationships that exist between these forms of existence. I show that there may be more than one type of ontological structure or nature within the one metaphysical system and, therefore, more than one ultimate reality.

7. For a discussion of this, see John Hick, *Interpretation of Religion* (New Haven: Yale University Press, 1989), 164, and chapter 2 of this work.

8. In the form of religious pluralism in which there is only one summit, followers of no more than one type of religious tradition can feel confident that they have a chance to achieve the soteriological conclusion they desire. In that model, there is only one mountaintop and it may not resemble any religious tradition. In this model, there are a number of mountaintops, and these different summits resemble a number of specific religious traditions. On this point, Raimundo Panikkar informs us that a true religion has to fulfill two conditions. I believe that

this proposal meets both of these conditions and his first condition mirrors the point being made here. The two conditions are as follows:

> It has to deliver the promised goods to its members. . . . It means, however, that those who follow the Commandments or the *Dharma* or observe the Four Noble Truths will reach the end or fulfillment of life that the particular religious tradition describes—independently of the many possible cosmological and anthropological interpretations of the same tenets. A true religion must serve its purpose for those who believe in it; it must achieve existential truth, honest consistency. . . . [and] It has to present a view of reality in which the basic experience is expressed in an intelligible corpus that can sustain intelligent criticism from the outside without falling into substantial contradictions. (Raimundo Panikkar, "Religious Pluralism: The Metaphysical Challenge," in *Religious Pluralism*, Leroy S. Rouner ed. [Notre Dame: University of Notre Dame Press, 1984], 99–100)

9. I explore this point in much greater detail, specifically with regard to the thoughts of John Hick and Raimundo Panikkar. It might be helpful at this point to note a few comments. For example, although there is a good deal of disagreement with the biases of R.C. Zaehner, few would disagree when he says: "That it is actually impossible to hold monistic and theistic opinions as both being *absolutely* true at one and the same time seems obvious" (R. C. Zaehner, *Mysticism: Sacred and Profane* [London: Oxford University Press, 1973], xv–xvii). This book illustrates how this is possible. Or, for example, few would disagree with Paul Griffiths in his analysis of Christianity and Buddhism.

> The representative intellectuals of most Christian religious communities have felt called upon to affirm that human persons do possess permanent souls. . . . [I]nterest in the soul and its nature is connected in intricate and complex ways with the view about salvation developed by the tradition, and, especially, with the views about God's nature and purposes. Much of traditional Christian metaphysics cannot stand if the Buddhist account of what constitutes a human person turn out to be correct. (Paul J. Griffiths, *An Apology for Apologetics* [Maryknoll, N.Y.: Orbis Books, 1991], 94)

My goal in this project is to show how essential soteriological issues can stand in both religions. Griffiths also says:

> It means, to take an example from Buddhism and Christianity, that ultimate reality must be such that it can be characterized *both* as a set of evanescent instantaneous events connected to one another by specifiable causes but without any substantial independent existence, *and* as an eternal changeless divine personal substance. While it may not be impossible to construct some picture of ultimate reality that meets these demands, it is far from easy to see how it might be done. (Ibid., 47)

The pluralistic model that I am presenting offers us exactly what Griffiths has contended is difficult to see.

10. John Cobb, one of the few to entertain such a possibility, puts it best when

he asks what is wrong with questioning the notion that there is only one ultimate reality: "What is wrong, I am told repeatedly, is that there can be only one 'ultimate reality.' I am left with the impression that those who affirm this doctrine regard it as self-evident and suppose a pluralistic metaphysics to be nonsensical. They may, of course, be correct. But is this supposition itself not subject to dialogue?" (John B. Cobb Jr., "Toward a Christocentric Catholic Theology," in *Toward a Universal Theology of Religion*, Leonard Swidler ed. [Maryknoll, N.Y.: Orbis Books, 1987], 87). I believe that this supposition is subject to dialogue even if it is more than a bit strange. But, is it any stranger than the notion that only one group of people in all of human history has gotten the truth and the rest has gotten it wrong? Or, is it any more bizarre than those positions that tell us that no religion has adequately described ultimate reality and therefore each is wrong in what it believes to be true?

11. If we used this metaphor, we would end up with a version of polytheism—different gods or different realities ruling different parts of the world. The model that is presented here does not end up with that position.

12.

> Holographic film typically has a resolution of 2,500 to 5,000 lines per millimeter ($10^{-3}$ meter), in contrast to standard photographic film, which has about 200 lines per millimeter. The higher resolution is achieved by using smaller grains of the photosensitive silver in the emulsion. The smaller grains are less sensitive to light and decrease the "speed" of the film substantially. (John Iovine, *Homemade Holograms: The Complete Guide to Inexpensive, Do-It-Yourself Holography* [Blue Ridge Summit, Pa.: TAB Books, 1990], 1)

13.

> These reconstructed images have a three-dimensional character because in addition to amplitude information, which is all that an ordinary photographic process stores, phase information also has been stored. This phase information is what provides the three-dimensional characteristics of the image, as it contains within it exact information on the depths and heights of the various contours of the object. ("Holography," *Encyclopaedia Britannica, CD 98*, 2)

14. Actually, it should be noted that a holographic image can be made to appear using any "reasonably coherent" light source as a reference beam. For example, the light from an ordinary lightbulb that is not in phase can be used to present a holographic image. The clarity of the image is better with a coherent light source.

15. The hologram that is described here was exhibited at the Franklin Institute (Philadelphia, Pa.) around 1980. My appreciation to the artist, who is unknown to me.

16. The use of these terms is indebted to David Bohm. His work is discussed extensively in chapter 4.

17. There are a number of places in this work that one may be tempted to draw comparisons to Hua-yen Buddhism. The entire domain of East Asian Buddhism has been left untouched in this work, but might be of future interest.

18. How the "same" implicate domain can be viewed simultaneously as being and becoming is explored in chapter 5. A review of this issue here would extend this introductory overview too far.

19. David Bohm, *Wholeness and the Implicate Order* (London: Routledge and Kegan Paul, 1980), 172.

20. The latter is known in Yogācāra as the imagined nature (*parikalpita*), and this nature is falsely imagined to be with subject and object. This nature is discussed in chapter 5.

21. In chapter 5, different versions of theism are distinguished.

22. For a discussion of this see Part 1 of Marcus J. Borg, *The God We Never Knew* (New York: Harper San Francisco, 1998).

23. In the review of different religious individuals in chapter 5, these individuals appear to have religious experiences that are ultimate and penultimate. For a discussion of this review, see by this author "A Holographic Analysis of Religious Diversity: A Case Study of Hinduism and Christianity," *Journal of Religious Pluralism* 2 (1993): 29–59.

24. The first two parts of this refrain are taken from a common Hindu *bhakti* statement comparing the nondualist perspective of Hinduism with the *bhakti* perspective. In the hopes of adequately including the third view of ultimate reality, I have appended the last part as a reference to Buddhism.

25. In all that follows, the positions of Gauḍapāda and Vasubandhu are presented as two different positions. This is certainly consistent with the traditions of each. This is not to imply that Gauḍapāda and the Advaita tradition are not greatly influenced by Mahāyāna thought. There is an enormous amount of scholarly literature and debate on this issue, specifically on the historical relation of these two thinkers and their respective traditions as well as on the philosophical connections between the different terms that each uses. This issue is addressed in chapter 5.

## *Chapter Two*

# Putting the Proposal in Context

### OVERVIEW

The holographic model for religious pluralism that is presented in the subsequent chapters needs to be placed in the context of other proposals for religious pluralism. This project was not conceived in a vacuum and will not be read in a vacuum. It is shown that this proposal shares few features with other proposals for religious pluralism. There are two major differences between this proposal and the proposals of some of the leading proponents of religious pluralism.

The first issue that we must confront concerns the contention that "real" religious pluralists cannot hold the position that there is more than one ultimate reality and more than one soteriological conclusion to human existence. It may seem natural to assume that a religious pluralist would hold such a position, but many religious pluralists find the notion that there can be more than one soteriological conclusion to human existence extremely problematic. As we shall see, they contend that such a notion leads to holding mutually exclusive worldviews.

The second issue that I examine concerns the role of models in the formulation and articulation of religious pluralism. On the one hand, pluralists contend that pluralism cannot be based upon a model or supersystem. I show that it is not only feasible to develop a model for religious pluralism, but it is also advantageous to the viability and comprehensibility of the project. On the other hand, critics of pluralism contend that pluralists are not really pluralists because the latter do have models. The critics claim that the alleged pluralists are either inclusivists or exclusivists. My position will curry favor with neither the alleged pluralists nor their critics since I openly acknowledge having a model.

In order to illuminate each of these two issues, I concentrate my attention on John Hick and Raimundo Panikkar. Each of these individuals has written extensively on this subject and their works have been reviewed and critiqued numerous times. While this presentation does not try to represent the totality of their respective positions, I do locate these two issues in the wider context of their works.

## ALTERNATIVES TO RELIGIOUS PLURALISM

Before turning our attention to religious pluralism, it is helpful to review three alternative positions to religious pluralism. In large measure, religious pluralism is a reaction to and rejection of exclusivism, inclusivism and reductionism. Each of these positions has various proponents and therefore different ways of being formulated. This is not the place to do any more than broadly define these terms. In addition, a few comments on relativism may help us avoid any confusion between that position and pluralism.

First, the exclusivist asserts that one religion, the exclusivist's religion, is the only true religion and the only way to achieve the ultimate end. For exclusivists, their particular religion is the ideal by which all other religions are judged, and all other religions are judged to be incapable of leading one to the Truth. Truth is singular in this perspective, and the possession of Truth is limited. Insofar as the articulation of these terms has been popularized by the Christian attempt to understand its relations with other religions, one can cite the classic Christian version of the exclusivist position—namely, "outside the Church, there is no salvation."[1] There is only one way to God and that is through the Church. This position builds upon the notion that Jesus is the Way, the only Way, and anyone not associated with that Way is excluded from salvation.[2] Other religious traditions have been equally as exclusivistic. For example, Śaṅkara, the great Hindu Advaitin, in his *Brahma Sūtra Bhāṣya* reviews a variety of rival Hindu and Buddhist schools and finds each of them lacking. He tells us that it is only Advaita Vedānta that has the truth.[3]

Inclusivists envision that the path (or paths) leading to salvation is wider than that imagined by the exclusivists. The inclusivist does not demand that individuals of other faiths convert to the "one" faith.

Rather, the inclusivist finds truth, or rays of truth, in a number of different religious traditions. For inclusivists, the power of salvation is most clearly articulated and contained in their tradition. However, other traditions may experience the "saving grace" expressed and contained in the inclusivist's religion because the God of that religion wants to save all. The inclusivist not only sees the possibility of God's activity in other religions, but contends that this activity can help illuminate the tradition of the inclusivist. Two examples of this position may be helpful. A classic Christian formulation of this position was devised by Karl Rahner, the noted Catholic theologian, who used the expression "anonymous Christian" to indicate that people of other faiths could be saved while remaining true to their own religion. Their salvation, whether they knew it or not, would be through Christ.[4] The *Bhagavad Gītā* also presents us with an inclusivist position when Krishna, the incarnation (*avatār*) of God, tells Arjuna that He will accept the devotion of any worshipper even if it is offered to another god. Krishna says:

> Robbed of knowledge by stray desires, men take refuge in other deities;
> observing varied rites, they are limited by their own nature. 7:20
> I grant unwavering faith to any devoted man who wants to worship any
> form with faith. 7:21[5]

In neither case is salvation limited to those who have professed an allegiance to only one particular God or religious tradition; however, the inclusivist's tradition embodies and understands the truth in ways that exceed that which is found in other traditions.

The third position, reductionism, tells us that religious truth is "nothing but *x*" and this *x* turns out to be whatever form of reductionism that group is professing as the ultimate answer. It could be economic, psychological or sociological truth. Each form of truth in the reductionist endeavor becomes the model by which each religion is subjugated and made to be the same. While these three positions are different in numerous ways, each presupposes that truth is singular and that they have the model to understand the nature of truth. In each of these cases, the utilization of a model for understanding the relationship between the different religions imposes a hierarchical ordering upon the different religions of the world. Any such hierarchical ordering of the different religions is antithetical to the spirit of pluralism. The pluralist must maintain the equality of more than one tradition.

Finally, relativism is the position that knowledge and moral behavior are relative to the culture in which they exist. In other words, there are no absolute standards or impartial points of view from which one arrives at knowledge or moral judgments. Outside of a particular culture, one cannot judge the moral behavior of an individual nor pass judgments on the cognitive statements of a particular culture. While there is a variety of versions of relativism, such as strong and weak forms of relativism, here, our chief concern is only to differentiate relativism from pluralism. The latter is aimed at establishing that there is more than one truth—that truth is plural; the former is aimed at informing us that we cannot know truth since all attempts are culturally bound. Relativists seek to avoid discussions about truth; they must bracket all questions of truth. The pluralist aims to uncover the truths.

## DEFINING PLURALISM

Yogi Berra is alleged to have said that 50 percent of baseball is 90 percent mental. With great trepidation for misrepresenting Yogi, I think one could say something similar about religious pluralism—namely, many of the disagreements are in the definitions. If we could agree on a definition of pluralism, we would all be standing at the same plate looking at the same pitch.

Before moving to a review of Hick's position, it would be instructive to cite a few of the definitions of pluralism that have appeared in the literature. We find, for example, Gavin D'Costa informing us that pluralism "is defined as holding that all the major religions have true revelations in part, while no single revelation or religion can claim final and definitive truth."[6] He goes on to say that pluralism maintains that all religions are roughly equal paths to salvation. While the latter notion has a great deal of resonance with John Hick's notion of different paths, the passage just quoted focuses upon the different revelations that each tradition has. In distinction from the position that we see Gerald Larson take, D'Costa also tells us that pluralism involves all the major religious traditions. When Gerald Larson defines religious pluralism, he simply tells us that it refers to more than one tradition: "Truth with respect to religions is neither singular (pertaining to one only) nor universal (pertaining to all together or some sort of unanimity). Truth with regard to religions is, rather, plural."[7] Here Larson is not focusing on the notion of revelation, but on the notion of Truth; and furthermore, he offers no assurance that all traditions have it. Paul Knitter, who has championed the notion of religious pluralism, not only gives us a different definition, but he also provides a distinctive title to his definition, calling his type of religious pluralism "unitive pluralism."

> Unitive pluralism is a unity in which each religion, although losing some of its individualism (its separate ego), will intensify its personality (its self-awareness through relationship). Each religion will retain it own uniqueness, but this uniqueness will develop and take on new depths by relating to other religions in mutual dependence.[8]

In addition, Knitter develops the notion of "soteriological effectiveness" by which a religion is judged by its ability to lead people to the overcoming of suffering and oppression. Each author emphasizes a different aspect of religion—from revelation to Truth to a religion's effectiveness in solving human problems[9]—and each sets the extent of the pluralism a bit differently. In what follows, we will see that John Hick, Raimundo Panikkar and I all use different definitions of pluralism emphasizing different aspects of religion. In light of that, one need not wonder why religious pluralists not only need to defend themselves against their critics, but also from other pluralists.

## JOHN HICK'S RELIGIOUS PLURALISM

John Hick is one of the leading spokespersons for religious pluralism. Hick's move to religious pluralism exemplifies the attempt to move away from the exclusivistic and inclusivistic trends within one's own religion and to avoid reductionism. Without the move toward pluralism, Hick says:

> We should have either to regard all the reported experiences as illusory or else return to the confessional position in which we affirm the authenticity of our own stream of religious experience whilst dismissing as illusory those occurring within other traditions. But for those to whom neither of these options seem realistic the pluralistic affirmation becomes inevitable.[10]

Hick goes on to add that the nonpluralistic trends within religions, particularly his own, have had problematic consequences. For example, "the dogma of the deity of Christ—in conjunction with the aggressive and predatory aspect of human nature—has contributed historically to the evils of colonialism, the destruction of indigenous civilizations, anti-Semitism, destructive wars of religion and the burning of heretics and witches."[11] Exactly what percentage of the preceding events can be traced to the nonpluralistic trends within Christianity, or exactly what percentage of similar problems involving other religions can be traced to their exclusivistic or inclusivistic trends, is a question far beyond the scope of this work.[12] We can, at least, say that the failure to treat human beings of other faiths as equals, because one sees their religion as inferior, has certainly not been conducive to interreligious harmony and world peace. As we proceed, one may question whether pluralism, specifically of the type Hick has in mind, is more conducive to openness between religions.

Hick's understanding of religious pluralism has been presented over a number of years and in numerous publications. It is itself a multifaceted philosophical system that runs the gamut from epistemology to ontology to theology. In order to understand how Hick can reject the notion that there can be more than one ultimate reality and still be a pluralist, some of these aspects are explored. For Hick, religious pluralism is that position that acknowledges there are a plurality of ways to conceive of ultimate reality and a plurality of ways to reach the final goal of human existence. Hick says:

> I want to explore the pluralistic hypothesis that the great world faiths embody different perceptions and conceptions of and correspondingly different responses to the Real from within the major variant ways of being human; and that within each of them the transformation of human existence from self-centeredness to Reality-centeredness is taking place.[13]

Here we see four of Hick's major points. First, there is the notion of "the Real," one Real. Second, this Real is understood by different cultures and different religions in different ways. Third, different religions with their different perceptions of the Real employ different practices to transform their lives. And finally, Hick contends that the major religious traditions in the postaxial age aim for the same transformation—a transformation from being centered on the ego/self to being centered on the Real.[14] This transformation, while utilizing different philosophical frameworks and employing different practices, aims at the same soteriological transformation.

In light of these four points, one can see that the pluralism that Hick is describing is not a pluralism of Reals—it is not a plurality of ultimate realities. There is only one Real. It is also not a pluralism of soteriological conclusions. There is only one soteriological conclusion. The pluralism that Hick develops is a pluralism of different conceptions of the Real and different paths to the Real. It is an epistemological pluralism—a pluralism of different ways of knowing the Real. It is also a pluralism of praxis; there are a number of paths that one can follow that are soteriologically effective.

In order to understand how Hick arrives at this notion of pluralism, we return to the idea of avoiding both exclusivism and inclusivism. Here we are faced with the problem of how to account for the multiplicity of different religious traditions. Clearly, any ranking of the traditions in some hierarchical schema would return us to an inclusivism or exclusivism and would destroy the pluralism that is sought. Alternatively, one could try to claim that the traditions are not really different. For example, one could try to claim that Islamic theism with its notion of a personal God is really the same as Advaita Vedānta with its notion that all is the nondual *ātman*/Brahman. Hick recognizes the immediate dangers in such a move. These traditions and so many others articulate positions that are too far apart. They have different gods, different conceptions of ultimate reality, different religious practices, and so forth. In spite of all their differences, Hick believes that he uncovers something that is common to all the major religious traditions since the postaxial period.

What is common to the different traditions is that each of these traditions seeks to transform the human person. The goal is some form of salvation or liberation. Although the soteriological hope of each tradition is understood in different conceptual schemes, Hick contends that each tradition seeks to transform the individual from one who is ego-centered to one who is Reality-centered. Hick says:

> The spiritual disciplines and the inner resolves and actions through which theists and nontheists change, and the interpretive frameworks in term of which they understand their own transformation are very different. And yet the transformation undergone within these diverse forms of life and systems of self-understanding is recognisably the same.[15]

For Hick, in spite of all the differences between traditions, each seeks the same transformation from ego-centered to Reality-centered. Hick contends that each tradition seems to have produced individuals who have undergone this process, and therefore each tradition has produced "saints."[16] As such, each tradition has been soteriologically successful. This latter point is central to Hick's understanding of the truth of religion.

Not only is there one form of transformation that underlies the variety of religious practices, but there is, as already indicated, one Real.

As we have seen previously, Hick postulates that each of the major religious traditions has a different conception and perception of the Real that is filtered through its theological and philosophical world-view. What is known of Reality is therefore always known through the lens of a particular religious tradition. In light of this and using a Kantian-type distinction, Hick distinguishes between the Real *an sich* and the Real as experienced and understood by different groups. The Real *an sich* is the Real in itself—the true and absolute nature of the Real. According to Hick, the Real *an sich* is beyond the grasp of human knowledge because our experience of the Real is always mediated by our human and cultural categories. This distinction allows Hick to claim that each religion only talks about and experiences the Real as humanly experienced and not the Real *an sich*.

While there are many different truth claims emanating from the different religions of the world, Hick concentrates on two types of claims that seem to dominate the religious landscape—namely, the Real as *personae*, as a personal I–Thou figure, and the Real as *impersonae*, as impersonal without any trace of individuality remaining within the individual or the Real. The former is associated with different forms of theism; the latter is associated with various sorts of nondualism. For Hick, these conceptions of the Real as personal and impersonal reflect the major theoretical divide in all postaxial religions. A concomitant divide exists within the notions of salvation. In the religious traditions that put forth the notion of a Real as *personae*, one longs for a salvation that entails the continuation of a personal existence in relation. On the other hand, in the religious traditions that put forth the notion of the Real as *impersonae*, one longs to overcome all personal existence and relations. For Hick, both of these major divisions as well as the multitude of subdivisions within each of these categories reflect the articulation of the Real *as experienced*.

These distinctions allow Hick to say that the conflicting truth claims about ultimate reality and about soteriology that arise between the different religions do not pertain to the Real *an sich*. Such conflicts pertain only to the Real as humanly experienced. This perspective allows Hick to maintain that the particular truth claims of a given religion can be reinterpreted in a nonexclusivistic and often in a nonmetaphysical manner. For example, we can see the impact of this point on Hick's understanding of Christianity. Specifically, he understands Jesus not as God the Son, but rather as the Son of God who is full of God's salvation. The former notion is clearly associated with the traditional metaphysics of Christian theology. However, Hick says, "It is also possible to understand the idea of divine incarnation in the life of Jesus Christ mythologically, as indicating an extraordinary openness to the divine presence in virtue of which Jesus' life and teachings have mediated the reality and love of God to millions of people in successive centuries."[17] Hick's perspective not only makes Christianity less exclusivistic and less inclusivistic, but it also becomes less Christocentric and more theocentric.

It must be noted that a number of scholars have criticized Hick on this point not only in relation to Christianity, but also in relation to other world religions.[18] In general, the complaint is that Hick's pluralistic approach diminishes the importance of the particularities of a specific tradition. It allows Hick to dismiss as not really true those facets of a religious tradition that impede his pluralistic platform—namely, that the only truth is the Real *an sich* and all other statements made by a religious tradition have to be reinterpreted as partial representations of that truth. Such statements have to be understood as expressions of the Real as humanly experienced. It seems to me that Hick's enterprise is liable to such attacks.[19] For example, for Hindus who have thought that they have realized Brahman as the Ultimate Reality and not as some partial representation of the Real *an sich*, Hick's position undermines the particularity of that religious tradition. Both the nondualistic Advaita Vedānta and the theistic, Viśiṣṭādvaita account of Brahman are understood by Hick to represent the Real as experienced; neither represents the Real *an sich* as each tradition asserts.[20] From this perspective, the fundamental contention of each tradition concerning the nature of Brahman is misguided.

Moving to Buddhism, Hick finds that there is a good deal in common between his Real *an sich* and the Mahāyāna Buddhist notion of *śūnyatā* (emptiness). However, he disagrees with the Mahāyāna notion that they can directly intuit ultimate reality since he maintains that one can only know the Real as experienced, not the Real *an sich*.[21] One may ask: if the Mahāyāna Buddhists do not really experience the Real as they claim, how did they arrive at their other notions to which Hick seems to have little disagreement? If you remove their claim to experience ultimate reality—to experience reality as it is—you alter the basis from which they formulate all other doctrines. These examples can be multiplied numerous times. Hick's notion of truth as the Real *an sich* becomes the measuring stick by which the statements of other religions are judged, and each appears to come up short.

The central focus of our discussion and the point to which all these issues return is the notion that John Hick wants to be a pluralist, but does not want to entertain the notion that there can be a plurality of ultimate realities and soteriological possibilities. Hick says:

> Why however use the term "Real" in the singular? Why should there not be a number of ultimate realities? There is of course no reason, *a priori*, why the closest approximation that there is to a truly ultimate reality may not consist in either an orderly federation or a feuding multitude or an unrelated plurality. But if from a religious point of view we are trying to think, not merely of what is logically possible (namely, anything that is conceivable), but of the simplest hypothesis to account for the plurality of forms of religious experience and thought, we are, I believe, led to postulate "the Real." For each of the great traditions is oriented to what it regards as the Ultimate as the sole creator or source of the universe, or as that which no greater can be conceived, or as the final ground or nature of everything. Further, the "truthfulness" of each tradition is shown by its soteriological effectiveness. But what the traditions severally regard as ultimates are different and therefore cannot all be truly ultimate. They can however be different manifestations of the truly Ultimate within different streams of human thought-and-experience—hence the postulation of the Real *an sich* as the simplest way of accounting for the data. But we then find that if we are going to speak of the Real at all, the exigencies of our language compel us to refer to it in either the singular or the plural. Since there cannot be a plurality of ultimates, we affirm the true ultimacy of the Real by referring to it in the singular.[22]

In this passage, there are several issues that we have already reviewed, such as the notion of the Real. In addition to the notion that there can only be one ultimate reality, there are two other points that we have not reviewed.

First, in the preceding passage, Hick informs us that he is looking for the "simplest hypothesis to account for the plurality of forms of religious experience," and the simplest hypothesis does not appear to him to be a plurality of ultimate realities. The simplest hypothesis is that there is one Real *an sich*. But, we must ask: Why should we be looking for the simplest hypothesis? I'm not sure that we should *a priori* look for either the simplest, the most complex or some theory in between. We could look for a hypothesis to accommodate the greatest amount of data possible from the various religious traditions or we could look for a hypothesis to account for the truth of one set of data from one religious tradition. The model that is developed in chapter 5 opts for the former position. (We will not account for all the data.) In light of Hick's statement it can also be noted that the holographic model is simple because it is observable, repeatable and explainable. There are fundamental principles that explain holography. One can observe a hologram and can correlate those observations with the ideas about religious pluralism that I present. Therefore, while I do not agree with his premise—namely, that we should look for the simplest hypothesis—the model that I am developing fits that criterion. However, this model yields more than one ultimate reality.

Second, Hick informs us that the truthfulness of a religious tradition is to be judged according to its soteriological effectiveness. It should be recalled that the soteriological effectiveness that Hick has in mind is the transformation from ego-centered to Reality-centered. While my holographic model for religious pluralism disagrees with Hick's notion that there is only one form of soteriological transformation, I do agree that the truthfulness of a religion is to be measured by its soteriological effectiveness. There is no doubt that religions perform a variety of functions for individuals. They assist people with life's moments of transition from birth to marriage to death. They help individuals form communities that organize social relations and functions. They educate and train people in all sorts of way. None of these functions need be denied in order to agree with Hick that the truthfulness of a religion is its soteriological effectiveness. Religions promise a lot of things, but what makes them distinct from other social organizations that can assist with life's transitions, create social orders or educate people is that these postaxial religions promise some form of soteriological conclusion to human existence. For the religious individual, the psychological, sociological, educational and economic functions of a religion are important, but one puts "faith" in the soteriological effectiveness of a religion.

The last issue to be noted from the previous quote brings us to the major point of this section. Hick declares that religious pluralism affirms that there is only one ultimate. Hick does not see how a plurality of ultimate realities is possible. How could each of the ultimates be ultimate if there is more than one? It seems axiomatic that ultimate is unique and therefore there cannot be two or more ultimates.[23] Hick cements his position by pointing out that that which the individual religions assert as ultimate are mutually exclusive. He says:

> But if the ultimate Reality is the blissful, universal consciousness of Brahman, which at the core of our being we all are, how can it also be the emptiness, non-being, void of Sunyata? And again, how could it also be the Tao, as the principle of cosmic order, and again, the Dharmakaya or the eternal Buddha-nature? And if it is any of these, how can it be a personal deity? Surely these reported ultimates, personal and non-personal, are mutually exclusive. Must not any final reality either be personal, with the non-per-

> sonal aspect of divinity being secondary, or be impersonal, with the worship of personal deities representing a lower level of religious consciousness, destined to be left behind in the state of final enlightenment?[24]

Herein lies the crux of the problem for religious pluralism—it seems contradictory to agree with the theological/philosophical proclamations of different religions. Either ultimate reality is theistic or nontheistic, personal or nonpersonal; either there is Being or Emptiness or something other, but how can there be Being and Emptiness?[25] Because these different descriptions appear to Hick to be mutually exclusive, he is left to conclude that religious pluralism cannot entail holding more than one of these positions. Therefore, Hick denies that any of these positions as put forth by the different religions pertain to the Real *an sich*. Rather, his notion of pluralism deals only with the different paths to the one Real *an sich*.

In response to Hick's position, I have two final issues to raise. First, must that which is mutually exclusive also be contradictory? I would agree that pluralism entails the acceptance of mutually exclusive claims to ultimate reality; however, I would disagree that pluralism need entail contradictory claims to ultimate systems.[26] The second issue concerns the problem of language and the definition of terms. Is part of our inability to conceptualize a pluralism of ultimate realities a linguistic shortcoming? Are Hick and others who have a difficult time imagining a plurality of ultimate realities trying to use a vocabulary designed for a nonpluralistic system to develop a pluralistic system?

The first issue requires that I explain how ultimate realities can be mutually exclusive, but not contradictory. With regard to a single individual at a given time, the claims of a theistic system in which one achieves final salvation in an I–Thou relationship with one's Creator and the claim of a nondualistic system in which liberation is achieved when all individuality is overcome are mutually exclusive. If I understand the terms *mutually exclusive* and *contradictory* correctly, we are being informed that that one "individual" cannot achieve both of these ultimate goals as distinct ultimate goals.[27] By analogy, an animal cannot be both a horse and a cow; horse and cow are mutually exclusive. It would be contradictory to say that *one* animal was both a horse and a cow, unless we were talking metaphorically about a third kind of animal. However, *one* animal can be a horse and *another* animal can be a cow. Returning to our issue, one individual cannot simultaneously achieve both a theistic salvation based upon notions of individuality and also a nondualist liberation based upon the complete overcoming of individuality. However, why cannot one individual achieve a theistic salvation and another individual achieve a nondualist liberation? These ultimate goals are mutually exclusive for a single individual, but they only become contradictory when we assume that all individuals must achieve the same goal. We must now ask if Hick's insistence on mutually exclusive and contradictory ultimate systems is a necessary element within pluralism or rather only an outgrowth of an alleged pluralism that is deeply rooted in a mind-set that sees all individuals with only one soteriological possibility?

This point brings us to our second issue. I raise this issue by first objecting to what I said previously and then dismissing the objection. The objection: What was said previously makes sense about horses and cows, but does not make any sense about ultimate realities. There are many different kinds of animals; but there cannot be two different metaphysical systems supporting two different soteriological conclusions. Two questions are in order. First, in order for one individual to achieve a theistic soteriological goal and a second individual to achieve a nondualistic goal, do we not have to have two different metaphysical systems? Second, is not the notion of two metaphysical systems a contradiction in terms? My answer to the first is no, and my answer to the second is yes.

The reason that I answered question one in the negative is, as I will illuminate, that it is conceivable that one metaphysical system can have a plurality of ultimate realities. In order to make this case, one must clearly distinguish the term *metaphysics* from the term *ultimate reality*. As long as these two terms are not distinguished, there is no possibility of developing a plurality of ultimate realities. These terms have been developed and used in nonpluralistic systems. If we continue to use these terms in the same way that they have been used in nonpluralistic systems, we are condemned to always thinking in nonpluralistic terms. On the other hand, if we distinguish these terms, we will be able to envision how there can be a plurality of ultimate realities within one metaphysical system.

I propose that with regard to *metaphysics* we follow the generally accepted understanding of this term. Therefore, we use the phrase "metaphysical system" as the most comprehensive term. It signifies being (or nonbeing) in all its forms and all the relations between all the forms of being or nonbeing. In this description, I have implied that there may be more than one form of *ontos*, but only one metaphysical system. On the other hand, I propose using "ultimate reality" to indicate a particular ontological structure capable of supporting a soteriological conclusion to human existence. It is that ontological structure or nature that allows an individual to achieve the goal that will release her from those conditions that are associated with the existential dilemma of being born. From this perspective, there can be only one metaphysical system, but that metaphysical system can have a plurality of forms of being/nonbeing, and each of these forms of being/nonbeing can be an ultimate reality if it can provide an effective soteriological conclusion to an individual's existence. Therefore, more than one soteriological conclusion can be realized.

By distinguishing metaphysics from ultimate reality, one can begin to see how these reported ultimates, personal and nonpersonal, can both be possible. From this perspective, the ultimacy of an ultimate reality does not refer to its singularity, such as the term *metaphysics* implies. Here the "ultimacy" of an ultimate reality does not mean uniqueness. Its ultimacy also does not imply that it must be *the* highest, that which is without equal, that which is above all else. Ultimacy in this latter sense demands that it be singular. Rather, in the metaphysical structure of this holographic proposal, "ultimate reality" means that it is an ontological condition for a soteriological conclusion to existence. It is an "ultimate" reality because it provides an ultimate solution to existence. Thus, in order for there to be more than one ultimate reality, I must show how there can be more than one ontological nature within a metaphysical system and how each of those ontological natures could be soteriologically effective.

Needless to say, all of this is extremely abstract and needs to be illuminated by a concrete analogy such as the holographic model that is being proposed. In chapter 5, I illuminate one holographic system with different domains—the implicate and the explicate—and different relations between these domains. The one system is compared to the one metaphysical system. Each of the domains and their relations are compared to the different ontological structures that constitute the different ultimate realities. I show how this model can be used metaphorically to envision the different soteriological descriptions that have appeared in the different religious traditions that are examined. As indicated, I compare the implicate domain to both forms of nondualistic ultimate realities. The implicate domain is shown to simultaneously exhibit the characteristics of Being and emptiness even though Being and emptiness are understood to be distinctly different. In addition, I compare the relation between the explicate domains and the implicate domain of holography to a theistic view of ultimate reality. The holographic structures that allow us to envision the last scenario are simultaneously existing and mutually interpenetrating with the holographic structures that allow us to envision both of the nondualistic ultimate realities. Therefore, all three ultimate realities can be envisioned as simultaneously existing within this one metaphysical system.

It appears to me that Hick's rejection of a plurality of ultimate realities is rooted in a philosophical picture in which metaphysics and ultimate reality are identified as singular and thus there can only be one form of soteriology concomitant with that single structure. Following that line of reasoning, it is not difficult to see why Hick and others have found the notion of a plurality of ultimate realities to be contradictory. On the other hand, my proposal (1) distinguishes metaphysical from ultimate reality, (2) illuminates, by analogy of holography, how there can be more than one ultimate reality within a metaphysical system, and (3) coordinates the different ultimate realities with different soteriological experiences found in a variety of religious traditions.

## PLURALISTS CANNOT HAVE MODELS; PLURALISTS DO HAVE MODELS AND THEREFORE THEY ARE NOT PLURALISTS; I WANT TO BE A PLURALIST WITH A MODEL!

While the heading to this section is far too long and would be a better country-and-western refrain, it does sum up the three major points that will be made. First, both pluralists and critics of pluralism agree that religious pluralism must stand on its own without devising a model from which to operate. Second, one of the chief criticisms of religious pluralists is that, contrary to their own disclaimers, they operate from an implicit model that undermines their pluralism. Finally, as the last line of the refrain hits a sorrowful pitch, this author acknowledges that his project is an explicit attempt to devise a model for religious pluralism in spite of all the advice to the contrary. If it is the case that in no way, shape or form can religious pluralists have a model, then this project is in *very* serious trouble!

For all their disagreements, most pluralists and critics of pluralism agree on one issue. They agree that one cannot be a pluralist if one has a model. The reasons seem fairly straightforward and noncontentious and can be summarized as follows. Pluralists assert that there is more than one true position and no one of these true positions is superior to any other true position. Therefore, one cannot be a pluralist if one devises a model that organizes the diversity of religious positions under its wing. The model or organizing system would preempt a pluralism of positions by claiming a place on top of all the individual positions. The model would hold a superior position. Having claimed a supreme position, such an organizing model would destroy the intended pluralism of positions. With few exceptions, there seems to be little doubt, among pluralists or among their critics, that pluralists cannot have a model.[28]

## PLURALISTS HAVE MODELS—CRITICS OF PLURALISM

In spite of the agreement that pluralists cannot have models, critics of pluralism have frequently noted that many self-avowed pluralists operate with an implicit model. Based upon uncovering an implicit model within the thoughts of a self-alleged pluralist, the critics have declared that these individuals are not really pluralists at all. Thinking that no one can operate without a model, Gavin D'Costa goes so far as to declare that there is no such thing as pluralism.

> I want to suggest that there is no such thing as pluralism because all pluralists are committed to holding some form of truth criteria and by virtue of this, anything that falls foul of such criteria is excluded from counting as truth (in doctrine and practice). Thus, pluralism operates within the same logical structure as exclusivism.[29]

Owen Thomas would agree with D'Costa that there is no such thing as pluralism since all pluralists operate from some "universal theory." He says, "It would seem that no coherent pluralistic theory is possible: there cannot be a theory of worldviews that is not also an interpretation from the perspective of one of the worldviews."[30] However, Thomas, in distinction to Owens, understands pluralists to be inclusivists, not exclusivists.

Not all critics of pluralism would go as far as D'Costa and Thomas in labeling all pluralists either exclusivists or inclusivists. Rather, some critics see some pluralists as exclusivists, while seeing other alleged pluralists as inclusivists depending on the type of implicit model the specific individual employs.[31] Gerald Larson's analysis of alleged pluralists goes so far as to place some of these thinkers not only in the camps of exclusivism and inclusivism, but he also places some individuals, who are referred to as "descriptive pluralists," in the camp of reductionism.[32]

Interestingly, not all critics of pluralism see the same individual in the same light. For example, in looking at the alleged pluralism of John Hick, we find critics who contend that Hick is an exclusivist and others who contend he is an inclusivist. Nonetheless, his critics seem to agree that he has a theory or model of religion from which he devises his entire understanding of the relations between religious traditions. (This is consistent with the preceding presentation of Hick.) For example, John Apczynski takes the position that Hick is an exclusivist. He sees in Hick's pluralistic willingness to accept the claims of all traditions a detachment from the substantive truth claims of each individual tradition. This detachment from the substance of each tradition leads Apczynski to the conclusion that for Hick none of the individual claims matters.[33] What ultimately matters is only Hick's formulation of the Real, all else being excluded from importance. On the other side is S. Mark Heim, who sees Hick as an inclusivist. Heim maintains that Hick does exactly what the inclusivists do in spite of Hick's disclaimers to the contrary and the latter's criticism of the inclusivist position.[34] Specifically, Heim says:

> Hick's approach does seem to be the classically inclusivist one he otherwise rejects when it is a Muslim arguing the Hindu's moral virtue is ultimately rooted in Allah, or a Buddhist arguing the Jew's ethical integrity is anonymous participation in the dharma. He exempts himself from the charge of being an inclusivist because he relativizes the ultimates of particular faiths not in favor of one among them, but in terms of something above and beyond them all: The Real. Of course, all religious pluralists also believe that the object of their faith is above and beyond the particularities of other religions—and often their own as well.[35]

Using different labels, both authors agree that Hick is not a pluralist because he invokes the notion of the Real that stands above each of the individual religions. While this Real is neither utterable nor knowable by any religious tradition, it is the theoretical model from which Hick makes all pronouncements and judgments concerning different religions. It is his metatheory from which he understands everything from ethics to soteriology to ontology; and whether it is labeled inclusive or exclusive, it is not pluralistic. The model renders all religious diversity superficial.[36]

## RESPONDING TO THESE CRITICS—A GLIMPSE AT THE HOLOGRAPHIC PROPOSAL

Among these specific criticisms of the alleged pluralist position that we have just seen, three points are relevant to my proposal and need to be discussed immediately. Without responding to these points, the holographic proposal will appear to fall into the same traps. First and foremost is the notion that one cannot have a model and be a religious pluralist. This is a very substantial point and is addressed in the following sections.

The second point that needs to be addressed was made by Owen Thomas (note 30) when he said: "There cannot be a theory of worldviews that is not also an interpretation from the perspective of one of the worldviews." The point here is that the worldview from which the interpretation of other worldviews is made would (1) become the ultimate worldview, and (2) destroy the ultimacy of the other worldviews. This holographic model is guilty of point 1, but not point 2. This holographic model does offer pieces of a worldview from which the different ultimate realities are understood. However, with regard to point 2, this holographic model does not destroy the ultimacy of the ultimate realities reviewed. The ultimate realities reviewed remain ultimate, but they lose their status of being a metaphysical system or a worldview. (Recall that I have distinguished ultimate reality from metaphysics, and here worldview would be associated with the latter.)

Furthermore, this holographic model does not offer an ultimate reality of its own. The only ultimate realities that this model offers are those that are uncovered in the religions of the world. Therefore, this model does not usurp the ultimacy of any of the ultimate realities.

(In addition, it should be noted that the holographic model offered here suggests only a few aspects of a worldview—specifically, that there can be more than one ultimate reality. However, this model does not provide anywhere near a complete worldview. This becomes evident as the problems to this proposal are reviewed in chapter 6 and most aspects of a worldview are left undetermined.)

The third point that needs to be addressed arises in response to Mark Heim's critique. In the passage quoted, he told us that "all religious pluralists also believe that the object of their faith is above and beyond the particularities of other religions—and often their own as well" (note 35). The religious pluralism that is being proposed in this work does not place one faith above and beyond the particularities of any other faith. The proposal being offered here does not offer any object of faith. It offers no soteriological position not already promulgated by some religious tradition. There is no holographic faith; no holographic soteriology apart from what appears in the religious traditions of the world. It cannot therefore claim that its faith is better than anyone else's faith. In fact, I argue that this model calls upon individuals to choose a particular religious tradition and practice. This model only shows that each of the faiths reviewed offers a distinct, yet equal, soteriological conclusion to human existence.

In light of what has been said, I must acknowledge that this proposal is not only pluralistic with regard to the different soteriological conclusions that can be attained, but that this proposal may be considered inclusivistic. It includes a variety of ultimate realities and soteriological conclusions under its umbrella. That is what a pluralist position must do, but this point must be openly acknowledged before it is attacked. As indicated, this proposal provides a framework in which we can conceptualize a plurality of ultimate realities within one metaphysical model. None of these ultimate realities are equated with the metaphysical structure. Each fits within it. However, the holographic model does not, itself, offer an ultimate reality and soteriological conclusion that is not found in one of the religious traditions. In that sense, this proposal does not fall within the traditional inclusivist position.

Traditionally, inclusivism meant that all people may be included in the one form of salvation brought about by *one* particular salvific agent even if they are unaware of such a salvific agent. In that sense, this proposal is not inclusivistic. I am certainly not proposing that there is only one form of salvation, nor only one path to salvation, nor one agent responsible for salvation. Different individuals get different salvations employing different means.

Confession number two: Yes, my proposal may be considered exclusivistic. It excludes any particular religious tradition with its view of ultimate reality from being the only ultimate reality. It also excludes a tradition from claiming that its view of ultimate reality and its concomitant soteriological conclusion are simultaneously metaphysical positions. Given that individual religious traditions have not only asserted that their view of ultimate reality is the only truth, but also that their view of ultimate reality is part and parcel of their worldview, this proposal excludes those truth claims made by the various religious traditions. Here, too, it seems to me that the pluralist position in order to be pluralist must exclude the exclusivistic position of the exclusivist. As such, it may be accused of being what it is refuting. However, my proposal does not exclude what the exclusivist says is ultimately true.

Once again, if we return to the notion of exclusivism developed in response, for example, to the Christian notion of "no salvation outside the Church," then my position is not exclusivistic in that sense. I am not saying that there is only one way to salvation and only one form of salvation. However, if, as some of the previous critics of pluralism seem to have done, we widen the notion of exclusivism to encompass any position whose principles exclude the principles of another position, then my holographic model is also exclusivistic. This metaphysical model excludes from the realm of metaphysical discourse the discourse of other traditions that equate their view of ultimate reality with the complete, total worldview.

## PLURALISTS CANNOT HAVE MODELS—PANIKKAR'S ANALYSIS

Having seen that pluralists have not always been successful in their attempts to avoid the use of a model, we should now see why pluralists, and in particular Panikkar, are so convinced that they cannot utilize a model in the development of their position.[37] Since this project is proposing a model for religious pluralism, I must face this issue directly.

With respect to the voluminous nature of Professor Panikkar's writing on the general subject of world religions, interreligious dialogue and religious pluralism, our review of his writings focuses upon this issue of models, utilizing two related points to provide the background to understand Panikkar's contention that religious pluralists cannot have models.

First, from Panikkar's perspective, the pluralist position rejects the notion that there is a universal, core rational process. Pluralists must reject the notion that there is one type of rationality or an underlying core to human reason that fits all philosophical systems and cultural types. Panikkar tells us that a universal form of rationality may allow for interchange between religions but it is essentially a reductionistic maneuver by which diversity gets transformed into a commonality. He sees this attempt to divine a single form of human rationality as a Western penchant and one that is antithetical to pluralism.[38] Whether or not this phenomenon is a peculiarly Western penchant, one can certainly agree with Panikkar that pluralism cannot be based upon one form of rationality. One form of rationality—one form of philosophical thinking—would eliminate the possibility of a diversity of religious systems, each with their own form of thinking, with their own ultimate reality and with their own soteriological vision.

Panikkar goes even further in this analysis by stating that pluralism entails "the dethronement of reason and the abandonment of the monotheistic paradigm."[39] By monotheistic paradigm, Panikkar does not have in mind a literally monotheistic system; but rather, any philosophical or theological system that tells us there is one and only one truth—such as, the one and only truth of nondualism. Again, I fully agree with him that pluralism is the "abandonment of the monotheistic paradigm." To maintain a pluralism of ultimate realities, one cannot tolerate any such monotheistic paradigm for ultimate realities.

On the other hand, I do not agree that pluralism need entail the "dethronement of reason." It seems to me that pluralism need only entail the dethronement of a single type of reason. We need to ask: Why can one not develop a model for religious pluralism that allows us to employ a variety of types of reason, different types of logic, different theories of negation? Different religious traditions with different views of ultimate reality utilize different forms of reason; they use different theories of negation.[40] If we reflect upon these different philosophical perspectives, we can see that each defines what is and what is not in its own way. Each position has a different form of rationality, a different logic, a different perception of what is real and what is not real.

These differences can be illustrated by example. Is not the conflict between monistic nondualism and classical theism precisely a conflict between different forms of rationality? What one defines as an illusion, the other defines as real. The former defines particularity and relations between particulars as not real; whereas the latter defines the real in terms of particulars and the relations between particulars. More concretely stated, in Advaita Vedānta, Brahman alone is real; all particularity and all relationship is *māyā*, an illusion. However, a theist such as Richard of St. Victor not only believes in the particularity of God and the individual souls, but he also believes that the relations that exist between the triune God and the individual souls are of the utmost significance in defining the nature of each. One might note here a third, and completely different, philosophical position that asserts that particulars are real, but not defined by relationship. In this last philosophical schema, all relationships are illusory impositions; they are that which is to be negated. Each of these systems defines what is and what is not in different ways. Each demands that we think in different ways and that we perceive the world in different ways.

As rational beings, we can use our generic rational capabilities to marginally understand each of the different positions. In that sense, I agree with Panikkar that pluralism demands overcoming this generic rational capability. However, a commitment, either religious or philosophical, to one of these systems of thought would demand a form of rationality that is at odds with each of the other systems. Such a commitment would demand that we think, imagine and perceive in the manner proscribed by the particular system. It is my contention that a pluralistic proposal would have to entertain more than one of these philosophical, rational systems. The holographic proposal does just that. A pluralistic proposal cannot be confined to one system of thought, but it need not abandon all rational thought.

A second issue that helps us understand Panikkar's position on pluralism is his rejection of the notion that Reality is totally comprehensible. This partial incomprehensibility is approached by Panikkar from two directions—from the anthropological side and from the metaphysical side. From the former perspective, human beings are contingent, contextualized creatures whose knowledge is constricted; and therefore, they cannot completely know Reality.[41] Moving to the metaphysical side, Panikkar says about this point:

> It contests one of the most widespread beliefs in the West as well as in the East—namely, that Reality is totally intelligible, that the *noesis noeseos* of Aristotle, the *svayamprakāsha* of the Vedantins, the self-intelligible and omniscient god of the Christians, the total reflection of many spiritualist philosophers, is really the case.[42]

Panikkar's assumption is that Reality, whether one calls it Being, Brahman, God, or something else, cannot completely know itself. Reality cannot be completely known because, for Panikkar, it cannot be completely equated with consciousness—Being is not consciousness. About this Panikkar says:

> The mystery of reality cannot be equated with the nature of consciousness. There "is" also *sat* (being) and *ānanda* (joy), the Father and the Spirit. They may be correlative and even coextensive with consciousness, probably because we cannot speak (think) of the one without the other, but certainly they cannot be all lumped together as ultimately one single "thing."[43]

All cannot be known because we are incapable of knowing it—the anthropological assumption—and it is incapable of being completely known—the metaphysical assumption. Panikkar refers to this unknown aspect as the "opaque remnant"[44] within Reality. It is the opaque remnant in which the variety of religious possibilities can be said to swirl. However, it must also be noted that this notion tells us that individual traditions have erred in their conception of Reality. Pluralism is established and the individual traditions are told that they do not know what they think they know; they do not know Reality as they have professed they know it. (We will return to this point and my confession to a similar offense.)

Drawing upon the two points outlined previously—namely, there is no core rational process and Reality is not totally comprehensible—it is not too difficult to see how Panikkar would never envision a model for religious pluralism. First, it would seem that any *one* model for religious pluralism would have to represent *one* type of rational process. From Panikkar's perspective, any model that was utilized for religious pluralism would reflect the enthronement of a particular type of rationality. Clearly, this would be unacceptable for a pluralist. Second, if Reality by its nature is not totally comprehensible, then any model that alleges to comprehend Reality must be false. In other words, if the goal of the model is to articulate its comprehension of Reality and Reality is not comprehensible, then the model must fail.

In response to Panikkar's point that Reality cannot be completely known, I would like to agree with some parts of this idea and respectfully offer an alternative rendering to other parts of his statement.[45] The simplest way to articulate my response is to refer to his example and to my holographic model. This holographic model does not challenge the Advaita notion that Being is Consciousness. In fact, it is designed to illuminate that notion. Panikkar seems to want to challenge that in order to allow for the notion that Reality is not totally intelligible. While this holographic model allows us to envision that Being is Consciousness, the model does not demand that we assume that Reality—the one metaphysical world—is totally comprehensible. Certainly, the argument throughout this book is that knowing that Being is Consciousness allows one to know the nature of all Being and therefore achieve liberation as professed by Advaita Vedānta. However, this model also contends that knowing that Being is Consciousness (*sat* is *cit*) does not allow one to know all the natures of Reality. For example, knowledge of *sat/cit* does not reveal the ultimacy of *śūnyatā* nor the ultimacy of the I–Thou relation in which the theist finds salvation. Thus, in response to Professor Panikkar, I would say that the Advaita notion of *svayamprakāsha* (the self-illumination of Being/Consciousness) can be retained in this model without assuming that Reality is completely revealed in all its natures. (Furthermore, it must be clearly acknowledged that this holographic model does not contend that it knows all ultimate realities or that it can adequately illuminate all ultimate realities. I am only trying to illuminate three ultimate realities as simultaneously existing and as equal.)

With these issues in mind, we turn to Panikkar's explicit rejection of the use of a model, a supersystem. He says:

> Pluralism in its ultimate sense is not the tolerance of a diversity of systems under a larger umbrella; it does not allow for any superstructure. It is not a supersystem. Who or what principles would manage it? The problem of pluralism arises when we are confronted with mutually irreconcilable world-views or ultimate systems of thought and life. Pluralism has to do with final, unbridgeable human attitudes. If two views allow for a synthesis, we cannot speak of pluralism. We speak then of two different, mutually complementary, although apparently opposite, attitudes, beliefs, or whatever. We do not take seriously the claim of ultimacy of religions, philosophies, theologies, and final human attitudes if we seem to allow for a pluralistic supersystem. . . . It is easy to be pluralistic if the others abandon their claim to absoluteness, primacy, universality, and the like: "We pluralists have allotted each system its niche; we then are truly universal." This, I submit is not pluralism. This is another system, perhaps a better one, but it would make pluralism unnecessary. We have a situation of pluralism only when we are confronted with mutually exclusive and respectively contradictory ultimate systems. We cannot, by definition, logically overcome a pluralistic situation without breaking the very principle of noncontradiction and denying our own set of codes: intellectual, moral esthetics, and so forth.[46]

Three key concepts can be highlighted from this passage. First, Panikkar definitively states that pluralism is not a supersystem. Second, pluralism demands that we take the different claims of ultimacy that religions profess seriously and that we do not ask them to abandon their claim to absoluteness. Third, we have a pluralistic situation only when we are confronted with "mutually exclusive and respectively contradictory ultimate systems." This third point has already been examined in the context of John Hick's work; and therefore, I shall address only the first two points.

First, we need to reflect a bit further upon Panikkar's declaration that pluralism does not tolerate a supersystem. We need to consider what impact the lack of a supersystem has upon the individual religious traditions. Each religious tradition believes that its view constitutes a supersystem. Individual religious traditions have not been historically pluralistic. Each tradition has seen itself as the articulator of the supersystem—the worldview that describes the ultimate reality and the soteriological conclusion to human existence. By declaring that there is no supersystem, Panikkar may try to avoid articulating the nature of that supersystem, but nonetheless he has told us what it is not. It is not the supersystem of any of the particular religious traditions that claim that they know the supersystem. Thus, we should be aware that such a notion of pluralism demands that the individual traditions relinquish their claims to be a supersystem. I acknowledge that my model does the same thing that I am accusing Panikkar of doing.

Second, I openly acknowledge that I am trying to create a model. However, I do not believe that a model as such destroys pluralism. Rather, it is how a particular model functions that can destroy pluralism. There are at least three ways in which a model can destroy religious pluralism. One, if a model presents its own version of ultimate reality and if that version of ultimate reality supersedes the different ultimate realities that are found in the world's religions, then such a model would destroy pluralism. Such a model would stand above the other religions. If a model, such as this holographic model, does not present its own version of ultimate reality, then it does not challenge the supremacy of the individual views of ultimate reality proffered by the different religions. In such a case, a model for pluralism would not *a priori* destroy pluralism. Next, if a model operates with one form/type of negation or one type of rationality, then it imposes a monotheism of thought and destroys pluralism. However, if the model can simultaneously illustrate a variety of forms of negation—a variety of forms of rationality—then it is by nature pluralistic. Such a model, such as this holographic model, would not destroy pluralism. Finally, if a model for pluralism can illuminate how mutually exclusive ultimate realities can be simultaneously accessible/attainable to different human beings so that different human beings can realize different ultimate realities, then such a model would not destroy pluralism. The problem is not that models *a priori* destroy pluralism; the problem has been that the models that have been proposed and/or refuted have all been rooted in a nonpluralistic frame of reference. Such models destroy pluralism. The goal in what follows is to develop a model that does not fall prey to these nonpluralistic tendencies.[47]

Finally, I completely agree with Panikkar that to be a religious pluralist one cannot deny ultimacy to other religious perspectives or somehow claim that one perspective is the most ultimate. On the other hand, his notion of the Real and our notion of a holographic model for religious pluralism seem to do exactly that! The metaphysical perch of this holographic proposal usurps the metaphysical position of the different religious traditions. However, the key point for this proposal is that I am making a distinction between metaphysics and ultimate reality. This proposal usurps their view of metaphysics, but not their view of ultimate reality.

I have acknowledged that when we speak of ultimate realities we are only talking about the final, ultimate conclusions to human existence. When we talk about metaphysics, we are talking about that most comprehensive view of existence/nonexistence that may include a number of ultimate realities and soteriological possibilities. Thus, this holographic model does try to usurp the traditional metaphysical stature that individual religious traditions have. It is proposing that parts of the different religious traditions be understood within the context of this holographic model. To use Panikkar's term, this model is a supersystem. However, as previously indicated, a complete worldview (supersystem) will not be developed here. That is not the intention of this project and there is no assumption that it is possible since Reality may retain an opaque remnant as noted previously. Furthermore, I must reiterate that the holographic model that is being proposed does not offer another form of "salvation"—another ultimate conclusion to be born into this world. This model does not operate on that level. It does not say that its ultimate reality is higher than anyone else's view of ultimate reality because this metaphysical model *offers no view* of ultimate reality beyond those that arise in the religious traditions of the world.

In this model, I am proposing that that which a religious tradition has experienced as ultimate may be truly ultimate. Its members may have experienced that which is soteriologically effective. This proposal for pluralism is only aimed at providing a model with which to conceptualize how there can be more than one soteriologically effective conclusion.

## NOTES

1. The Council of Florence, 1438–1445, declared:

> It firmly believes, professes, and proclaims that those not living within the Catholic Church, not only pagans, but also Jews and heretics and schismatics

> cannot become participants in eternal life, but will depart "into everlasting fire which was prepared for the devil and his angels" [Matt. 25:41], unless before the end of life the same have been added to the flock; and that the unity of the ecclesiastical body is so strong that only to those remaining in it are the sacraments of the Church of benefit for salvation. (*The Sources of Catholic Dogma*, Roy J. Deferrari trans., from the Thirtieth Edition of Henry Denzinger's *Enchiridion Symbolorum* [St. Louis: B. Herder Book Co., 1957], 230)

2. For an interesting nonexclusivistic interpretation of this passage, see Diana Eck, *Encountering God: A Spiritual Journey from Bozeman to Banaras* (Boston: Beacon Press, 1993), 94 ff.

3. With reference to Śaṅkara's refutation of other religious positions, one can see his *Brahmasūtrabhāṣya* II: 2, 1–45. In these sections, Śaṅkara not only refutes the positions of rival Hindu schools such as Sāṁkhya, but also different Buddhist schools as well as the Jain position. For example, in conclusion to his comments on Buddhism, Śaṅkara says:

> To be brief, from every point of view that this Buddhist doctrine may be examined for finding out some justification, it breaks down like a well sunk in sand; and we do not find any the least logic here. Hence also all behavior based on the Buddhist scripture is unjustifiable. Moreover, Buddha exposed his own incoherence in talk when he instructed the three mutually contradictory theories of the existence of external objects, existence of consciousness, and absolute nihilism; or he showed his malevolence towards all creatures, acting under the delusion that these creatures would get confused by imbibing contradictory views. The ideas is that the Buddhist view should be abjured in every way by all who desire the highest good. (*Brahma-Sūtra-Bhāṣya of Srī Śaṅkaracārya*, Swami Gambhirananda trans. [Calcutta: Advaita Ashrama, 1965], 426)

With regard to Śaṅkara's view of those who believe in God, in his commentary to the *Bṛhadāraṇyaka Upaniṣad* (I.iv.10), he says: "While he, one who is not a knower of Brahman, who worships another god, a god different from himself, approaches him in a subordinate position, offering him praises, salutations, sacrifices, presents, devotion, meditation, etc. . . . He, this ignorant man, has not only the evil of ignorance, but is also like an animal to the gods" (Śaṅkarācārya, *The Bṛhadāraṇyaka Upaniṣad with the Commentary of Śaṅkarācārya*, Swami Madhavananda trans. [Calcutta: Advaita Ashrama, 1965], 171).

4. For a fuller discussion of Rahner's position along with the position of Hans Kung and that of Vatican II, one can see Paul Knitter, *No Other Name?* (Maryknoll, N.Y.: Orbis Books, 1990), ch. 7.

5. *The Bhagavad Gita*, Barbara Miller trans. (Toronto: Bantam Books, 1986), 73.

6. Gavin D'Costa, "The Impossibility of a Pluralist View of Religion," *Religious Studies* 32 (1996): 224. It should be noted that D'Costa is not a pluralist; he is an inclusivist describing the position of the pluralists.

7. Gerald Larson, "Contra Pluralism," *Soundings* 73 (1990): 313. In this article, Larson is presenting a critique of Panikkar and not his own position.

8. Paul Knitter, *No Other Name?*, 9.

9. See Paul Knitter in "Toward a Liberation Theology of Religions," in *The Myth of Christian Uniqueness*, John Hick and Paul F. Knitter eds. (Maryknoll, N.Y.: Orbis Books, 1987), 187 ff.

10. John Hick, *An Interpretation of Religion* (New Haven: Yale University Press, 1989), 249.

11. Hick, *Interpretation of Religion*, 372.

12. Paul Knitter ("Toward a Liberation Theology of Religions," 182) echoes part of this issue when he tells us that the Third World is leery of Rahner's "anonymous Christian" and Kung's "critical catalyst" because they are seen as promoting a "crypto-colonialist theology of religion."

13. Hick, *Interpretation of Religion*, 240.

14. By "postaxial religions" John Hick, referring to the work of Karl Jaspers, means those traditions arising between 800 and 200 B.C.E. whose focus shifts away from one's identification with the group and toward a concern for the salvation of the individual. See *Interpretation of Religion*, 32 ff.

15. Hick, *Interpretation of Religion*, 279.

16. With regard to this issue, Hick maintains that the superiority of a religion has to be posed in empirical terms, specifically which tradition has produced more saints. Hick finds no reason to suppose that one tradition is superior with regard to this test. See: "The Non-Absoluteness of Christianity," in *The Myth of Christian Uniqueness*, 23 ff.

17. Hick, *Interpretation of Religion*, 372.

18. Some of the scholars who have criticized Hick on this issue are John V. Apczynski, "John Hick's Theocentrism: Revolutionary or Implicitly Exclusivistic?" *Modern Theology* 8 (1992): 39–52; Kenneth Surin, "A Certain Politics of Speech: Religious Pluralism in the Age of McDonald's Hamburger," *Modern Theology* 7 (1990): 67–100; Paul J. Griffiths, "The Uniqueness of Christian Doctrine, in *Christian Uniqueness Reconsidered*, Gavin D'Costa ed. (Maryknoll, N.Y.: Orbis Books, 1990), 161 ff; and S. Mark Heim, *Salvations: Truth and Difference in Religion* (Maryknoll, N.Y.: Orbis Books, 1995), ch. 1.

19. In what follows, the reader will have to judge whether the criticism leveled against Hick is also valid against my proposal. While I explore this issue in subsequent chapters, I would preliminarily say that my pluralistic, holographic proposal is less liable to these charges than Hick's proposal. My proposal elucidates a plurality of ultimate realities and a plurality of soteriological possibilities thereby not having to diminish the particularities of a given religious tradition as much.

20. Hick, *Interpretation of Religion*, 282–283.

21. Hick, *Interpretation of Religion*, 292–293.

22. Hick, *Interpretation of Religion*, 248–249.

23. For the notion of uniqueness see J. Z. Smith, *Divine Drudgery: On the Comparison of Early Christianities and the Religions of Late Antiquity* (Chicago: University of Chicago Press, 1990), 36 ff.

24. Hick, *Interpretation of Religion*, 234.

25. A discussion of Jain logic and their view of *anekāntavāda* may prove a useful tool in further examining this pluralistic model and the issue under discussion.

The Jain theory may help us reflect upon how each of the three ontological perspectives is limited. On the other hand, as we will see the limitation of each is not soteriologically crippling, I will leave this comparison for a later date.

26. This section dealing with the notions of mutually exclusive and contradictory ultimate realities was presented at the annual meeting of the American Academy of Religion, 1992, Interreligious Dialogue Section. In that paper, I made the point that one individual could not achieve both forms of salvation—personal and impersonal—but different individuals could achieve different forms of salvation since there could be different ultimate realities. This holographic model accommodates the notion that an individual can experience different ultimate realities as penultimate, and, as we will see in chapter 6, a nonpluralistic model would allow us to envision how one individual could experience more than one ultimate reality as ultimate. S. Mark Heim makes a very similar point:

> So, for instance, Hick will say that nirvana and communion with God upon death are contradictory beliefs. Then he contends we have only three options. All such religious faith is nonsense; one is true and the others false; or the true content of religion is on a plane far above the terms of such contradictions. But this all depends on a nonpluralistic assumption. Nirvana and communion with God are contradictory only if we assume that one or the other must be the sole fate for all human beings. True, they cannot both be true at the same time of the same person. But for different people, or the same person at different times, there is no contradiction in both being true. (S. Mark Heim, *Salvations: Truth and Difference in Religion*, 149)

27. As is discussed in the final chapter, a nonpluralistic system could entertain the notion that one individual can realize both ultimate realities.

28. An exception to this notion may be found in the work of a few scholars who have begun to entertain such a possibility. For example, see Lonnie D. Kliever, "Moral Education in a Pluralistic World," *Journal of the American Academy of Religion* LX (1992): 122–123; John Cobb, *Beyond Dialogue* (Philadelphia: Fortress Press, 1982), 110 ff; and "Toward a Christocentric Theology of Religion, " in *Toward a Universal Theology of Religion*, Leonard Swidler ed. (Maryknoll, N.Y.: Orbis Books, 1987), 94 ff.

29. Gavin D'Costa, "The Impossibility of a Pluralist View of Religions," *Religious Studies* 32 (1996): 225–226.

30. Owen C. Thomas, "Religious Plurality and Contemporary Philosophy: A Critical Survey," *Harvard Theological Review* 87 (1994): 200.

31. Kenneth Surin, "A Certain Politics of Speech," 81. In an interesting article, Surin refers to the ideology of pluralism as a component of hegemonism.

32. Gerald James Larson, "Contra Pluralism," 314–315.

33. Apczynski, "John Hick's Theocentrism," 39–52.

34. S. Mark Heim, *Salvations: Truth and Difference in Religion*, 102 ff., offers one of the finest analyses of this subject. He also presents a synopsis of the positions of W. C. Smith and Paul Knitter and the metatheories that underlie each of these positions.

35. Heim, *Salvations*, 30.

36. Heim, *Salvations*, 7.

37. For two excellent reviews of Panikkar's work, see Gerald Larson, "Contra Pluralism"; and Thomas Dean, "Universal Theology and Dialogical Dialogue," in *Toward a Universal Theology of Religion*, Leonard Swidler ed. (Maryknoll, N.Y.: Orbis Books, 1987), 162–174. With regard to the former, Larson examines Panikkar's work from the perspective of the logic of its truth claims. He says:

> I believe that Panikkar's formulation of the problem of *theoretical* pluralism is basically correct. Unfortunately, when so formulated, the notion of pluralism becomes unintelligible in a two-valued (truth–falsehood) logic, inasmuch as the principle of the excluded middle is violated. The notion of pluralism so formulated is as self-defeating as any formulation of relativism and as tripped up by the problem of self-referentiality as any formulation of universalism or absolutism. (312)

38. Raimundo Panikkar, "Invisible Harmony: A Universal Theory of Religion or a Cosmic Confidence in Reality," in *Toward a Universal Theology of Religion*, Leonard Swidler ed. (Maryknoll, N.Y.: Orbis Books, 1987), 122. While I would certainly agree that Western culture has been more successful in imposing its type of reasoning upon other cultures and more successful in denying that there is any other form of reason than its own, I would not be so quick to say that other cultures did not see their own form of rationality as the universal form of rationality.

39. Panikkar, "Invisible Harmony," 125.

40. For a further analysis of this issue, one should see Krishnachandra Bhattacharyya, considered to be one of the greatest twentieth-century Indian philosophers. Bhattacharyya ("Some Aspects of Negation," in *Studies in Philosophy*, volume II [Calcutta: Progressive Publishers, 1958]) contends that there are four fundamental types of logic reflecting four different types of negation that underlie the variety of philosophical systems. Each system can be analyzed by the type of negation it utilizes. He says:

> There are certain ultimate modes of logical thought embodying types of negation which are really incommensurable and that all philosophical dispute resolves itself in the final analysis into a conflict between such types. Every system of philosophical thought or religion has its own logic and is bound up with one or other of the fundamental views of negation. (207)

This fourfold theory of logic and negation leads Bhattacharyya to conclude: "Not that, however, subjectivism or scepticism is the necessary consequence: all the types may be true and truth may be manifold. It is necessary to formulate, if possible, the logic of this view of the manifoldness of truth" (206). Positions such as subjectivism employ one of the four types of negation. In light of the density of Bhattacharyya writings, I offer his synopsis of these four positions.

> In view (i), the particular simple beings are ultimately given and are not in any way determined by negation or the indefinite. In view (ii), both the beings and their negations are given as particular and so all relations are also given as facts. In view (iii), particularity is not given but posited or constituted by definite absolute negation. This however does not abolish their dual-

> ism: their identity and their difference remain as inexplicabilities, though not as given beings. In view (iv) finally, being is abolished and absolute negation alone remains, not only as inexplicably definite but also as inexplicably self-related or self-negating i.e., as a free function or activity. (210)

It is beyond the scope of this work to further explicate this fourfold theory of negation; however, in this context, it should be noted that one may also wish to examine the work of Stephen Pepper, *World Hypothesis: A Study of Evidence* (Berkeley: University of California Press, 1972), who proposes that there are four fundamental root metaphors that underlie the variety of philosophical positions. The four positions that Pepper proposes—namely, mechanism, formism, organicism and contextualism—can be compared to the four types of negation that Bhattacharyya explicates.

41. Panikkar, "Invisible Harmony," 128–129, 131.

42. Panikkar, "Invisible Harmony," 129.

43. Panikkar, "Invisible Harmony," 130.

44. Panikkar, "Invisible Harmony," 130.

45. My comments in this section are indebted to a correspondence from Professor Panikkar on an earlier draft of this material. Needless to say, this does not mean that I have adequately represented his response or that he would agree with my analysis.

46. Panikkar, "Invisible Harmony," 125.

47. In this context, it can be added that I do not believe that one can think (at least clearly) without some model, at least implicit. The criticisms of religious pluralists that we examined in the beginning of this section indicate that the pluralist attempt to avoid using models has been deemed unsuccessful. They have models and seem unable to avoid it. Our thinking is symbolic; our symbolic thinking about metaphysics is metaphorical; and our use of metaphor, as we see in chapter 4, is only a short jump to some model, especially when one is attempting to articulate the issues surrounding such an abstract notion as religious pluralism.

*Chapter Three*

# The Debate within the Philosophy of Mysticism

## INTRODUCTION

Mystical experience, broadly understood, is an immediate experience or awareness of ultimate reality, of God, of Brahman, of the Tao, of the nature of "self," and so forth. Such mystical experiences are extremely important to our subject matter because these experiences are one of the ways in which individuals and traditions lay claim to not only having experienced the ultimate, but also to having uncovered the soteriological conclusion to human existence.[1] If mystics have experienced ultimate reality and uncovered a soteriological conclusion to human existence, then it seems that all we need do is ask them what they have uncovered and we would resolve the central issue of this book—is there one soteriological conclusion or more than one and what might they/it be? In response to such an apparently simple question, the philosophy of mysticism enters the fray with a variety of epistemological and ontological questions. For our purposes, we are directly confronted with the following questions. Are all mystical experiences really the same? Is each mystical experience different from the next experience? What accounts for all the differences or alleged differences among mystical experiences? And finally, what are the epistemological and ontological issues that must be considered in unraveling the nature and truth of mystical experiences? While these questions may raise doubts about the veracity of these experiences, there is no doubt that individuals and traditions have used these experiences as part of the foundation for their views of ultimate reality and their soteriological goal.[2]

In this chapter I address some of these concerns by turning to the work of Steven Katz and those who have contributed to his three volumes on mysticism. Their work and the responses to their work have been at the center of the debates within philosophy of mysticism for the past two decades. Professor Katz and those who worked with him have brought a contextualist approach to the foreground of the study of mysticism. Katz's basic premise is that there are no unmediated experiences, no uninterpreted experiences. All experiences, including all mystical experiences, are mediated by the background of the individual having the experience. This position leads Katz to the notion that there is no single, core mystical experience and that mystics of different traditions are different. Jewish mysticism is not the same as Christian mysticism and neither is the same as Hindu mysticism. This position is opposed by all those who hold that there is an underlying core experience to mysticism as well as those who hold that there is an underlying typology to this diversity.

Consistent with the proposal of this book and with Katz's position, my contention is that there is not one core experience that underlies all mystical experiences. Rather, the claim is that there is a diversity of mystical experiences. Again consistent with Katz's position, I would say that different religious traditions look for different experiences; they train individuals in different ways with different beliefs and different practices to have different experiences. However, I find myself at odds with the Katz position, since the diversity of mystical positions seems to correspond to the diversity of soteriological positions, which stands as the underlying assumption of this work. Such ontological diversity does not seem to be the underlying assumption of the Katz work. Specifically, we will see that this diversity of mystical experiences corresponds to the diversity of positions on the nature of the self that was articulated in the opening chapter—namely, (1) an experience of a self (soul) in relationship to an ultimate Other; (2) an experience that there is no other, only the One Self; and (3) an experience that there is no self, nor Self, just the processes of interdependent existence. Consistent with our knowledge of the impact of diverse epistemological backgrounds upon mystical experience, we will also see that these typological groupings cannot be homogeneous. They vary from mystic to mystic and from religious tradition to religious tradition. Those, like Katz, who rule out the possibility of a typology of mystical positions on the grounds that there is diversity within each typological group forget the contextualist epistemological principle from which they began—namely, that experience is contextual; and as such, each typological grouping must exhibit variations.

## THE CONTEXTUALIST APPROACH

Katz's analysis of mysticism is grounded in the long and well-established tradition, in both philosophy and psychology, of epistemological constructivism. Before examining Katz's claim with regard to mystical experience, the underlying constructivist epistemology concerning normal waking experience must be clear. In general, a constructivist position begins with the notion that individuals come to an experience with a particular background—a worldview, a culture, a language(s), a personal history, and so forth. This background influences different stages of the process. First, these personal and cultural factors influence the way people attend to their environment and therefore to those aspects of their environment that are the focus of their individual experiences. (This selection process is not only a personal and cultural phenomenon, but also varies from species to species.) Second, these personal and cultural factors also supply the individual with the categories through which a given aspect of one's environment is filtered. The third aspect of this process involves the interpretation of the experience. Personal and cultural factors provide the categories and structures in which the experience is interpreted and remembered. In other words, what is selected, how it is processed and how it is recalled are all mediated processes that influence our normal waking experiences.

Katz contends that mystical experience must be understood in a similar light. Mystical experiences do not occur to individuals who have lived their entire life in a vacuum. There are no such individuals. Each person has a cultural/religious background that has provided her with a set of linguistic terms and a worldview. Such is the case for an individual raised within a religious tradition and it is also the case for an individual raised without a religious tradition. As we see later, an individual raised within a given religious tradition learns the language, the ideas and the practices of that tradition. The Christian does not think about the Tao; the Taoist does not think about God. Each tradition provides its adherents with the filters by which and in which mystical experience occurs.

Individuals raised without affirming a specific religious tradition are nonetheless raised within a particular culture.[3] An individual raised with no particular religious tradition in India of the fourth century C.E. has a different worldview than an individual with no particular religious tradition who was raised in Europe in the fourteenth century C.E. Similarly, someone raised in contemporary New York has a worldview different from that of both those individuals. Each worldview sets the individual's sense of identity, time, space, logic, value and so forth. Thus, each of these individuals may have a different sense of time, maybe linear or cyclical; a different sense of space, maybe flat earth or round; a different set of values, human suffering is instructive or merely painful. Our cultural, linguistic, religious background shapes who we are and how we experience the world. Katz's point is that these backgrounds affect not only our ordinary experiences, but our mystical experiences as well.

At the beginning of the second volume, Katz summarizes the position on mystical experience that he took in the first volume:

> The question I tried to answer was: "Why are mystical experiences the experiences they are?" And in order to begin to answer this query, I adopted as a working hypothesis the epistemic thesis that there are *no* pure (i.e. unmediated) experiences. Neither mystical experience nor more ordinary forms of experience gives any indication, or any grounds for believing, that they are unmediated. That is to say, all experience is processed through, organized by, and makes itself available to us in extremely complex epistemological ways. The notion of unmediated experience seems, if not self-contradictory, empty at best. This seems to me to be true even with regard to the experiences of those ultimate objects of concern with which mystics have intercourse, e.g., God, Being, nirvāna, etc., and this "mediated" aspect of all our experience seems an inescapable feature of any epistemological inquiry, including the inquiry into mysticism. . . . We must recognize that a right understanding of mysticism is not just a question of studying the reports of the mystic after the experiential event but also of acknowledging that the experience itself, as well as the form in which it is reported, is shaped by concepts which the mystic brings to, and which shape, his experience.[4]

Katz is particularly concerned that we acknowledge that mystical experience is not only contextualized by the interpretative categories through which one remembers the experience and in which one conveys that experience to others, but also that the *experience itself* is shaped by the cultural and personal background that the mystic brings to the experience. Mystics of a given religious tradition are trained to look for a particular type of experience. Hindus expect to experience Brahman; Christians expect to experience God. They are tutored in all the theological concepts that are appropriate to an experience of that particular sort. Thus, Hindus of a given school are told what the nature of Brahman is according to that school; likewise, Christians are told what the nature of God is according to their Christian theology. Each type of mystic is also trained in a series of practices that are appropriate to having an experience of a particular sort. They are led to expect a particular type of experience and the experience is framed by the interpretative categories that the mystic brings to the experience. In addition, their theological training provides them with the appropriate categories by which to explain their experience to others. In this light, the mystic's experience is contextualized and mediated by that context at the various stages of the "experiential process." Interpretation is not just a postexperiential factor.

## ANALYSIS BY ABSTRACT TERMS

In order to develop Katz's position beyond the preceding sketch, five additional points will be discussed. First, Katz cautions us about utilizing a list of abstract qualities, such as "ineffable," "noetic," and "paradoxical," to develop a cross-cultural typology of mysticism. Philosophers and psychologists of mysticism, from William James to Abraham Maslow, have devised lists of qualities that they believe represent the cross-cultural characteristics of mystical experience. The assumption has been that these terms mean the same thing when used by different mystics. For example, if mystic A says his mystical experience is paradoxical and mystic B says her mystical experience is paradoxical, there has been a tendency to assume that both mystics have had the same "paradoxical" experience. However, Katz asks, why should one assume that there is only one paradoxical experience to which the mystics could be referring? Similarly, if ten mystics have experiences that each labels "ineffable," one should not assume that the ten individuals have the same experience.[5] They could have had ten different ineffable experiences. And furthermore, Katz adds, "If the terms 'paradoxical' and 'ineffable' mean anything, do they not cancel out all other descriptive claims, thus undermining any and all attempts at a phenomenological typology of mystical experience based on post-experiential reports?"[6] Katz's analysis on this point and his last question should make us cautious before proceeding down a path in which we do cross-cultural comparisons based upon these types of terms. However, Katz's analysis should also make us leery of saying that the experiences of different mystics are not the same.[7] If we can't say that these experiences are the same because we can't say anything at all, then we can't say that they are different.

## COMPARING PHILOSOPHICAL CONCEPTS

Second, Katz urges us to be equally careful when comparing philosophical and theological concepts that appear in the writings of different mystics. Katz highlights this point by discussing the notion of "nothingness." Different mystics in different traditions have described their mystical experience as an experience of "nothingness." Katz cautions us about making comparisons between the nothingness (*ayin*) of the Jewish mystic who believes in a personal God as the highest ultimate reality and the nothingness/emptiness (*śūnyatā*) of the Buddhist, for whom the notion of an all powerful, personal, creator God is a hindrance to liberation. Building on this point, Katz adds:

> Again, it is often, but in my view erroneously, argued that the Christian mystical tradition of Dionysius the Areopagite and his heirs which talks of the "nothingness," as *nichts* in Eckhart's language, is the same as Buddhist *Mu*, for the Christian mystic such as Eckhart seeks the re-birth of his soul now purified through its immersion into the *Gottheit*, whereas the Buddhist seeks *śūnyatā* as the transcendence or liberation from all selfhood.[8]

It is not difficult to agree with Katz that the doctrines of nothingness, or of any other such concept, found in each of these traditions must be understood contextually so that any comparisons must be based upon solid textual and linguistic analyses. However, we must also exercise caution that we do not overcontextualize the mystical experience, as may occur by conflating issues.[9]

In reference to the preceding passage, nowhere in this work would I argue that the Christian notion of salvation entailing the rebirth of the soul is the same as the Buddhist experience of overcoming the soul. In fact, the point of this book is that these are different soteriological experiences. However, I believe that we should be cautious that we do not conflate the two distinct soteriological experiences with the "ontological" descriptions of nothingness found in each tradition. For example, one may find that the Christian description of nothingness, as described by Richard of St. Victor (chapter 5), while definitely not to be understood as part of his final soteriological vision, may nonetheless be compared with the Buddhist description of *śūnyatā*. (These descriptions are offered in chapter 5, and the reader may then judge.) The philosopher of mysticism should neither remove from the mystics' reports statements that provide contextualization nor should the philosopher of mysticism add to the mystics' reports ideas that provide additional contextualization.

## DEVELOPING TYPOLOGIES

Consistent with the first two points, the third issue to be noted is Katz's antipathy toward the different typologies of mystical experience. He reviews three typologies and rejects all of them. In general, his rejection of these three typologies rests on two interrelated points. On the one hand, he rejects these typologies because they do not respect the diversity of experience that he uncovers; and on the other hand, he finds that these typologies lack the epistemological sophistication to handle adequately the notion that mystical experiences are contextual experiences.

The first position rejected by Katz claims that "all mystical experiences are the same; even their descriptions reflect an underlying similarity which transcends cultural or religious diversity."[10] At this point, it should be obvious that any position that tries to claim all mystical experiences to be the same is going to be rejected by one whose basic principle is a call for the recognition of diversity. Second, Katz rejects the claim that, although all mystical experiences are the same, the reports by the mystics are contextually grounded and therefore make the experiences of the mystics appear different. This position, which implies that all conceptualization takes place after the experience, fails to recognize the significance that one's prior cultural and religious experience play in shaping the experience. This type of position is exemplified by W. T. Stace, who says:

> We see that the very words of the faithful Catholic are almost identical with those of the ancient Hindu, and I do not see how it can be doubted that they are describing the same experience. Not only in Christianity and Hinduism but everywhere else we find that the essence of the experience is that it is an *undifferentiated unity*, though each culture and each religion interprets this undifferentiated unity in terms of its own creeds or dogmas. . . . The answer is that concepts such as "one," "unity," "undifferentiated," "God," "Nirvana," etc., are only applied to the experience *after* it has passed and when

> it is being remembered. None can be applied during the experience itself. (Italics in original)[11]

That which Stace italicized is exactly what Katz would highlight, but for opposite reasons. Stace does not recognize the role that one's practices and beliefs have in shaping the experience. He wants to assert that all such interpretative categories come into play only after the experience. This position is absolutely at odds with Katz's position, with the model that we are developing, and with a constructivist epistemology in general.[12] These positions acknowledge that context influences the experience that one has.

Finally, Katz rejects those philosophers of mysticism who have maintained that mystical experience should be divided into a small number of cross-cultural types. This latter position is associated with individuals such as R. C. Zaehner, W. T. Stace and Ninian Smart.[13] In general Katz rejects this last position by contending that they force "multifarious and extremely variegated forms of mystical experience into improper interpretative categories which lose sight of the fundamentally important differences between the data studied."[14]

Katz's specific criticisms of Zaehner are worth noting since they further illuminate Katz's position and provide us with the foundation from which to suggest that a typology of mystical positions is a reasonable position. In reviewing Katz's criticism of Zaehner, in particular, we see that it is possible to construct a typology of mystical experiences that is in absolute agreement with Katz's criticisms, but that draws a different conclusion from these criticisms. Our conclusion not only stresses epistemological contextualism, but also illuminates its relevance in explaining how there must be a variety of experiences within each type. In maintaining that the variety of experiences within each type mitigates against the construction of a typology, Katz actually fails to heed his own warning. Given the warning that each experience is contextualized, we should expect diversity as well as similarity within each group of the typology.

Zaehner describes three types of mystical experience—monistic, theistic and naturalistic or pan-en-henic. He recognizes that these types cut across the boundaries of religious traditions. A given religion such as Hinduism should not be imagined to embody only one type of religious experience, such as the monistic. In the following passage, in which Zaehner articulates this point, we glimpse one of his underlying presuppositions: "Thus when I argue that the monist completely misunderstands the position of the theistic mystic rather than vice versa, so far from arguing against Hinduism as such, I am arguing against a trend in *all* religions."[15] Zaehner not only indicates that monistic mysticism appears in a plethora of religious traditions, but he also indicates his preference for the theistic form of mysticism. In addition, he elsewhere makes his commitment to Roman Catholicism very clear. Katz and others have criticized Zaehner on this point.

The most crucial point in regard to the development of this project is Katz's criticism that Zaehner's threefold typology, while better than many others, is still inadequate because it is simplistic and reductionistic.[16] Specifically, Katz tells us that there is not just one form of theistic mysticism, nor is there one form of monistic mysticism.

> For example, both Jewish and Christian mystics are for the most part theistic in the broad sense, yet the experience of Jewish mystics is radically different from that met in Christian circles. And again, the "theism" of the Bhagavad Gita or of Ramanuja is markedly different from the theism of Teresa of Avila, Isaac Luria, or Al Hallaj.[17]

There is much that I agree with in the preceding passage. Our epistemological analysis has progressed sufficiently far that I would certainly agree with the notion that *Jewish theistic mysticism* is different from *Christian theistic mysticism* and that both are different from the theistic mysticism of the Bhagavad Gītā. I would also agree that the *theism of Rāmānuja* is different from the *theism of Isaac Luria*. However, we need to be cautious about the scope of our comparisons. If we are examining the mystical experience of one mystic, we need to compare it to the mystical experience of a second mystic and not to the entire mystical theology of a second mystic. In comparing mystical experiences, we should not compare "the theism of the Bhagavad Gītā" with "the theism of Teresa of Avila." There is no doubt that the theism of each of these is very different. The particular beliefs of each of these vary enormously, but is this variance not wider than the variance in their reported mystical experiences? The theisms of each of these individuals certainly influenced the mystical experiences that each individual had, but the theism of each is also far broader and more encompassing than the particular mystical experiences and, I think we can see, shows far greater variance. Here we are once again pointing to the problem of overcontextualization leading to increased awareness of particularity.

Let me restate this point so as to avoid misinterpretation. In this section, we are discussing mystical experience. More specifically, we are interested in the view of ultimate reality that individual mystics hold.

We are not comparing theisms; nor are we involved in comparing Christian mysticism and Jewish mysticism in the broad sense of these terms. In the broad sense of these terms, Christian mysticism, Jewish mysticism and so forth refer to a whole range of phenomena that certainly influences the mystical experience of the Christian, Jew and others, but which go beyond the experience. Any one form of mysticism would include the theology of that mystical tradition, the particular practices of that specific tradition, the hagiographies of that tradition, as well as the reports of the mystical experiences from mystics of that tradition. While we have agreed that one cannot isolate a mystical experience from the mystical tradition in which that experience develops, we should also be careful not to conflate the mystical experience of ultimate reality with the complex totality of beliefs, practices, hagiographies, scriptures and so forth that comprises the entire tradition.

Returning to the previous passage (at note 17), there are two phrases that I find rather revealing of Katz's position, and they illuminate the points just made. Katz said: "Both Jewish and Christian mystics are for the most part theistic *in the broad sense*, yet the experience of Jewish mystics is *radically different* from that met in Christian circles" (emphasis added). Katz's use of these two italicized phrases indicates that for him any similarities are far outweighed by the radical differences in their individual positions. The radical difference that Katz stresses certainly shows up in his discussions of the particular theologies of each tradition and the mystics that represent these traditions. For example, he informs us that only Jewish mystics would have been schooled in the notion that the covenant between God and His people is expressed "in the act of circumcision and the giving of the Torah."[18] However, this "radical difference" between theistic traditions seems to fade if one were to compare that which Katz describes as the ultimate goal of Jewish mystical practice with the ultimate goal of some theistic mystics of other traditions such as Rāmānuja. It must be reiterated that our real concern is with the different ultimate goals. Thus, our comparisons can be limited to this point. Katz says:

> Jewish mystics envisioned the ultimate goal of mystical relation, *devekuth*, not as absorption into God, or as unity with the divine but rather as a loving intimacy, a "clinging to" God, a relation which all the time is aware of the duality of God and mystic, i.e. which *experiences* God as Other rather than Self. All Jewish mystical literature reflects this teaching of *devekuth* as the goal to be sought and, even more importantly, all Jewish mystical testimonies conform to this pattern.[19]

Katz is emphatic that this understanding of the ultimate goal of Jewish mysticism applies not just to one particular Jewish mystic in one particular branch of Jewish mysticism, but that this pattern applies to all Jewish mysticism. (Its universality within Judaism, I leave to Katz and other scholars of Judaism.)[20] For our purposes, we can accept that this statement accurately represents the ultimate goal of at least one major type of Jewish mystical experience. With regard to one religious tradition, we have established an experience of ultimate reality that cuts across geographical borders and historical boundaries that have scattered Judaism. Katz's contextual analysis, at least in this one instance, has not particularized the discussion so much that he could not make the previous typological descriptions concerning the ultimate goal of the Jewish mystic—(1) it is not absorption in God; (2) it is a loving intimacy; (3) it is a clinging to God; and (4) it is an awareness of the duality of God and the mystic.

With this description in mind, I believe we can begin to unfold a different perspective on this problem. The ultimate goal of Jewish mystics that Katz describes can be compared to the ultimate goal of other theistic mystics. For example, his description is not far removed from the vision of the ultimate goal as described by Hindu *bhaktis*. We find the following description of Rāmānuja's (1017–1137) notion of ultimate reality.

> Rāmānuja's God was a personal being, who was full of love for his creation. . . . The individual soul, made by god out of his own essence, returned to its maker and lived forever in full communion with him, but was always distinct. It shared the divine nature of omniscience and bliss, and evil could not touch it, but it was always conscious of itself as an I, for it was eternal by virtue of its being a part of godhead, and if it lost self-consciousness it would cease to exist. It was one with God, but yet separate, and for this reason the system of Rāmānuja was called *viśiṣṭādvaita*, or qualified monism.[21]

Rāmānuja did not envision a separation of God and the individual soul; nor is he looking for an experience of unqualified unity. He argued vociferously against the latter as found in Advaita Vedānta. His entire religious practice and theology were centered around a devotionalism (*bhakti*) in which the notion of an unqualified identity of God and the soul was an anathema. The *bhakti* is certainly looking for a clinging to God.[22] The Hindu *bhakti* longs to be in communion with God in a loving relation with God, a relation of *śesa* and *śesī* (of master and server).[23]

There is no question the Jewish mystic and the *viśiṣṭādvaita* mystic have different names for God and some very different notions about the nature of God and the roles that God has played in the world. They also have different notions of time and space, of messiah or *avatār*, and a whole host of other theological differences. In spite of all that, there seems to be a similarity in the way each envisions the ultimate goal of mystical experience, which is understood to be a relation of self to Ultimate Other. Katz's description of Jewish mysticism and the description of Rāmānuja's system, both seem to envision the ultimate goal as a personal relation between the individual and God, a nonabsorptive relationship, a loving intimacy between God and the individual.

Following his discussion of Jewish mysticism, Katz also makes the point that Jewish mystical experience is different from the Buddhist mystical experience. Here, we are in absolute agreement. As we have seen, the former is a relational experience and the latter is a nonrelational experience. I agree with Katz's thesis when he says that "there is no intelligible way that anyone can legitimately argue that a 'no-self' experience of 'empty' calm is the same experience as the experience of intense, loving intimate relationship between two substantial selves, one of whom is conceived of as the personal God of western religion and all that this entails."[24] If we accept, as Katz and I are willing to do, that these two experiences are different, then we are led to two conclusions. First, not all mystical experiences are the same. Second, there appears to be at least two types of experience revealing two types of ultimate realities. On the one hand, there appears to be a relational mystical experience in which the individual finds fulfillment in a personal encounter with a personal Other. While Katz describes this experience as the essence of the Jewish mystical tradition, we have seen that this experience cuts across cultural and religious boundaries. On the other hand, from what Katz himself has said and from what we will see as we discuss Buddhism, there is a second type of ultimate experience associated with the Buddhist notion of *nirvana*, which is a nonrelational experience of a particular sort—namely, a nonmonistic sort.

At this point we should note that Katz himself raises a third type of mystical experience, revealing a third view of ultimate reality. In his discussion of Christianity, he tells us that there are two types of mystical experience in Christianity—a nonabsorptive experience and an absorptive experience. The former type corresponds to that in Jewish mysticism.[25] (Of course there are also differences as Katz notes, and we would expect such differences given our epistemological position.)

The latter type of mystical experience entails the overcoming of all distinctions between God and the self. This unitive mystical experience reveals a nondualistic ultimate reality. Katz goes on to tell us that Christian absorptive mysticism is unlike any other type of mysticism because of the Christological elements. Certainly, we would expect there to be a variety of ways that this third type of mystical experience is sought and that what is anticipated by different mystics in different traditions will also be different. Furthermore, the experience as the mystic herself understands that experience would have to vary from mystic to mystic within traditions and across traditions. Finally, the way that the experience is explained varies from mystic to mystic. All of this illustrates the epistemological point from which this chapter began. Given the contextual nature of mystical experience, we must anticipate that the articulation of the mystical experience of a given type will show variations from tradition to tradition, from mystic to mystic. To expect a homogeneity of experience is to lose sight of the original point of departure—namely, epistemological contextualism. The fact that differences appear within a given type of mystical experience does not negate the existence of that type of experience. It merely highlights that each typology exhibits common elements and diverse elements.

At this point, an additional reason for proceeding with the tripartate typology of this book needs to be stated. As indicated, my presentation of the holographic model for religious pluralism is drawn from three specific religious thinkers from three different religious traditions. Given what I have said previously and the way that I and others perceive the history of world religions, a typology of ultimate realities seems a reasonable way to organize these phenomena. However, even if this typological structure were to be declared absolutely bankrupt, this proposal would proceed on the merits of devising a model for a religious pluralism that integrates the positions of an Advaita Vedāntin, a Yogācāra Buddhist and a Christian theist. From these three religious thinkers, we have three different views of ultimate reality and each of these views can be understood individually by employing a holographic model. Furthermore, all three of these allegedly mutually exclusive and contradictory views can be simultaneously illuminated using this holographic model for religious pluralism. It is in light of this that I proceed with this proposal for ontological pluralism and soteriological diversity.

I conclude this discussion of our third point with a brief overview. First, we have come to agree with Katz that all mystical experiences are not the same. There is too wide a spectrum of mystical experience to conclude that there is only one type of experience. But, as Katz himself acknowledges, there are different types of experiences. We have agreed with Katz that within each of these different types of mystical experiences there are variations. For Katz, these variations indicate that the typology is defective. He maintains that difference far outweighs similarity and comparisons/typologies across religious traditions are problematic. For me, these variations within a given type of mystical experience illustrate the principle of epistemological contextualism. As we see in the next section, Katz does not doubt that mystics are experiencing some "object" or "state of affairs," even though they may not be experiencing the same "object" or "state of affairs." In light of what Katz says later about different types of mystics claiming to experience mutually incompatible ultimate realities and what has been said previously concerning the diversity of experiences that contextualism demands, I believe that we will be in a position to understand that different mystics experience and understand different ultimate realities in different ways.

## THE GOAL OF MYSTICAL PRACTICE

The fourth point within Katz's analysis that needs to be elucidated deals with the goal of mystical practice. The constructivist analysis of mysticism leads Katz to question the often-stated notion that mystical practice and experience is a deconditioning experience. According to the latter position, mystical practice aims at having individuals transcend their contextual situations by developing a state of pure consciousness. In rejecting that position, Katz says:

> For it is in appearance only that such activities as yoga produce the desired state of "pure" consciousness. Properly understood, yoga, for example, is *not* an *un*conditioning or *de*conditioning of consciousness, but rather it is a reconditioning of consciousness, i.e., a substituting of one form of conditioned and/or contextual consciousness for another, albeit a new, unusual, and perhaps altogether more interesting form of conditioned-contextual consciousness.[26]

This is a very important point and one that has raised the eyebrows of a number of scholars who contend that yoga and other mystical techniques lead to a state of unconditioned consciousness—a state of pure consciousness.[27] Some of those who have sought to rebuff Katz on this point have pursued epistemological analyses. Leaving for others to judge the success of the epistemological debates between Katz and his opponents, I would like to examine one of the presuppositions that underlie Katz's analysis and move this discussion in an ontological direction, consistent with the general direction of this project.

Examining the underlying presupposition becomes rather important in light of Katz's contention that his analysis allows us to deal with all the data that come from the different mystics and that this analysis does not assert the truth or normative nature of one tradition over other traditions. Katz also tells us that his approach is nonreductionistic. Believing that his approach does not force the evidence into any preconceived metaphysical notions and that his epistemological pluralism is ontologically neutral—open to all ontological worldviews, he says:

> Our account neither (a) overlooks any evidence, nor (b) has any need to simplify the available evidence to make it fit into comparative or comparable categories, nor (c) does it begin with *a priori* assumptions about the nature of ultimate reality—whatever particular traditional theological form this metaphysical assumption takes (such *a priori* assumptions are common to almost all the non-pluralistic accounts).[28]

The following discussion concerning the goal of mystical practice raises a doubt about the alleged metaphysical neutrality of Katz's position, because his position seems to rule out certain positions.

Returning to the first quote in this section (at note 26), even if we agree with Katz that some interpreters of mysticism assume that yoga, for example, leads to a deconditioning of consciousness, it would be problematic to assume that all of the yoga traditions of India hold that position. For example, the Sāṁkhya school of Indian philosophy, which Katz discusses immediately following the passage quoted previously, does not think that yoga leads to a deconditioning of consciousness. Consciousness for Sāṁkhya is never conditioned.[29] According to the Sāṁkhya school, consciousness is always pure, never an object. Consciousness is one of two primordial forms of existence—matter (*prakriti*) and consciousness (*puruṣa*). For the Sāṁkhyan, mind and mental processes are part of the material world, the world of *prakriti*. Consciousness is an eternally distinct entity that never needs to be deconditioned or purified. Mind and all *prakriti* are always constituted by the three *guṇas* (the three qualities in varying amounts that constitute all matter). As such, the goal of the Sāṁkhya school with regard to mind is to recondition the mind so that it is dominated by the lightest, the brightest *guṇa*, namely the *sattva guṇa*. In this regard, Katz and Sāṁkhya are in complete agreement.

For the sake of clarity it should be noted that the Sāṁkhya dualism is different from the dualism that is often presupposed in Western thought, in which the dualism is between mind/consciousness on the one hand and matter on the other hand. In that context, it makes sense to talk about "reconditioning consciousness" (or a reconditioning of mind). However, such is not the case in the Sāṁkhya school or in other schools of Indian thought such as the Yoga school or the Advaita Vedānta school.[30] In spite of the disagreements between Sāṁkhya, Yoga and Advaita about the nature of self and ultimate reality, consciousness is said to be eternal, pure and unchanging.[31] It is the mind (*antaḥkaraṇa, manas*) and the body that can be reconditioned by yoga and meditation, but consciousness cannot be deconditioned or reconditioned.

This distinction is not mere sophistry—not just a case of getting technical. Rather it is a question of disclosing one's presuppositions before one builds an argument. Certainly, the Sāṁkhya, Yoga and Advaita schools would agree with Katz when he tells us that yoga leads to the reconditioning of the mind. These schools would also agree with the notion that yoga does not decondition the mind.[32] They would agree with his constructivist epistemological analysis of mind. However, based upon their different ontological presuppositions, these schools of thought would disagree with Katz's apparent conflation of consciousness and mind. They would therefore reject the idea that a constructivist epistemological analysis is applicable to *puruṣa*, to *cit*, to consciousness. They would reject the idea that yoga aims at deconditioning consciousness since, ontologically, they maintain that consciousness is always unconditioned. Thus, until we have resolved all the controversies surrounding the mind/consciousness/matter quandary and have agreed upon the same ontological presuppositions, an epistemological analysis of mysticism will always be suspect. We must recognize the philosophical presuppositions that underlie this aspect of Katz's analysis of mysticism and the limitations it places upon his conclusions regarding the impossibility of pure consciousness.

Before jumping from the Katz bandwagon to the bandwagon of those who have been proponents of the "pure consciousness experience" and critical of Katz's epistemological constructivism, we should examine at least one such proposal. Robert Forman has not only edited a volume entitled *The Problem of Pure Consciousness*, whose focus is a response to the position developed in the Katz volumes, but he has also written a number of other articles on this issue.

One aspect of Forman's proposal to explain the pure consciousness experience (PCE) evolves out of neurophysiological studies reported by the psychologist Robert Ornstein and others.[33] In an attempt to understand the meditative practice and the results that such practice produces, Ornstein reviews the experimental research on individuals who have a visual image stabilized on their retina by means of a retina-stabilizing device. Ornstein also reviews the research done with individuals who have experienced a ganzfeld—a completely patternless visual field. In both cases, one is producing a situation in which the individual is presented with a complete lack of *diverse* visual stimuli. In both cases, there are visual stimuli but the stimuli are completely homogeneous. When this occurs, the individual reports a lack of visual experience. Ornstein compares this situation to concentrative meditational practices in which one focuses one's attention on a particular point. Neurophysiologically, this type of concentrative meditation, like the experience of the ganzfeld and the stabilized image on the retina, entails a recycling of the same neural subroutine over and over again. From this perspective, regardless of whether the meditational practice involves visual, auditory or tactile repetition, the different practices aim at producing constant stimuli and these constant stimuli will produce a state of mind that is no longer cognizant of the stimuli. Building upon this information, Forman says:

> Not merely does the recycled stimulus itself ultimately fade, but there is a complete disappearance of any sense of thinking, perceiving, and so on. All perception and mental activity come to be forgotten. A vacuous state of emptiness, a nonresponsiveness to the external world, is evoked in the central nervous system by the catalytic action of the continuous subroutine. Such an emptiness, it should be clear, is not like remembering something and applying it to form or reform visual information, rather it is more akin to a massive forgetting.[34]

And later, Forman adds: "If something is utterly forgotten, it does not form or cause or mediate or construct an experience. Hence, a formless trance in Buddhism may be experientially indistinguishable from one in Hinduism or Christianity."[35] We must ask if this common neurophysiology leads us to conclude with Forman, and against Katz, that there is a pure consciousness experience of the sort that mystics of various traditions would be happy to affirm? The response to this latter question enables us to see the shortcoming of Forman's position and revisit the problems with Katz's analysis.

Before proceeding to respond to Forman, the complexity of the neurophysiological data needs to be explored, otherwise Ornstein may be misunderstood. Having addressed this issue previously, I quote:

> Ornstein seems to say that by using the physiological techniques which can produce the same subroutine over and over again in the nervous system, that is, a ganzfeld and the stabilised image on the retina, the psychology and physiology of the mediator have been reproduced. But in actuality he does not say this. Neither does he say that to shut off visual perception one necessarily would shut off all perception of the external world. He says that this process leads to a decrease in awareness of the external world and this is analogous to the meditator's situation. It should be noted that in two separate studies of stabilized images on the retina—one by Roy M. Pritchard and the other by D. Lehmann, G. W. Beeler, and D. H. Fender—no mention is made that the subjects of the experiments lost anything but visual contact with the external world.[36] The reticular system does not have just one cutoff point but is connected to each of the sense organs. Thus to shut off one sense organ is not necessarily to shut off all awareness of the external world.[37]

This comment does not invalidate the neurophysiological analysis of meditation; it only indicates that the meditational process is a bit more complicated than the studies with the ganzfeld and stabilized image. If one is to produce a state of mind that is completely unaware of the external world, the meditational process must incorporate all sense modalities. What Ornstein and by extension Forman seem to have in mind is that one needs to focus all of one's attention into one sense modality and then that sense modality needs to be neurologically recycled over and over again. Ornstein says: "It seems that a consequence of the structure of our central nervous system is that if awareness is restricted to one unchanging source of stimulation, a 'turning off' of consciousness of the external world follows."[38] With this provision, we return to Forman's critique of Katz.

Forman's response to Katz shows that the neurophysiology and neuropsychology of experience must be taken seriously. While each individual has a different epistemological history and therefore mediates experience in different ways, it is also true that human beings have common neurological structures and processes, which can be compared cross-culturally. If the neurophysiological data teach us that, in spite of all their cultural differences, mystics in different traditions are not only neurophysiologically doing the same thing, but also producing the same neurophysiological state which is unimpeded by external stimuli, then we may be led to temper our epistemological contextualism.

The philosophical presuppositions that underlie Forman's position must also be exposed. First, Foreman states that if one follows his analysis, which includes Ornstein's research on the neurophysiology of meditation, then "this model swings the pendulum back toward the perennial philosophy camp, that mysticism is alike from one culture to another."[39] The neurophysiology of meditation may swing the pendulum back to the notion that mysticism, at least one form, is alike in different cultures, but it will not swing the pendulum back to perennial philosophy as I understand that position. Perennial philosophers not only contend that mystical experience is cross-culturally alike, but they also believe that this cross-cultural mystical experience is an experience of the One, of the nature of Reality. However, the neurophysiological research on meditation does not lead us to the One, to Reality. Rather, this research leads Ornstein to acknowledge that meditational experience is not something esoteric but a matter of applied psychology. Ornstein says:

> So we can say (within our frame of reference) that concentrative meditation is a practical technique which uses an experiential knowledge of the structure of our nervous system to "turn off" awareness of the external world and produce a state of blank-out or darkness, the "void," the cloud of unknowing. The techniques of concentrative meditation are *not deliberately mysterious or exotic but are simply a matter of applied psychology*. (emphasis added)[40]

At this point, we must ask ourselves: Are we left to conclude that while mystical experience is cross-culturally alike, it yields only an experience of one's own neurophysiological structures and states? Certainly, that would be the conclusion of any philosophical or neuropsychological materialist. Anyone holding an identity theory of mind/brain in which all conscious states are reducible to brain states would not conclude from the neurophysiological data that the mystics have an awareness of the One or Reality. This information on meditation presents us with a brain state in which external stimuli is not recognized at a conscious level because its repetitiveness indicates that it is not significant for the conscious mind.[41] These data cannot be used to establish the perennial philosopher's understanding of the "pure consciousness experience." Before one leaps to the conclusion that there is a pure consciousness experience that yields knowledge of ultimate reality, one must make specific ontological assumptions about the nature of matter, brain, mind and consciousness. The same problem that confronted Katz must be confronted by Forman.

Before concluding this section, a brief comment about the epistemologically mediated character of the pure consciousness event is warranted. If, as some of the Indian schools suggest, consciousness is independent of brain/mind and therefore consciousness can be "experienced" without the mediation of mind, then we must still recognize that when one returns to a state of mind from no-mindedness, one's mind would mediate the knowledge of the pure consciousness experience to oneself. This conclusion may leave neither of the two camps happy.

## OBJECT OF EXPERIENCE

The fifth point that needs to be raised is Katz's position on the objective referent of the different mystical experiences. Not wanting his readers to misunderstand his view concerning "the 'known' aspect of mystical experience,"[42] Katz moves the discussion in a different direction by acknowledging that

> mystical experience is not (putatively) solely the product of the conditioned act of experience as constituted from the side of the experiencer, but is also constituted and conditioned by what the *object* or "state of affairs" is that the mystic (believes he) "encounters" or experiences. To say, "Smith experiences *x*" is also to recognize that this experience is in part dependent on what *x* is.[43]

Consistent with his presentation, Katz does not spell out what *x* is. He does not even say whether the *x* is a state independent of the physiology/neurophysiology of the mystic, although that does not seem to be the direction in which he is going. Earlier in the article, in the midst of his epistemological discussion of Stace, he tells us that mystics of different traditions present incompatible visions of Reality (of *x*). He says:

> Every system and every mystic had made claims to ultimate objectivity and to discovered Reality, but the claims are more often than not mutually incompatible. For example, while objectivity or reality (Reality) in Plato and Neoplatonism is found in the "world of Ideas," these characteristics are found in God in Jewish mysticism and again in the *Tao*, *nirvāna*, and Nature, in Taoism, Buddhism, and Richard Jefferies respectively. It seems clear that these mystics do not experience the same Reality or objectivity, and therefore, it is not reasonable to posit that their respective experiences of Reality or objectivity are similar.[44]

In these two passages, Katz tells us three things: (1) there is an *x* upon which the experience of the mystic is dependent; (2) claims about Reality by different mystics are mutually incompatible; and (3) mystics do not "experience the same Reality." Unless the last statement referring to the lack of an "experience of the same Reality" does not refer to *x*, but rather to a completely epistemological, contextualized experience, Katz seems willing to entertain the possibility that different mystics trained in different ways with different expectations experience different realities, "objects" or "states of affairs."[45] This notion is consistent with his plea for the recognition of epistemological diversity. It is also consistent with the diversity of experiences that we uncover within specific mystics.

Mystics of various traditions have long recognized that there is more than one mystical experience.[46] However, each of these mystical traditions has also declared that its particular religious tradition knows which of these is the ultimate experience and which are at best penultimate. As we see in chapter 5, during our discussion of specific mystics, the penultimate experience of one theistic mystic, Richard of St. Victor, shows striking similarities to the ultimate experience of the nondualistic mystic found in the Advaita Vedānta tradition. The converse seems also to be true.[47] Thus, it may be that the debate is not over whether different realities are experienced. The debate may be over the ranking of the experiences as long as one understands these ultimate realities as mutually incompatible. However, if we return to the epistemological assumption from which we began—namely, that each tradition trains its members in a particular theology and that this training influences what they look for, what they experience and how they interpret that experience—then we should not be surprised that the theist ranks theistic experiences as ultimate and other experiences as penultimate. Likewise, we should not be surprised that nontheistic mystics, of whatever sort, devise a different ranking. This diversity of mystical experience with a variety of rankings leaves us in a position to return to the original question from which this book began—namely, is it possible that there is more than one ultimate reality? Is it possible that we do not have to rank these different experiences declaring one true and the rest not really true? Is it possible that these experiences are not mutually incompatible?

## OVERVIEW

The contextualist position as put forth by Steven Katz and others warranted a serious review not only because it represents a creative and fine piece of scholarship on mysticism, but also because this position poses a serious challenge to some of the essential components of the pluralistic proposal that is presented in this work. Specifically, Katz and company present two challenges that must be confronted. One, they challenge the notion of a pure consciousness experience on the grounds that such experiences cannot be unmediated, as alleged. I have tried to show that the epistemological arguments for and against this position rest upon particular ontological assumptions. Recognizing that the ontological assumptions are not resolved leaves the question of the "unmediated nature" of the pure consciousness experience unresolved.

The second challenge that Katz's work presents focused upon his attack on the development of typologies. I agree with many of his criticisms of Zaehner, Stace and Smart. Specifically, it seems that the fundamental criticism of these typologies is that they either mask an underlying position stressing the unity of experience (Stace and Smart) or express a hierarchical ordering of the experiences (Zaehner). Either of these moves is antithetical to the position that is being developed here—a plurality of equal and ultimate mystical experiences. My disagreement with Katz was that while he acknowledged that there were different types of mystical experiences, he objected to the diversity that each typology exhibited. On the contrary, it seems to me that the diversity that we uncover within each typology is consistent with the basic epistemological principle of contextualism from which we began this chapter. In fact, given this epistemological principle, one should expect diversity within each typological position.

## NOTES

1. In addition to mysticism, there are other ways that religious traditions claim to ascertain such information, such as revelation, scripture and prophesy.

2. About this issue Steven Katz says: "Whatever validity mystical experience has, it does not translate itself into 'reasons' which can be taken as evidence for a given religious proposition. Thus, in the final analysis, mystical or more generally religious experience is irrelevant in establishing the truth or falsity of religion in general or any specific religion in particular" (Steven T. Katz, "Language, Epistemology, and Mysticism," in *Mysticism and Philosophical Analysis*, Steven T. Katz ed. [New York: Oxford University Press, 1978], 22). Robert Gimello (same volume, 177) makes a similar point: "The truth of an interpretation of a mystical experience, be that interpretation theistic or monistic or whatever, cannot be established on the basis of the mystical experience itself." I certainly agree that, for those

engaged in the academic study of religion, mystical experience does not prove to be the evidence for establishing the truth or falsity of a religion. As we see in this chapter, the ontological referent of these experiences cannot be verified. For that matter, neither does any other aspect of religion from revelation to sacred scripture serve such purpose for those engaged in the academic study of religion. However, for the mystic and for those who follow the mystic, these mystical experiences do turn out to be reasons to follow a religion and to claim that it is true.

3. I raise this issue in the context of Robert Forman's work. Forman says that "it is not unusual to hear of an untrained and uninitiated neophyte who has a mystical experience without any deep preconditioning" (Robert K. C. Forman, "Introduction: Mysticism, Constructivism, and Forgetting," in *The Problem of Pure Consciousness*, Robert K. C. Forman ed. [New York: Oxford University Press, 1990], 20). Certainly some people are more steeped within a tradition than others, but everyone who has a language has some background in a culture and its traditions.

4. Steven T. Katz, "The 'Conservative' Character of Mystical Experience," in *Mysticism and Religious Traditions*, Steven T. Katz ed. (New York: Oxford University Press, 1983), 4.

5. Ninian Smart, "The Purification of Consciousness and the Negative Path," in *Mysticism and Philosophical Analysis*, Katz ed., 123–124, takes an alternative tack on this subject:

> The indescribability of the pure state of consciousness which I postulate to be at the core of mysticism is not *strict* indescribability. For to call consciousness-purity "blank," "empty," "indescribable" is to say that it cannot be described by any of the usual terms to signify items in or phrases in the *usual* flow of consciousness, which teems with thoughts and feelings and inner and outer pictures. Second, such terms as "indescribable," "ineffable" and so on are themselves performatives also, and help to *express* an off-scale sublimity beyond the usual rungs of the ladder of value and joy. There is nothing specially mysterious in all this; limitations on description and expression are widespread: how do you describe the sublime taste of artichokes?

6. Katz, *Mysticism and Philosophical Analysis*, 55–56.

7. Christopher Chapple, "The Unseen Seer and the Field: Consciousness in Sāṁkhya and Yoga," in *The Problem of Pure Consciousness*, Forman ed., 69–70, makes this point which essentially counterbalances Katz's proposal.

8. Katz, *Mysticism and Philosophical Analysis*, 53.

9. Sallie B. King, "Two Epistemological Models for the Interpretation of Mysticism," *Journal of the American Academy of Religion* 56 (1988): 260 ff., raises a similar issue. In reference to a discussion of the nirvana and *devekuth*, she criticizes Katz's treatment of this comparison by saying: "But this is a comparison of doctrine and does not clarify for us anything about the experiences themselves. Surely this is a case of reducing mystical experience to doctrine."

10. Katz, *Mysticism and Philosophical Analysis*, 23.

11. Walter T. Stace, *Teaching of the Mystics* (New York: Mentor Book, 1960), 21.

12. Specifically, Katz criticizes Stace for his "failure to appreciate the complexity of the nature of 'experience' with its linguistic, social, historical, and concep-

tual contextuality, and the severe limitations of his concentration on a naively conceived distinction between experience and interpretation" (Katz, *Mysticism and Philosophical Analysis*, 29).

13. In light of the discussion of Stace, it should be noted that his typology is based upon the distinction between extrovertive mysticism and introvertive mysticism. As the terms indicate, the primary distinction lies in the manner in which the mystic seeks the mystical experience. In the former, one looks outward through the senses and in the latter, one looks inward and seeks to shut down the senses. This difference does not preclude for Stace that "both culminate in the perception of an ultimate Unity—what Plotinus called the One—with which the perceiver realizes his own union or even identity" (W. T. Stace, *Mysticism and Philosophy* [London: Macmillan, 1961], 61). See also W. T. Stace, *Teachings of the Mystics*, 10, 14. This paring away of the distinction between these two types of experience is certainly not going to bring an endorsement from Steven Katz.

14. Katz, *Mysticism and Philosophical Analysis*, 25.

15. R. C. Zaehner, *Mysticism: Sacred and Profane* (London: Oxford University Press, 1973), xv.

16. Ninian Smart and others are also critical of Zaehner. Smart recognizes that Zaehner's notion of monistic mysticism is too broad an umbrella including as it does such diverse positions as nondualistic Advaita Vedānta, pluralistic Sāṁkhya and the no-self position of the Buddhists. Interestingly, Smart's comment upon this situation also reveals his underlying position: "So Zaehner should not have two but many baskets—or alternatively one, ascribing differences of description to doctrinal interpretation" ("Understanding Religious Experience," in *Mysticism and Philosophical Analysis*, 14). This criticism of Zaehner must be taken seriously and will not be part of any typological position developed in this work. With regard to Smart, we can see his inclination to one ultimate experience that becomes differentiated by doctrinal differences.

17. Katz, *Mysticism and Philosophical Analysis*, 32.

18. Katz, *Mysticism and Philosophical Analysis*, 33.

19. Katz, *Mysticism and Philosophical Analysis*, 35–36.

20. See for example, Moshe Idel, "Universalization and Integration: Two Conceptions of Mystical Union in Jewish Mysticism," in *Mystical Union in Judaism, Christianity, and Islam: An Ecumenical Dialogue*, Moshe Idel and Bernard McGinn eds. (New York: Continuum, 1996), 27–58.

21. A. L. Basham, *The Wonder That Was India* (Calcutta: Fontana Books, 1971), 335. Compare also Rāmānuja's *Vedārtha Saṃgraha* 91:

> When a person . . . has become wholly turned toward the supreme Person as a result of taking refuge at his lotus-feet . . . when the darkness veiling his inner self is dispelled by the grace of the supreme Person, who is supremely compassionate is pleased with the continual acts of worship such as praising, pondering, glorifying, saluting, striving after, exalting, listening to and declaring his perfections, meditating, worshipping and prostrating before his presence, and so on—then he will be able to attain the supreme Person by means of his devotion, which takes the form of a direct vision of supreme clarity, and which is directed constantly to him alone, who hold it to be pre-

> eminent and most precious. (Quoted from Eric Lott, *Vedantic Approaches to God* [New York: Barnes and Noble Books, 1980], 182)

Furthermore, see Rāmānuja's *Gītābhāṣya* 9:34 and J. A. B van Buitenen's analysis of this material in *Rāmānuja on the Bhagavadgītā* (Delhi: Motilal Banarsidass, 1974), 21 ff.

22. John Braisted Carmen, *The Theology of Rāmānuja* (New Haven: Yale University Press, 1974), 190, says:

> From the side of the devotee, this relationship with God is one of utter dependence and reliance on God for support. There is, in the first place, the intellectual realization that all intelligent and material entities, in all conditions whatsoever, are dependent on the Supreme Person with respect to their essential nature, existence, and activity (*svarūpa-sthiti-pravṛtti*). The highest kind of devotee applies this knowledge also to himself: "I am a śesa of Vāsudeva, with my essential nature, existence, and activity under His control, knowing that He is superior to all others because He possesses countless auspicious attributes."

23. For a discussion of these two terms see chapter 11, John Carmen, *The Theology of Rāmānuja* and Rāmānuja's *Gītābhāṣya*, 9:14: "Because of their intense love for Me, they discover that it is impossible to support their souls [*ātmadhāranam-alabhamānaḥ*] for even an infinitesimal part of a moment without being engaged in singing My names, or in holy exercise, or in obeisance to Me" (quoted from Carmen, 191).

24. Katz, *Mysticism and Philosophical Analysis*, 39–40.

25. Katz, *Mysticism and Philosophical Analysis*, 41.

26. Katz, *Mysticism and Philosophical Analysis*, 57.

27. See the collection of essays in Robert K. C. Forman ed., *The Problem of Pure Consciousness*.

28. Katz, *Mysticism and Philosophical Analysis*, 66.

29. For a discussion of this issue, see Gerald James Larson and Ram Shankar Bhattacharya eds., *The Encyclopedia of Indian Philosophies: Sāṁkhya: A Dualist Tradition in Indian Philosophy* (Princeton: Princeton University Press, 1987), 73–83.

30. For a discussion of this subject with regard to Advaita Vedānta, see Karl Potter ed., *Encyclopedia of Indian Philosophies, Volume III, Advaita Vedanta* (Delhi: Motilal Banarsidass, 1981), 92 ff.

31. It should be noted that although there are similarities between the pure consciousness experience of Advaita Vedānta and Sāṁkhya, there are also rather large differences between these systems. Advaita is a nondualistic system that declares that all is *ātman*, Brahman, the Ultimate Reality. Sāṁkhya contends that there is a plurality of selves (*puruṣas*). I am not claiming that these two systems are the same; nor am I claiming that their alleged mystical experiences are the same and interpreted differently. This proposal is attempting to develop a model that is willing to contemplate that each of these experiences is different.

32. In order to understand the Advaita position on the debate between the deconditioning or reconditioning of mind, one should examine the Advaita debate concerning the *jīvanmukti*—one who is liberated while alive. Advaita Ved-

ānta while generally endorsing this notion of a *jīvanmukti* had trouble with this notion because the liberated person had a mind which by its nature still experienced the world in dualistic categories associated with ignorance (*avidyā*). From this we can see that they held that the experience of liberation did not completely decondition the mind; it certainly reconditioned the mind and that process is, relative to the unenlightened individual, a deconditioning process. For a full description of the issues surrounding the notion of *jīvanmukti,* see Andrew O. Fort and Patricia Mumme eds., *Living Liberation in Hindu Thought* (New York: State University of New York Press, 1996).

33. Note that Robert Ornstein fundamentally maintains a constructivist epistemology, which he explains in detail. See Claude Narranjo and Robert Ornstein, *On the Psychology of Meditation* (New York: Viking Press, 1974), 171–189.

34. Forman, *Problem of Pure Consciousness*, 37.

35. Forman, *Problem of Pure Consciousness*, 39.

36. D. Lehmann, G. W. Beeler, and D. H. Fender, "EEG Responses during the Observation of Stabilized and Normal Retinal Images," *Electroencephalography and Clinical Neurophysiology* 22 (1967): 136–142; Roy M. Pritchard, "Stabilized Images on the Retina," *Scientific American* 204 (June 1961): 72–78.

37. My response to their positions is drawn from an article that reviewed and critiqued the neurophysiological data on meditation that I published earlier: "An Appraisal of a Psychological Approach to Meditation," *Zygon* 13 (1978): 88.

38. Robert Ornstein, *On the Psychology of Meditation*, 168–169.

39. Forman, *Problem of Pure Consciousness*, 39.

40. Ornstein, *On the Psychology of Meditation*, 167.

41. In the aforementioned volume, Ornstein discusses the notion that these meditational processes assist in (1) allowing us to be conscious of faint signals that arise from the autonomic system that we normally do not attend to (221), and (2) breaking down some of the normal categories by which we attend to external stimuli. He concludes the book by noting that Western science is only beginning to explore a number of more radical issues such as the physical or nonphysical nature of consciousness (233).

42. Katz, *Mysticism and Philosophical Analysis*, 64.

43. Katz, *Mysticism and Philosophical Analysis*, 64.

44. Katz, *Mysticism and Philosophical Analysis*, 50.

45. I should note that I was part of a panel presenting papers at the annual convention of the American Academy of Religion (1986) responding to Katz's work. At that time, I presented an early draft of my pluralistic, ontological response to Katz's epistemological pluralism. In light of Steven Katz's response to my work, I think it is safe to say that a plurality of ultimate realities is not what he had in mind.

46. For a discussion of the importance of this issue in understanding mysticism, see Peter Moore, "Mystical Experience, Mystical Doctrine, Mystical Technique," in *Mysticism and Philosophical Analysis*, Katz ed., 120 ff.

47. See Stephen Kaplan, "A Holographic Analysis of Religious Diversity: A Case Study of Hinduism and Christianity," *Journal of Religious Pluralism* 2 (1992): 29–59.

## *Chapter Four*

# Models, Holography and Bohm's Holographic Model

## INTRODUCTION

In the next chapter, the holographic model for religious pluralism is developed. In order to present this model there are a number of issues that must be addressed. Clearly, the development of such a model demands that we are familiar with holography. To that end, this chapter not only reviews the general principles of holography, but also reviews the history of its use as a model in both physics and comparative religions. Our focus in this review is upon David Bohm, who is eminently responsible for stimulating the entire discussion of holography as a model applicable to certain aspects of physics and to certain aspects of comparative religions.[1] In addition to understanding holography, we must also clarify our use of the term *model*. There is a wide variety of schools of thought within the sciences and the humanities regarding the notion of models. While this text is not the place to rehash those debates, the perspective on models that is adopted here must be clear to the reader.

## THE WHEEL AS MODEL—MODEL OF WHAT?

I begin this discussion of models with a concrete example in order to illuminate a number of issues concerning the use of models in general and the specific use of models in this work. The example that we will use is the rather straightforward artifact, the wheel. Unlike a computer, a hologram, an electric motor, the solar system, or a hydraulic system, everyone is familiar with a wheel. Everyone knows what a wheel looks like and everyone knows how it works. Not everyone understands how a computer works or knows what the inside "guts" of a computer look like.

The wheel has been used countless times as a metaphor and as a model. One way of understanding a model is as an extended or sustained metaphor. Sallie McFague describes this relationship:

> In the continuum of religious language from primary, imagistic to secondary, conceptual, a form emerges which is a mixed type: *the model.* The simplest way to define a model is as a dominant metaphor, a metaphor with staying power . . . For our preliminary purposes, however, the main point is that models are a further step along the route from metaphorical to conceptual language.[2]

Images or artifacts, such as the wheel, which have been used as metaphors are often also used as the basis for models. Some of the characteristics that emerge in models arise in metaphors.

Turning to the wheel as a metaphor, we are familiar with such expressions as the "the wheel of life" and the "wheel of fortune." In the latter, the qualities of a wheel are applied to fortune. Wheels turn round and round just as an individual's fortune turns round and round. The movement of such a wheel is understood in this metaphor to be constant, completely arbitrary and beyond the control of the individual. Similar wheel-like qualities or attributes can be applied to an individual's life. The "wheel of life" as a metaphor tells us that our lives keep changing, and this change is beyond our control. While the "wheel of life" and the "wheel of fortune" are different metaphors, the image or understanding of the wheel that is being employed in both of these cases is similar.

The wheel has been used in a variety of other metaphors that invoke different images from those mentioned previously. For example, coming from the Spanish proverb, "A fifth wheel to a cart is but an incumbrance," we get the metaphor of a "fifth wheel." A "fifth wheel" gives us the image of something unnecessary—four wheels are certainly sufficient. One does not want to be a fifth wheel nor be referred to by one's acquaintances or coworkers as a fifth wheel. Moving to a new metaphor, one does not want to "reinvent the wheel" or be asked to serve on a committee whose only outcome is reinventing the wheel. While the metaphors of the "fifth wheel" and "reinventing the wheel" both have negative connotations, they do not provide the same metaphorical image and they are certainly different from the notions of "wheel of life" and "wheel of fortune."[3] Before rolling on to new material, we would be remiss not to mention the "wheel of fire." It has been used as a metaphor for unending psychic suffering as well as a metaphor for the illusion that constitutes suffering (*saṃsāra*).[4]

The wheel as a metaphorical image has a great deal of plasticity and this plasticity makes the wheel ripe for a variety of uses. The wheel goes round, makes things turn around, gets in the way if there is too much going round and has been around for such a long time that we need not reinvent it. Other artifacts or images that are used as metaphors often have these multivalent natures. One could, for example, contemplate the variety of metaphorical images that surround the notions of father, mother, book and moon. In each of these instances the metaphorical vehicle has an open-endedness that provides it with a richness that allows it to be used in a variety of ways.

This quality of openness that we find in metaphors we also uncover in models. This should not be surprising since we have seen that models are understood to be extended or sustained metaphors.[5] While models are stepping stones from a metaphorical image about something to a theory about something, we see that the familiar system upon which the model is based can be as multivalent as the metaphorical image. The familiar system may be sufficiently open-ended to allow several different models to be drawn from it. Whether it be a wheel, a computer or a hologram, the object from which the model is drawn can be understood in a number of ways.

In what follows, we are interested in theoretical models as opposed to scale models or mathematical models.[6] These models are developed by utilizing some artifact or theory that is fairly well known to explain something that is less well known—the explanandum. Mary Hesse provides us with the following explanation.

> Basically, the theoretical model exploits some other system (such as a mechanism or a familiar mathematical or empirical theory from another domain) that is already well known and understood in order to explain the less well-established system under investigation. The latter may be called the explanandum. What chiefly distinguishes theoretical models from other kinds is a feature that follows from their associating another system with the explanandum. This is that the theoretical model carries with it what has been called "open texture" or "surplus meaning," derived from the familiar system. The theoretical model conveys associations and implications that are not completely specifiable and that may be transferred by analogy to the explanandum; further developments and modifications of the explanatory

> theory may therefore be suggested by the theoretical model. Because the theoretical model is richer than the explanandum, it imports concepts and conceptual relations not present in the empirical data alone.[7]

In devising a model, one takes the familiar system and one applies by analogy some aspects of that system to the less familiar situation. There is no preestablished, one-to-one correspondence between the familiar system and the explanandum. Given that the familiar system has a surplus of meaning, only parts of the familiar system can be and will be correlated with the unfamiliar system. Other parts will be ignored. It is this process of coordinating selected aspects of the familiar system with the unfamiliar system that allows us to see that a given familiar system can be used to develop multiple theoretical models.

Two points help elucidate this issue. First, in the formation of a model, three different types of analogies are postulated. They are referred to as the positive analogies, neutral analogies and negative analogies. Positive analogies are those aspects of the known system that are initially coordinated with the explanandum and are essential for the initial formation of the model. The negative analogies are those parts of the familiar system that are inappropriate for use in the model, such as the color of a billiard ball in the billiard ball model of gases. The neutral analogies refer to those aspects of the familiar object that are not immediately recognized as either positive or negative for the initial development of the model. This aspect becomes fertile ground for further development of this specific model. In developing a model, one must establish the positive, neutral and negative analogies. They do not appear in neon lights, already prelabeled, in front of the creator of the model. The creator of the model must make these correlations. While this should be terribly obvious, it is important to note as we highlight the plasticity of the object that is used to develop the model. Different aspects of the original artifact may be selected to serve as the positive analogies or as the negative analogies. Ian Barbour reinforces this notion saying: "Theoretical models are novel mental constructions. They originate in a combination of analogy to the familiar and creative imagination in inventing the new. They are open-ended, extensible and suggestive of new hypotheses."[8] As we see in the following, this flexibility in the selection process ensures that an object may be used in different ways to create different theoretical models.

The second point that must be stressed is that the theoretical model refers to the familiar object/process in conjunction with an explanation that elucidates at least some part of that object/process. The familiar object without the theory is not a theoretical model. It is just a familiar object—for example, a billiard ball. The theory without the familiar object is not a theoretical model. Following Mary Hesse, it is only this combination of the familiar object and the theory that we refer to as a theoretical model. She says:

> We can therefore make a distinction between the model as exhibited by the familiar system and the model as it is used in connection with the theory. The latter is a conceptual entity arrived at by stripping away the negative analogy, and it is only this that can plausibly be identified with the theory. It is only this that we shall in future speak of as the theoretical model proper.[9]

Since a theoretical model comprises these two aspects, we must be careful about referring to a model solely by employing the name of the familiar system.[10] Such a designation may lead us to overlook the possibility that there may be more than one theoretical model to be drawn from a single familiar system. For example, if we talk about the wheel model of the universe, one might infer that there is only one wheel model of the universe. We must recognize that one artifact can be combined with two or more theories to create two or more theoretical models.

The plasticity of the familiar system to yield more than one model can be illuminated by returning to the wheel. The wheel has been used as a model in a number of different ways by adherents of different religions. For example, the wheel is used by both Buddhists and Hindus for very different purposes. The Hindu wheel is a wheel of Being; the Buddhist wheel is the wheel of becoming; and, one might add a third wheel that would depict a theistic worldview.

The Buddhist worldview does not include an all-powerful God who creates the universe out of nothing and saves human beings out of grace. Buddhists understand the created worlds to be without a creator and without a beginning. The world is a beginningless cycle on which we are trapped by our own ignorance and desire until we overcome the latter and see the world as it is. Seeing the world as it is is seeing the world as a "wheel of becoming." For the Buddhist, the wheel is a model for constant change, for continuous flux. Just as the wheel keeps turning, so also all things within the world keep changing. There is nothing that is permanent; all things are constituted by momentary events (*dharmas*) that are related to each other in a series of cause-and-effect relationships. Dependent origination (*pratītya samutpāda*) is the law that explains the arising and cessation of all things. It is the twelvefold chain of causation, and this law of change and continuity is depicted by a wheel. The wheel is so clearly the dominant metaphorical image as well as the theoretical model of all things and processes in the universe that the three gems of Buddhism—the Buddha, the *dharma* (teaching) and the *saṅgha* (community) are iconographically represented by three wheels. Śākyamuni is the *cakravartin* (the wheel turner or wheel king), and the first sermon that the Buddha gave is known as "Turning the Wheel of Dhamma." The *mudrā* (hand posture) that informs us that the Buddha is teaching is known as the *dharmacakramudrā*. The wheel as a model in Buddhism is so dominant that one can almost forget that other religions utilized this object to create a very different model.

For Hindus, the wheel is not understood as a model of becoming; but rather it is a model of being. In the Upaniṣads, Hindus use the image of a wheel as a model to explain the relationship between Brahman, *ātman* and the world. Here, as in Buddhism, the world is not created by an all-powerful God out of nothing—*ex nihilo*. For the Hindu, the world is a part of the eternal Brahman/*ātman*. Just as one should not mistake the rim and the numerous spokes of a wheel as being separate and independent entities, so also one should not conceive the multitude of things that appear before us in this world as independent of Brahman. *Ātman*/Brahman is the self of all. *Bṛhadāraṇyaka Upaniṣad* 2.5.14–15 tells us:

> This self is the honey of all beings, and all beings are the honey of this self. The radiant and immortal person in the self and the radiant and immortal person connected with the body (*ātman*)—they are both one's self. It is the immortal; it is *brahman*; it is the Whole.
>
> This very self (*ātman*) is the lord and king of all beings. As all the spokes are fastened to the hub and the rim of a wheel, so to one's self (*ātman*) are fastened all beings, all the gods, all the world, all the breaths, and all these bodies (*ātman*).[11]

Here the metaphor of a wheel is easily extended into a theoretical model that provides its adherents with a worldview that includes an image of the nature of ultimate reality, the relationship between the world and ultimate reality, and how in misunderstanding the nature of an individual part one is trapped in the cycle of rebirth.[12]

It should be noted that in the *Upaniṣads* the wheel analogy seems to unfold in two ways consistent with the latter development of Hindu thought—in a more nondualistic manner and in a more theistic, qualified nondualistic manner. In the former, all is part of Brahman; there is nothing but Brahman. Brahman is the wheel and all are part of this wheel. In the latter sense, Brahman or *ātman* is the innermost self to which all things are attached; it is the innermost self of all.[13]

This latter sense of the wheel model also appears in Western theology. In such a case, the spokes represent the individuals and the hub of the wheel represents God. All beings in this model are drawn to the God as all spokes are connected to the hub of the wheel. Abraham Heschel expresses this model as follows:

> We do not step out of the world in a different setting. The self is not the hub, but the spoke of the revolving wheel. In prayer we shift the center of living from self-consciousness to self-surrender. God is the center toward which all forces tend. He is the source, and we are the flowing of His force, the ebb and the flow of His tides.[14]

Suffice it to say that in this theistic model, the rim and the spokes of the wheel are never separated from the hub of the wheel, but the hub of the wheel is not of the same nature as the rim and the spokes.

In the preceding cases, we have one familiar system—a wheel—and have produced several different religious models of the universe. The wheel is multivalent. It can be used by analogy in a number of diverse ways. In each case, the features that become the positive analogies are different. One model focuses upon the wheel as symbol of change; another focuses upon the wheel as a symbol of the unity of being; and the third focuses upon the wheel as a symbol of the relation of diverse natures. Inversely, the features of the wheel that become the negative and neutral analogies differ in each case. For example, since Buddhists do not envision the world as nondual being, they ignore the analogy that can be developed between the apparent parts of the wheel and the unity of the wheel. In addition, although change is not the primary feature of the Hindu perception of the wheel, it does appear as a neutral or, in this context more appropriately phrased, a secondary feature in certain Hindu contexts. For example, the *Śvetāśvatara Upaniṣad* (6:1) refers to the wheel of Brahman going round.[15] Here the wheel of Brahman which is not other than Brahman refers to the world, and this world/wheel is made to turn by the power of Brahman. In this case, the wheel is invoked as a model of change, but this change, while important, is secondary to the unity of Being/Brahman that the wheel represents. The wheel, like other metaphors extended into models, can be understood in a number of ways.

Understanding the multivalent nature of metaphors and models is essential to understanding the holographic project that follows. The point of the preceding discussion has been to highlight the fact that the familiar system upon which a model is based can often be used to develop a number of different models. The wheel as a metaphor and the wheel as a model are both multivalent. Holography is as multivalent as the wheel. It will be shown that holography can be used as the familiar system from which different theoretical models of the universe can be developed. Holography does not present us with a single model. In fact, holography does not present us with anything. Rather, different individuals can use holography to devise different models of the universe in the same way that different individuals and different religious traditions can use the wheel to devise different models of the universe.

Saying that holography, like the wheel, is an artifact/system that can be viewed in a number of different ways does not entitle one to disregard the basic principles of holography. If one is to use holography as a model for understanding the relation between religions, one must accurately reflect the basic principles of holography. Assuming the latter point as a basis, we are also recognizing that there are a variety of perspectives that can be taken in how the artifact/system of holography—from the production of holograms to the reproduction of holographic images—can be perceived. One can order and organize these relations in a variety of ways and each way can serve as the basis for a different model.

## NOT A SCIENTIFIC MODEL; A MODEL FOR RELIGIOUS DIVERSITY

Before engaging in an endeavor that tries to illustrate that holography can be multivalent and that different models can be drawn from holography, the direction of this project needs to be clarified. First, it must be clear that this project is not presenting a scientific model. There is *absolutely no presumption* that the holographic model that is presented in this work is a scientific model of the nature of the universe. The explanandum for this model is not scientific descriptions of the structure of the universe. Second, the explanandum to which this model is directed is the diversity of ultimate realities and soteriological positions that one finds in the religious traditions of the world. Different views of salvation appear in the different religions of the world. The model that is developed is aimed at explicating how a plurality of those views can be simultaneously possible. Both of these points need to be elaborated.

With regard to the fact that this project does not develop a scientific model, I am not denying that scientists who wrestle with the unresolved issues of science are continually involved in developing models to elucidate these areas. However, this project does not attempt to resolve any such quandary. There is no intention in this project to tackle scientific problems.

Because of its importance, let me reiterate this point with specific reference to holography. The holographic model that is developed here is not going to be applied to quantum physics. A physicist may wish to argue that holography can or cannot be used as a model to understand the hidden structures of the universe. Specifically, David Bohm looked for the correlations between the principles of quantum physics, relativity theory and the mathematics of holography. This is certainly a legitimate endeavor. Bohm's work, along with those who have followed suit, should be and will be debated in the halls of science. It must be clear that I am not arguing against such a practice. I am only stating that I am not engaged in such an endeavor; and in fact, I show that I am engaged in a very different endeavor.

Furthermore, just as I do not believe that the model developed here can be applied to scientific issues, so also I do not utilize the "holographic" scientific model developed by David Bohm and apply it to religious and philosophical issues. Other writers have taken Bohm's work on holography and used this material to extrapolate a philosophical perspective—a worldview.[16] There are two reasons that I am not engaged in such an endeavor. First, I do not have the qualifications as a mathematician or a physicist to judge the validity of Bohm's scientific analyses. The scientific community has not come to a consensus on this matter such that I could utilize that consensus to develop a scientific model. Second and even more significant, the nondualistic model that Bohm has developed is at odds with the diversity of ultimate realities that is found among the religious traditions of the world. This project begins with this diversity and ends with a holographic model that allows us to conceptualize how this diversity can be maintained.

It should be acknowledged that if a holographic, scientific model of the universe were to be successful, it would have, in all probability, a significant impact on other areas of thought, specifically on religious thought. It would take our thinking in new directions. We have seen this spillover effect from science to religion numerous times. For example, the impact of Copernicus's and Darwin's ideas on religious ideas are well known to all. As profound an effect as these two major revolutions in scientific thought have had on religious thinking, it must be noted that neither has resulted in a single accepted religious perspective. Certainly, the theory of evolution has transformed our understanding of the origin of the human species, but it has not led to an agreed-upon theological or metaphysical position. This theory has led some to abandon all theological declarations and to reject the notion that there is a God who created human beings. Others have not rejected God, but rather have reinterpreted how this God created human beings, abandoning the notion of a creation on the sixth day. Still others have used this information to transform their notion of God, creating a process model of God. A scientific model/theory as powerful as evolution has had a profound effect on religious discourse; however, no such theory has ever been the silver bullet that resolved all discrepancies within religious thought or that produced a single religious/philosophical perspective to which all have agreed.

This point may seem terribly obvious, but it sometimes appears forgotten, especially among the popular literature. We find books that utilize a modern scientific theory, in conjunction with a religious worldview, notably the "wisdom of the East," to produce the new scientific-religious worldview. We should not imagine that this material comes stamped with an imprimatur that will be accepted by all or that this new theory will not be old and replaced before too long. Likewise, if a holographic, scientific model of the universe were to prove successful, the debates over the metaphysical implications of such a theory would only just begin. This becomes more evident as we review Bohm's work and note some of the divergent philosophical interpretations of his work that have already appeared.

It should also be stated that if a holographic, scientific model of the universe were to prove *unsuccessful*, it would not alter this proposal. The explanandum for this project is not the scientific structure of the universe. Therefore, a refutation of a holographic scientific model of the universe would not affect this proposal. The explanandum for this model is the divergent and allegedly conflicting views of ultimate reality that are found in different religious traditions. Whether one's ultimate solution to being born into this world is to be discovered in one's soul, in One Soul or in no-soul is not an issue that the scientific community is apt to resolve. In addition, I am not about to prove, in a scientific fashion, that any one of these religious views of ultimate reality is correct. And, I am certainly not about to prove, in a scientific fashion, that more than one of these views is correct. I am only trying to devise a model by which we can imagine how more than one of these views of ultimate reality can be simultaneously possible. If all of these views of ultimate reality were, somehow, to be proven false or if only one of these views of ultimate reality was to be proven true, then this proposal would be *useless*. I say *useless* and not false because there is no assumption that what this model is attempting to develop can ever be classified as true. This model can be a useful way to understand the relationship between different views of ultimate reality. This proposal is more akin to a logical puzzle, not a scientific problem.

## UNDERSTANDING HOLOGRAPHY

Holography refers to the technique by which three-dimensional optical images are produced. It is the technique by which a light source reflected off an object can be stored on photographic film and subsequently can reproduce an image of the object three-dimensionally. A hologram refers to the film upon which the information necessary to reproduce the complete image of an object is recorded. It is derived from the Greek words *holos*, meaning complete or whole, and *gramma*, meaning to write. A hologram thus writes the whole, or we may say that it contains the whole picture. It contains the whole picture in the sense that the image of the object that is reconstructed has all the visual properties of the original scene. It appears solid and tangible. It appears to be located in the midst of space just like any other object might appear to us.

Holography was invented in 1947 by Dennis Gabor. Gabor was trying to improve the resolution of the electron microscope by devising a system that did not need to utilize lenses. His lensless method, however, needed a coherent light source to be really effective. In 1965, Emmett Leith and Juris Upatnieks utilized the recently invented laser, a coherent light source, to develop holograms. Subsequently, Gabor was awarded the Nobel Prize for physics (1971) for his work on holograms. Holograms and holography are now a part of contemporary society—from the logo on your credit card, to the scanning devices in supermarkets, to devices used to measure minute industrial stress in metals and other objects, to holographic art.

A holographic image does not resemble a photographic image. The former is not backed by a piece of paper or projected upon a two-dimensional surface. Holographic images exhibit the optical properties of our three-dimensional perceptual world. For example, holographic images exhibit parallax effect. In other words, if a hologram contains two images, an anterior image that partially conceals a posterior image, one can change one's vantage point in order to see around the anterior image and thereby view the entire second image. This multitude of perspectives cannot be obtained from photography or cinematography. A photograph is exhibited upon (two-dimensional) paper or flashed upon a (two-dimensional) screen. It is flat—it has height and width, but by the nature of its two-dimensionality, it has no depth. Without depth, there cannot be a variety of perspectives within a single photographic image. The lens captures an image from one perspective and records that image in a point-to-point correspondence on the film. As we will see, there is no point-to-point correspondence on a hologram.

A brief description of how holograms are produced will help illuminate the characteristics of holography. In order to create a hologram, a laser beam is aimed at a half-silvered mirror, which splits the beam. Lasers, and not ordinary light, are used to produce holograms.[17] Lasers are coherent light sources and do not contain the multiplicity of frequencies that compose ordinary light. Once the laser beam is split, half of the laser is used as a reference beam. The reference beam does not reflect off the object, but rather is directed toward the film. At the film the reference beam converges with the other half of the laser, which is reflecting off the object—the object or scene beam. The convergence of these two beams of light on the film creates interference patterns. These interference patterns are like the ripples created by throwing stones into a pool of water. The waves interact with each other, setting up patterns of neighborhood interactions known as superposition. The superposition—the interference patterns of the two halves of the laser beam—is recorded on the film. This is the hologram. The interference patterns that the hologram records appear meaningless. No discernible object can be discovered by looking at the hologram. (In this regard, it is also unlike a photograph in which, on the negative, an image of the object can be seen.)

In order to reconstruct an image of the original object, a laser beam of the same frequency as that which was used to construct the hologram is directed at the holographic film.[18] This illumination of the hologram produces an image of the original object by reconstructing the original wave patterns that were reflected off the object. That which was originally coded onto the hologram in the form of interference patterns can be decoded from the hologram by passing a reference beam through the holographic plate. Theoretically speaking, we can say that the superposition of wave fronts onto a film can be mathematically analyzed by convolutional integrals. These equations, such as Fourier equations, which code the original interference patterns, are reversible equations; and therefore, they can also decode the interference patterns of the film. This occurs when the hologram is illuminated by a coherent light source of the same frequency as that of the original beam. As Philip R. Westlake puts it:

> The first equations describing the hologram construction are basically nothing more than a standing wave or stationary wave interference equation. The photographic process was shown to leave the interference pattern essentially unchanged in information content. The second equations, those of the reconstruction, simply state that if the recorded wave-interference pattern is illuminated by either of the two original interfering waves, the second wave will be reconstructed in a form which is combined with the first. Thus, when the interfering radiation which originally existed in the plane of a window is reconstructed, it will propagate from the surface of the hologram T in a manner which would have taken place had the hologram plate not blocked the window surface. If the optical conditions of the construction and reconstruction are suitable, e.g., geometrices, lenses, etc. this reconstruction will propagate in a manner which will result in the construction of real and virtual images of the original sources.[19]

Philip Westlake's description makes reference to the distinction between "real and virtual images of the original sources." Real and virtual images are two types of images that can be reconstructed from a hologram. The distinction between the real image and the virtual image depends upon the nature of the light that is present in the place at which the holographic image appears to the viewer. If, at the spot at which the viewer sees the image, there exists a light source already reconstructed from the hologram, then the image is said to be a real image. A photographic film placed in the location at which the real image is seen would produce a photograph of the image. If, at the spot at which the viewer sees the image, there does not exist any light source already reconstructed from the hologram, then the image is said to be a virtual image. Photographic film located at that position would be blank.[20]

The distinction between real and virtual images reveals one of the interesting properties of holography. In holography, the image always appears separated from or at a distance from the hologram. The reconstruction of a holographic image necessitates that the image appears in a location other than where the hologram is located. It should be recalled that although the hologram contains all of the necessary elements to reproduce the entire image, the manner in which it is stored—in interference patterns—does not resemble, in the slightest degree, the image of the object that it has recorded and that it can reproduce. Therefore, the image can never be seen on the hologram since the image does not exist on the hologram. The image must always be reconstructed from the interference patterns that are recorded on the hologram. This reconstruction of the image is a projection.

The term *projection,* when normally associated with optics such as movie film, may signify either the casting of the image upon a screen or the image which is cast upon the screen. In order to appreciate holography on its own terms and not assimilate it into the model of photography, we must delineate its idiosyncrasies. First, the image is not projected from the film onto a screen as in a movie film. Any projection onto a screen would imply that the image is two-dimensional. In holography, the image appears to be in space; it appears three-dimensionally. In addition, literally, we should not say that the image is projected from the hologram. The image, as we see it, is not on the hologram. Interference patterns are located on the hologram and they in no way resemble the image that we see or the object that was recorded on the hologram. The image does not exist in any form until it appears.

A second property of a hologram that must be noted is its ability to store multiple images. Different images can be stored on the same plate by coding them at different frequencies. In other words, by using coherent light sources of different frequencies one can record, on successive exposures of a hologram, different images. One subsequently can retrieve each image by illuminating the hologram with the reference beam of a wavelength identical to that which produced it. Various images can also be stored on a hologram by changing the angle at which the interference patterns are recorded on the hologram. This capacity of a hologram to store multiple images in the same location is currently being explored as a means to enormously increase data storage in the computer/information industry. In addition, this capacity becomes very important in chapter 5, where the holographic model for religious pluralism is developed. In that chapter, the notion that different objects can be enfolded into one holographic-like implicate domain is used to postulate how different realities can be simultaneously existing.

Another fascinating characteristic of a hologram is its redundancy.

Holographic redundancy can be illustrated by the following fact—namely, one can tear a hologram in half, throw away one half, illuminate the other half and reconstruct the entire image. In fact, an image can be reconstructed from far less than one-half of the original. (Note that when smaller and smaller sections of the original film are used to reconstruct the image, one decreases one's possible vantage points from which to view the image and one will lose some detail while the depth of focus increases.)

> A 2″ × 2″ corner is cut from the 8″ × 10″ film, and the larger piece is set aside. The complete image is still visible through the smaller film, as if through a small hole in a wall. Next a 1/4″ hole is punched out and held with tweezers in front of the laser beam, projecting it onto a large screen. The image is not three-dimensional, but you can see the entire figurine. Any randomly chosen spot from the original 8″ × 10″ film will project the entire image.[21]

Each part of the hologram can be used to reconstruct the entire image because the material needed to reconstruct the entire image is contained in all parts of the hologram. This redundancy of information occurs because of the manner in which the light is reflected from the object and recorded on the hologram. It has been

> demonstrated that holograms can be constructed with diffuse illumination of the object, which has some very interesting advantages. Diffusing the light that illuminates the object effectively causes each point of the object to radiate a spherical wave, hence the information concerning each point of the object is spread out over the whole hologram. Therefore, each point of the hologram now contains information about the whole object.[22]

Thus, the whole hologram can illuminate each part of the original scene and each part of the hologram can illuminate the whole of the original scene. The information on the hologram is therefore distributed throughout the entire hologram, allowing each part of the hologram to represent the whole hologram and the whole hologram to structure each part. David Bohm states the issue:

> It is clear that there is no one-to-one correspondence between parts of an "illuminated object" and parts of an "image of this object on the plate." Rather, the interference pattern in each region R of the plate is relevant to the whole structure, and each region of the structure is relevant to the whole of the interference pattern on the plate.[23]

This characteristic of holography offers us a different model by which we can understand the nature of a whole and its parts. We are accustomed to assume that the whole is the sum of its parts; or maybe that the whole is somehow greater than the sum of its parts. The chair upon which I am sitting has arms, legs, a back and a seat. The whole chair is the conglomerate of its parts; or one may say that as a whole it has qualities that the parts as parts do not have. It is the whole upon which I sit or throw my jacket. When I have only one leg of the chair, I do not have the whole chair; when I see only one leg, I do not see the whole chair. Our logic and the structure of our thinking preclude us from envisioning that a part can contain the whole. Our experience has always revealed to us a world where each part of an object is other than every other part and where every object is spatially and temporally distinct from every other object. However, holography is a system that does not record its impressions, nor therefore define its parts, in our normal three-dimensional spatial categories. Holography records frequencies and phase relationships as they converge into interference patterns; and the characteristics of this frequency domain are not the characteristics of our three-dimensional spatial world. In this domain, each part is not self-enclosed and each part does not stand in direct contradistinction to every other part only to be united as elements within the whole. Rather, each part embodies the structure of the whole.

## AN ENTRY INTO THE WORK OF DAVID BOHM

The holographic situation, as just described, consists of (1) the object filmed, (2) the film and (3) the reproduced, three-dimensional image of the object. This situation presents us with two distinct domains. David Bohm calls these domains the implicate order and the explicate order. The implicate order refers to the film. Specifically, it refers to the unusual manner in which the information is recorded on the film. The explicate order refers to the object that is filmed and the reproduced image of that object. Each domain has characteristics that are strikingly different from the other. Given their importance, these characteristics are reviewed subsequently.

The explicate order is that order with which we are most familiar. It is that order in which objects and images appear four-dimensional—they have height, width, depth and exist in time. The explicate order is the spatial-temporal world in which each thing is distinct from the next thing. Things are separate; boundaries between things are explicit. Explicit entities can be measured and analyzed. Explicit entities can be divided into parts and the sum of these parts constitutes the entire entity. Each part is different from the next part just as each entity is distinct and different from every other entity. Insofar as they are distinct and different, they can be relational. Distinctness, difference and relationality are the chief characteristics of an explicate domain. The explicate domain is a domain in which objects and persons are defined in distinction to other objects and persons. Each object is not only defined as existing at a particular place, but each object is defined as existing at a particular time.

The implicate order, on the other hand, is not constituted by entities that are defined by particularity or by spatial-temporal relationships. Particularity and its concomitant spatial-temporal relations are enfolded—folded within the *entire* implicate domain. There are not separate and distinct entities within the implicate order. Rather, in the implicate domain each "piece" contains the whole, yet each part of the hologram is a relevant element in the reproduction of one, and only one, image of the whole. Here it makes no sense to talk about a subject who stands over against a world of objects. Nonduality, nonrelationality and wholeness are terms appropriate for the implicate domain.

David Bohm utilizes the implicate domain in order to arrive at his model for undivided wholeness. While Bohm is first and foremost a physicist trying to resolve a problem within physics, we see that he is also well versed in the language of philosophy. He moves freely between both disciplines. Among his numerous publications, some are strictly scientific in nature and others exhibit varying combinations of physics and philosophical reflection. While this book is not the place to review Bohm's career in physics or even to try to present an extensive outline of his work on holography, an overview of his thoughts on these subjects must be presented before presenting the pluralistic holographic model in the next chapter.

In a 1985 article in *Zygon*, Bohm traces his own intellectual development from his book *Quantum Theory* (1951) to his development of the holographic model. He informs us that this early work was an attempt to explain quantum physics from Niels Bohr's view on complementarity.[24] This work led him to consider the similarities and the differences between quantum theory and relativity theory. While these theories are very different and not compatible, Bohm found both theories had the notion of wholeness in common. Bohm describes this as follows:

> The basic orders implied in relativity theory and in quantum theory are qualitatively in complete contradiction. Thus relativity requires strict continuity, strict causality and strict locality in the order of the movement of particles and fields. And as we have seen throughout this book, in essence quantum mechanics implies the opposite. . . . Would it not be possible that the present contradiction between the basic concepts of relativity and quantum theory could similarly lead to a qualitatively new idea that would open the way to resolve all these difficulties?
>
> As a clue to what this new idea might be, we could begin by asking, not what are the key differences between these concepts, but rather what they have in common. What they have in common is actually a quality of *unbroken wholeness.*[25]

With the notion of unbroken wholeness in mind, Bohm found himself contemplating a new form of technology that had come to his attention—namely, holography and, specifically, the implicate domain.[26] He began to explore the possibility that quantum theory could be explained in terms of the enfoldment and unfoldment of a wave function similar to that of the implicate domain of holography. This holographic image allowed Bohm to consider that

> the whole universe not only determines and organizes its subwholes; it also gives form to what have until now been called the elementary particles out of which everything is supposed to be constituted. What we have here is a kind of universal process of constant creation and annihilation arranged into a world of form and structure, in which all manifest features are only relatively constant, recurrent, and stable aspects of the whole.[27]

As we see in what follows, Bohm's notions of physics and his insights from holography converge into a view of a dynamic universe whose undivided wholeness, which enfolds space (and time), becomes the ground from which particularity emerges.

In the context of this discussion, it is essential to see that wholeness has been the major presupposition of Bohm's work or as he puts it, "the underlying theme" of his work. For example, Professor Bohm commenced the final chapter of his book *Wholeness and the Implicate Order* with the following:

> Throughout this book the central underlying theme has been the unbroken wholeness of the totality of existence as an undivided flowing movement without borders.
>
> It seems clear from the discussion in the previous chapter that the implicate order is particularly suitable for the understanding of such unbroken wholeness in flowing movement, for in the implicate order the totality of existence is enfolded within each region of space (and time). So, whatever

> part, element, or aspect we may abstract in thought, this still enfolds the whole and is therefore intrinsically related to the totality from which it has been abstracted. Thus, wholeness permeates all that is being discussed, from the very outset.[28]

From this it is very clear that wholeness is, and has been, the central organizing concept to Bohm's thought. His vision of the universe—of all that is—is one of wholeness, a wholeness modeled upon the implicate domain of holography.

His notion of wholeness is distinct from other views of wholeness such as might be derived, for example, from the model of an organic body. The latter is a model of wholeness in which the individual parts are united in one interrelated, organic entity. The parts of the entity still retain a sense of identity and individuality in spite of their lack of independence.[29] The implicate domain of holography presents a different view of wholeness—namely, one in which the parts do not have any sense of individuality or identity as a part of the whole. Rather, each part can reproduce the whole.

This notion of wholeness from which Bohm is working has another important consequence for his overall project. He sees it as undermining the mechanistic perspective that has dominated science for the past two centuries. The mechanistic worldview is the methodological disposition for reducing the world to primary elements. It puts primary emphasis on the independent reality of the parts and is therefore in conflict with the notion of wholeness. Bohm contends that one needs to give primary emphasis to one of these two poles—either parts or wholes. He chooses wholes. Thus, he wants to reverse the mechanistic disposition with a disposition that moves in the opposite direction.

> In the prevailing mechanistic approach, however, these elements, assumed to be separately and independently existent, are taken as constituting the basic reality. The task of science is then to start from such parts and to derive all wholes through abstraction, explaining them as the results of interactions of the parts. On the contrary, when one works in terms of the implicate order, one begins with the undivided wholeness of the universe, and the task of science is to derive the parts through abstraction from the whole, explaining them as approximately separable, stable and recurrent, but externally related elements making up relatively autonomous sub-totalities, which are to be described in terms of an explicate order.[30]

Instead of reducing the whole to the parts, Bohm would have us reduce the parts to the whole. The universe is not for him a collection of parts, but rather an undivided whole from which parts emerge and into which parts return. It must noted that Bohm's approach avoids a mechanistic reductionism, only to lead us to a reductionism to the whole. In the pluralistic model that follows, neither the part nor the whole become the sole interpretative category for all experience. Bohm's model leaves us with one interpretive category—undivided wholeness.

In spite of Bohm's desire to remove all the tensions surrounding the use of the holographic model, he understands that holography and the hologram will be unable to do this. They are metaphorically limited.[31] There are negative analogies between the hologram/holography, on the one hand, and the issues that he is trying to describe, on the other hand. Three limitations of the holographic model need to be reviewed in order to give us a better sense of the particular model that Bohm is actually developing.

First, given the world of physics that Bohm has in mind—quantum mechanics and relativity theory—the hologram is far too static an image of the world. The hologram is a recording of a specific scene. Once that scene is recorded on the holographic film, it remains fixed. The world that Bohm is describing is a world of flux, a world of constant change. In order to accommodate this dynamic view of reality, Bohm says that we must replace the notion of a static hologram with the notion of holomovement. The latter refers to the fundamental implicate order of enfoldment and unfoldment. It should be noted that the interference patterns that constitute a hologram are dynamic, flowing wave patterns. They become static when they are encoded onto a piece of film. For Bohm, who envisions the entire universe structured in the manner of an implicate domain, there would not be a static piece of film. Such a piece of film would be a negative analogy in his holographic model of the universe. It must also be noted that in the holographic model for religious pluralism, I follow Bohm on this particular issue. Furthermore, it must be added that Bohm sees this dynamic structure as enfolding all space and time and, as such, as being timeless. (These last two ideas are discussed further in chapter 5.)

For Bohm, this holomovement is the fundamental order of existence. The explicate domain is derived from this implicate domain of holomovement in a manner not analogous to the hologram analogy. In the final chapter of *Wholeness and the Implicate Order*, Bohm says:

> In chapter 6 we called this totality by the name *holomovement*. Our basic proposal was then that *what is* is the holomovement, and that everything is to

> be explained in terms of forms derived from this holomovement. Though the full set of laws governing its totality is unknown (and, indeed, probably unknowable) nevertheless these laws are assumed to be such that from them may be abstracted relatively autonomous or independent subtotalities of movement (e.g., fields, particles, etc.) having a certain recurrence and stability of their basic patterns of order and measure . . .
>
> Up till now we have contrasted implicate and explicate orders, treating them as separate and distinct, but as suggested in chapter 6, the explicate order can be regarded as a particular or distinguished case of a more general set of implicate orders from which latter it can be derived.[32]

Here we see that Bohm not only declares that all that is is the holomovement, but he also makes it clear that the explicate order is to be understood in terms of the implicate order. The implicate order is fundamental and the explicate order is derived. The implicate order is the order of undivided wholeness; it is the dynamic ground from which the explicate domain is unfolded.

Related to the preceding point, we can see the second negative analogy of the hologram model according to Bohm. In holography, the object or scene that is recorded has an independent existence. It appears to have a structure that is independent of any other domain. If one makes a hologram of a rock, then the rock first exists as an independent entity whose image can then be enfolded on the holographic film. The rock is not dependent upon its being recorded on the holographic film. Nor is the existence of the rock dependent on it being unfolded from the holographic film. For Bohm, since the holomovement is fundamental and all order enfolds from that domain, the notion of independent entities provides an asymmetry between the model of holography and the world of physics as he is portraying it.[33] This point is expressed by F. A. M. Frescura and B. J. Hiley in their analysis of Bohm's work.

> In other words, in the optical analogy, special significance is given to the object being hologrammed. But in a description where process is taken to be basic, there is no a priori concept of a material object and therefore there is no substantive object to be hologrammed. As we have remarked above, in our approach a material object is to be abstracted from the basic movement and will appear as no more than a quasistable form which would arise from a reprocessing of basic movements which rise and fall (are "created" and "annihilated") giving direct meaning to some natural underlying periodicities, a notion which has considerable appeal, particularly when we recall things like vacuum polarization, sub-quantum media, etc.[34]

Bohm's position here is consistent with his position on reversing the mechanistic trends within science. Maintaining that either the parts or the wholes must be emphasized and having chosen the wholes, one of the negative analogies of holography for this understanding of physics is the persistence of explicate entities—namely, the parts—that appear real to us.[35]

The third point that needs to be clarified about this holographic model is that the implicate domain of holography does not do justice to the complexity that arises when different levels of physics are all brought to the forefront. One implicate domain is simply insufficient. Moving from the classical field, Bohm suggests that "when this field is quantised, a further kind of implicate order is introduced. We shall call this the super implicate order. The super implicate order is related to the implicate order as the implicate order, in particle theories, is related to the particles."[36] Bohm goes even further than the notion of a second implicate domain by suggesting that there can be a third implicate domain which implicates the second implicate domain. In fact, he wonders if it is possible to have an indefinite number of implicate orders.[37]

Just as there may be more than one implicate domain, in this context we should reiterate that there may be more than one explicate domain enfolded in an implicate domain. We have already noted that more than one holographic image may be recorded on the same piece of film by varying either the frequency of the coherent light source or by changing the angle of the film. In this model, we get a series of domains that are implicated into another domain in which its wholeness becomes the encompassing structure for all that has been enfolded.

Bohm's interest in undivided wholeness was not limited to physics. It reappears in his philosophical positions, specifically in three areas—philosophy of language, philosophy of mind and philosophy of religion. With regard to the first, he examines the relationship between our forms of linguistic expression and our understanding of reality. In this context, Bohm sees a connection between our linguistic reliance on nouns and our fixation with reified objects—with static objects, with a philosophy of being. He maintains that our perception of the world as constituted by static objects is concomitant with our linguistic penchant for nouns that present ideas as reified objects.[38] Entering the debates within the philosophy of mind, Bohm locates the problem of the mind/matter dichotomy within the context of the universal flux, the holomovement. All such alleged dichotomies such as mind/matter are only a projection from the underlying reality. Bohm states it succinctly:

> Intelligence and material process have thus a single origin, which is ultimately the unknown totality of the universal flux. In a certain sense, this implies that what have been commonly called mind and matter are abstractions from the universal flux, and that both are to be regarded as different and relatively autonomous orders within the one whole movement.[39]

In these issues Bohm is moving beyond the issues of quantum physics and relativity that originally formed the core of his work. Here he is engaging in the subjects of traditional philosophy. Nonetheless, it should be clear that the notion of undivided wholeness is still the operative interpretative category. One can see this in his understanding of religion as a quest for wholeness and a quest for the holy. The latter term he sees as etymologically related and philosophically connected to the notion of wholeness. It is not only the search for the hidden variables in physics that turn up the notion of undivided wholeness, but an individual's religious search also turns out to be a search for wholeness/holiness.[40]

Two additional subjects need to be mentioned—namely, Bohm's view of God and his notion of soteriology. While Bohm offers no sustained and systematic discussion of God, it does seem clear that his notion of God is not the traditional theistic position of an everlasting Being who is separate from creation. Rather, he seems more comfortable with the notion of "a universal spirit creating and underlying everything. But this is also most deeply just what is meant by the word God."[41] According to Bohm, this universal spirit would be without predicates, and as such without particularity or personality. It appears that his notion of the holy comes closest to his notion of the super implicate domain. He says:

> There is at least an analogy between how the super-implicate order organizes and even forms and creates the first implicate order and the way in which God is regarded as creating the universe (at least as this is put in many religions). I myself would prefer to regard this as no more than an analogy or a metaphor, that may be useful for giving insight, but that should not be taken too literally. After all knowledge is limited. We may use scientific knowledge to make an intuitive leap that is part of an unending process of exploration. But I do not think that to do this can provide certainty about the ultimate ground. . . . I cannot escape feeling that this ground enfolds a supreme intelligence. Although it is not quite so evident, I would say also that this intelligence is permeated with compassion and love.[42]

While the traditional theistic notion of an eternal Being who is separate from the universe does not seem to be what Bohm has in mind, what exactly he has in mind is not explicitly clear. In part, he says that this is the nature of the subject. However, he also seems to lean in a number of directions.[43] On the one hand, he seems to identify the holy with the super implicate domain, which is without particularity and without any predicates. On the other hand, he seems to say that this super implicate order is connected with a supreme intelligence that is characterized by love and compassion. While the latter is not a full-blown personality and being of the sort one might traditionally associate with a theistic god, it is also a bit more personal than the strictly nondualistic positions found in such traditions as Advaita Vedānta and Yogācāra Buddhism.

In a recorded conversation with Renee Weber, Bohm reflects upon soteriology. Consistent with his notion of undivided wholeness, he does not believe that salvation is a personal or individual affair. He says:

> Individual salvation actually has very little meaning, because, as I have pointed out, the consciousness of mankind is one and not truly divisible. Each person has a kind of responsibility not, however in the sense of answerability or guilt. But in the sense that there's nothing else to do, really, you see. That there is no other way out. That is absolutely what has to be done and nothing else can work. . . . You can see that this view may be all wrong but if what I said is right then there is nothing else possible but that.[44]

Bohm's comment about salvation is related to his views about consciousness. As we have seen, his views on the latter are derived from his views on undivided wholeness. David Bohm's interests cover a great deal of territory and his views on each of these topics are interrelated; they all seem to begin and end in the notion of undivided wholeness.[45]

Before concluding this chapter, it is pertinent to indicate that while some have followed Bohm down the path of nonduality,[46] others have objected to the implications of Bohm's notion of undivided wholeness. For example, Ted Peters, who is critical of Bohm's nondualism, offers a theistic position. First, he questions the relation of part to whole and whole to part with regard to the dichotomy between animate and inanimate. He asks: "If life is characteristic of the whole but not the inanimate subtotality, then how can the whole be wholly present in the subtotality? Is life left out? Or is it just not manifest? Does he mean to say that life is present implicately even when only inanimate matter is explicate? If so how do we know? By faith?"[47] Second, the notion of nondualism minimizes the distinction between God and the creation that Peters sees as an important part of the Christian position.[48] Finally, he sees Bohm's understanding of causality as minimizing the importance of history.[49] With regard to this issue, Bohm contends that causation proceeds through the implicate domain. Causation is not a relationship between explicate entities since these entities unfold from the implicate domain. Rather, causal connections between explicate entities, if such may be said to exist, are to be understood as occurring in the implicate domain. Peters finds this notion of causality too ahistorical and as such not in line with the historical nature of the Christian message. In light of these criticisms, Peters substitutes the notion of *proleptograms* for holograms. The former anticipates wholeness rather than presents wholeness. With this notion of future wholeness in mind, Peters suggests a notion of God. He says: "It is at the point of this defining whole in the final future that we will find God. All events are moving ahead to meet a common future, a common future that is the reality of God. There is no whole at present."[50] Peters is not enamored with Bohm's nondualistic position; rather, he is interested in reworking Bohm's insights into a theistic format. In the following chapter, I utilize holography to present a model that neither seeks to reduce all existence to undivided wholeness nor claims that the only form of salvation lies in an I–Thou relationship.

## OVERVIEW

In the preceding discussion of models, two points were stressed—(1) artifacts used for models are multivalent, and (2) the type of discourse employed in the use of a model must be clearly delineated. With regard to the first notion, I have stated that my use of holography varies from those, notably David Bohm, who use holography as a model for undivided wholeness. With regard to the second point, scientific models must be distinguished from religious or philosophical models. We have seen that Bohm was interested in resolving the problem that arises between relativity theory and quantum physics. The model that I present is aimed at providing a pluralistic perspective upon the different soteriological claims that appear in the religions of the world. These are very different enterprises. They are trying to solve different enigmas. The former tries to resolve two "contradictory" theories within science. The latter tries to explain how more than one soteriological vision can be true and yet not the same.

## NOTES

1. Beginning in the 1970s, David Bohm and Karl H. Pribram, the neuropsychologist, simultaneously worked on holographic models within their respective disciplines and applied these models to a range of issues including philosophy of mind. Among Pribram's numerous publications, see *Languages of the Brain: Experimental Paradoxes and Principles in Neuropsychology* (Pacific Grove, Calif.: Brooks/Cole Publishing Co., 1977).

2. Sallie McFague, *Metaphorical Theology: Models of God in Religious Language* (Philadelphia: Fortress Press, 1982), 23.

3. Other such wheel metaphors that one may consider are "big wheel" and "a squeaky wheel gets oiled."

4. The first reference derives from Shakespeare in which the wheel of fire dramatized King Lear's unendurable psychic suffering—"I am bound upon a wheel of fire." William Shakespeare, "King Lear," in *William Shakespeare, The Complete Works*, Alfred Harbage ed. (New York: Viking Press, 1969), Act 4, Scene 7, ll. 46–47. This image can be traced back to Ixion, who was bound to a wheel in Hades forever. The second reference derives from Indian thought in which a whirling firebrand produces the illusion of a continuous wheel of fire. For example, see *Māṇḍūkya Kārikā*, 4:47–51.

5. McFague, *Metaphorical Theology*, 83.

6. For a discussion of the different types of models, Max Black (*Models and Metaphors: Studies in Language and Philosophy* [Ithaca, N.Y.: Cornell University Press, 1962]) still offers a very clear presentation with sufficient examples to illuminate the different types.

7. Mary Hesse, "Models and Analogy in Science," *The Encyclopedia of Philosophy*, vol. 5, Paul Edwards ed. (New York: Macmillan and Free Press, 1967), 356.

8. Ian Barbour, *Myths, Models and Paradigms: A Comparative Study in Science and Religion* (New York: Harper and Row, 1974), 47–48.

9. Hesse, "Models and Analogy in Science," 356.

10. Ian Barbour's description of models presents this issue as follows:

> A theoretical model, then, is an imagined mechanism or process, postulated by analogy with familiar mechanisms or processes and used to construct a theory to correlate a set of observations. I will call the source of the analogy "the familiar system," where "familiar" means better understood rather than everyday. The model drawn from the familiar system suggests a theory. It also suggests possible relationships between some of the terms of the theory and some observation terms; these correlations linking theory and observation are called "rules of correspondence." A theoretical model, in short, is used to generate a theory to explain the behaviour of an observable system. (Barbour, *Myths, Models and Paradigms*, 30–31)

It seems that what Hesse and I are referring to as the theoretical model—namely, "the model as it is used in connection with the theory"—is what Barbour refers to as the familiar system postulated by analogy to an unfamiliar system.

11. Patrick Olivelle trans., *Upaniṣads* (Oxford: Oxford University Press, 1996), 32. See also *Kauṣītaki Upaniṣad*, 3.8.

12. With regard to this last point, see *Praśna Upaniṣad* 6.6: "In whom the parts are fixed, as spokes on a hub—You should know that person, who is to be known, so that death may not disturb you" (Olivelle, *Upaniṣads*, 287).

13. One can consult a number of passages, such as *Śvetāśvatara Upaniṣad* 1:4 and the *Muṇḍaka Upaniṣad* 2.2.10, that utilize the wheel metaphor. The interpretation of these passages is often debated.

14. Abraham Heschel, *Quest for God: Studies in Prayer and Symbolism* (New York: Crossroads, 1982), 7.

15. *Śvetāśvatara Upaniṣad* 6.1: "It is rather the greatness of God present in the world by means of which this wheel of *brahman* goes around" (Olivelle, *Upaniṣads*, 263).

16. See, for example, Robert M. Anderson Jr., "A Holographic Model of Transpersonal Consciousness," *Journal of Transpersonal Psychology* 9 (1977): 119–128; John A. Schumacher, "Prolegomena to Any Future Inquiry: A Paradigm of Undivided Wholeness," *International Philosophical Quarterly* 21 (1981): 439–457; Jennifer Wade, *Changes of Mind: A Holonomic Theory of the Evolution of Consciousness* (Albany: State University of New York Press, 1996); and Michael Talbot, *Beyond the Quantum* (Toronto: Bantam Books, 1988). Other authors who have utilized holography are discussed in this chapter and in the next.

17. It should be noted that there are several different types of holograms. The methods of production and reproduction vary according to exact type. My purpose here is only to give an overview.

18. Actually, it should be noted that a holographic image can be made to appear using any "reasonably coherent" light source as a reference beam. For example, the light from an ordinary lightbulb, which is not in phase, can be used to present a holographic image. The clarity of the image is better with a coherent light source.

19. Philip R. Westlake, "The Possibilities of Neural Holographic Processes within the Brain," *Kybernetik* 7 (1970): 136.

20. For a discussion of how these two types of images are produced, see Stephen Kaplan, *Hermeneutics, Holography and Indian Idealism* (Delhi: Motilal Banarsidass, 1987), 18 ff.

21. "Notes on Holography," Lawrence Hall of Science (Berkeley, California, 1978), 1.

22. Howard K. Smith, *Principles of Holography* (New York: Wiley-Interscience, 1969), 21–22.

23. David Bohm, "Quantum Theory As an Indication of a New Order in Physics: Part B," *Foundation of Physics* 3 (1973): 145.

24. Bohm describes the history of his intellectual development in "Hidden Variables and the Implicate Order," *Zygon* 20 (1985): 111–117; and "Quantum Theory As an Indication of an New Order in Physics. Part A: The Development of New Orders As Shown through the History of Physics," *Foundations of Physics* 1 (1971): 368–379.

25. D. Bohm and B. J. Hiley, *The Undivided Universe: An Ontological Interpretation of Quantum Theory* (London: Routledge, 1993), 351–352.

26. Bohm also contemplated a device he had seen on a British Broadcasting Corporation television program in which ink drops are placed in a cylinder of glycerine and then turned a number of times. The ink drops become spread throughout the cylinder upon the turning of the device. When the device is turned in the opposite direction the ink drops are reconstituted. The ink drops in both states illustrated for Bohm a sense of order that he also uncovered in holography. "Hidden Variables and the Implicate Order," 117–118.

27. Bohm, "Hidden Variables and the Implicate Order," 120.

28. Bohm, *Wholeness and the Implicate Order* (London: Routledge and Kegan Paul, 1980), 172.

29. This notion of wholeness has been used to develop theistic models. We have seen this in our discussion of Rāmānuja.

30. Bohm, *Wholeness and the Implicate Order*, 178–179; see also Bohm's comments on mechanism in "The Implicate Order: A New Approach to the Nature of Reality," in *Beyond Mechanism: The Universe in Recent Physics and Catholic Thought*, David L. Schindler ed. (Lanham, Md.: University Press of America, 1986), 35.

31. In light of the previous discussion of models, it should be noted that Bohm holds the position that the use of metaphors and models in science is a legitimate endeavor. He says: "However, in science it is essential to unfold the meaning of the metaphor in even greater and more 'literal' detail, while in poetry the metaphor may remain relativity implicit" (David Bohm and F. David Peat, *Science, Order, and Creativity* [Toronto: Bantam Books, 1987], 33).

32. Bohm, *Wholeness and the Implicate Order*, 178.

33. This limitation of the holographic model is also a limitation in the other model that Bohm often draws upon—the ink drops in the glycerine. He says:

> It must be pointed out that the specific analogies of the ink drop and the hologram are limited and do not fully convey all that is meant by the implicate order. What is missing is the fact that the parts or subwholes not only unfold from the whole, but they unfold in a self-organizing and stable way. On the other hand, in both these models, there is no inner principle of organization that determines the parts of subwholes and makes them stable. In fact, the order enfolded in the whole is obtained from pre-existent, separate, and extended elements (objects photographed in the hologram or ink drops injected into the glycerine). (Bohm, "Hidden Variables and the Implicate Order," 119)

34. F. A. M. Frescura and B. J. Hiley, "The Implicate Order, Algebras, and the Spinor," *Foundations of Physics* 10 (1980): 14.

35. This issue reappears in the next section in which the pluralistic model of holography is presented. A pluralistic holographic model cannot be developed unless both the parts and the wholes are given equal status. It should be noted that there are a number of other scholars who have been critical of Bohm's perspective of this point. For example, see Robert John Russell, "The Physics of David Bohm and Its Relevance to Philosophy and Theology," *Zygon* 20 (1985): 145–147. Russell questions how well Bohm's perspective handles issues related to gravitational physics, cosmology, evolution and the direction of time. Ted Peters, "David

Bohm, Postmodernism, and the Divine" (same volume as preceding), also raises questions related to the distinction between the animate and the inanimate (202) and what he sees as a reversal of the composition fallacy—"namely, the fallacy of division when the properties of the whole are attributed without warrant to the parts" (208). In light of these points, Peters says:

> What Bohm wants to affirm is unity, wholeness. Whatever unity or wholeness there is, then, is a quality that by definition belongs not to the parts but to the whole. The parts even just formally cannot contain all the qualities of the whole. It seems that the holographic model might be leading Bohm away from his target, because this model implies that all of the qualities of the whole are exhaustively present in the part. (208)

While I would be hesitant to agree with Peters that holography is leading Bohm away from Bohm's own target or notion of wholeness, I would agree that the notion of wholeness that Bohm articulates presents problems. The pluralistic holographic model takes a very different perspective on this issue.

36. D. Bohm and B. J. Hiley, *The Undivided Universe: An Ontological Interpretation of Quantum Theory* (London: Routledge, 1993), 379.

37. Bohm and Hiley, *The Undivided Universe*, 380.

38. For a discussion of this, see Bohm, *Wholeness and the Implicate Order*, ch. 2.

39. Bohm, *Wholeness and the Implicate Order*, 53.

40. Bohm, *Wholeness and the Implicate Order*, 3.

41. David Bohm, "Fragmentation and Wholeness in Religion and Science," *Zygon* 20 (1985): 131–132.

42. Bohm, "Hidden Variables and the Implicate Order," 123–124.

43. David Griffin believes that Bohm is expressing three different views on this subject ("Bohm and Whitehead on Wholeness, Freedom, Causality, and Time," in *Physics and the Ultimate Significance of Time*, David Griffin ed. [New York: State University of New York Press, 1986], 136–140). This lack of clarity also seems to spill over to the interpretation of Bohm's views by different scholars. For example, Kevin Sharpe ("Holomovement, Metaphysics and Theology," *Zygon* 28 [1993]: 53) is critical of Robert John Russell's interpretation of Bohm. The original lack of clarity may arise in Bohm himself. For Robert John Russell, see: "The Physics of David Bohm," 135–157.

44. Bohm, "The Enfolding-Unfolding Universe: A Conversation with David Bohm," conducted by Renee Weber, *RE-VISION* 1 (1978): 41.

45. An issue not discussed in this chapter that needs to be mentioned is the notion of timelessness and freedom. If there is no time—if time is enfolded—then how can we account for freedom? These issues are extensively discussed in a series of articles collected in David Griffin ed., *Physics and the Ultimate Significance of Time*.

46. See note 16.

47. Ted Peters, "David Bohm, Postmodernism, and the Divine," *Zygon* 20 (1985): 202.

48. Peters states: "The problem with monism in all its forms is that it denies the Christian belief in a radical distinction between God and the creation. This

distinction functions to affirm divine ultimacy. God transcends the world. This means among other things that the creature can never become totally divine" (Peters, "David Bohm, Postmodernism, and the Divine," 212).

49. Peters, "David Bohm, Postmodernism, and the Divine," 212. On this issue, see also Robert John Russell, who says: "What is the basis for time and time's arrow, an explicitly asymmetric feature of the explicate order, if the dominating ontology is the highly systematic implicate order? Surely such asymmetries as time, history, evolution, entropy, and so on, are more than mere distortions of an underlying massive symmetry" (Russell, "The Physics of David Bohm," 145).

50. Peters, "David Bohm, Postmodernism, and the Divine," 215.

## *Chapter Five*

# A Proposal for a Pluralistic Ontology and Soteriology

### REFLECTIONS UPON THE FIRST FOUR CHAPTERS

In this chapter, I intend to lay out the holographic model for religious pluralism. As indicated, this model illuminates how there can be a plurality of ultimate realities and a concomitant plurality of soteriological experiences. In other words, I hope to illustrate how different people can achieve different ultimate goals. These ultimate goals are sustained by a pluralism of ontological possibilities. Individuals with different religious beliefs engage in different religious practices, expect different experiences, report having different experiences and seek different soteriological goals. This proposal is an attempt to illuminate how, at least, some of this diversity could be simultaneously true and equal.

Once again, this proposal does not guarantee that these different positions are true. I am only trying to illuminate how these diverse positions found among the different religious traditions of the world can be integrated into one system. Each of the individual religious traditions from which the different soteriological positions are drawn asserts that only its vision is true. They may all be true; they may all be false. One may be true and the others all false. All or some may contain some level of truth and some level of error. The truth or falsity of any religious tradition is beyond the knowledge of this author. My goal in this project is not to make pronouncements of truth, but rather to present a model in which the truth of one religious tradition need not demand that the truths of other traditions are false.

As we have seen, the notion that different individuals achieve/realize different ultimate realities is, to say the least, an idea without a great deal of support. While many seem to find some form of epistemological pluralism, such as is offered by Professor Hick, intriguing, the notion of ontological pluralism seems to strike people as bizarre, as contradictory, as simply not feasible. However, it strikes me that the alternatives are also odd. Essentially, the alternatives are (1) to claim that one religious tradition has the truth and the vast majority of people in the world are wrong; or (2) that no one is truly right and therefore all religious individuals are wrong. That people find it more comforting to think that all of the people are wrong or that the vast majority of the people are wrong than to think that more than one group of people could be right strikes me as very interesting. Therefore, as I begin to lay out the possibility that there is more than one ultimate truth, I ask the reader to entertain the possibility that the universe may allow for more diversity and more truths than traditionally imagined.

In the preceding chapters, I have tried to lay the foundation for this proposal. In chapter 2, we saw that the notion that there can be more than one ultimate reality need not be contradictory. By distinguishing ultimate reality and metaphysics, I have raised the possibility that there can be more than one ultimate reality in a given metaphysical system. In addition, we saw that it would be possible to develop a model for religious pluralism as long as that model utilized more than one form of reason and so long as the model did not itself become a higher form of ultimate reality and soteriology. Since the holographic model that is presented does not itself offer a view of salvation or liberation in addition to those found in the religious traditions of the world, one need not worry that this model usurps the ultimacy of those positions. Finally, our analysis of the contextual nature of mystical experience led us to the conclusion that there was not a single underlying core experience to all mystical experience. Furthermore, in the rejection of the core experience notion, I came to the conclusion that there are a number of different types of mystical experiences. Each type of mystical experience exhibits a diversity of expressions since each experience incorporates the contextual situations from which it arose. Thus, the contextualist position does not destroy the possibility of a typology of mystical experiences, but rather, it illuminates the diversity that is found within each of the typological positions.

## REFLECTIONS ON OTHER ANALOGIES

Before developing this holographic model, several issues related to other models must be clarified. First, it must be reiterated that a hologram is no more metaphysical than a wheel. It may serve as the basis for a model about any number of things from metaphysics to poetry to neuropsychology to quantum physics. Second, like the wheel, a hologram presents us with a concrete yet fluid image from which one can articulate a number of metaphysical models. Just as the wheel has been employed by both Hindu *ātmavādins* and Buddhist *anātmavādins* and can serve as a model for theists as well, a hologram may be employed in different ways. A hologram, like the wheel, is multivalent. Third, it is my contention that a hologram is a more powerful image for this model than the wheel.

In the following, the discussion is not limited to the hologram—to the film on which the information is stored. While incorporating the hologram, our discussion includes the process of holography. As in the development of other models, not all aspects of holography and the hologram are equally emphasized.

Three characteristics of holography that appear to make it a more potent analogy than the wheel can be noted. First, holography provides us with the unusual characteristic of redundancy whereby each piece of the film can reproduce the entire image. This notion is radically different from a wheel, where each piece of the wheel is different from the next piece and no piece can reproduce the whole. This characteristic of holography is effective in understanding some of the characteristics of the *ātmavāda*, nondualistic position in which there is only one Self in spite of the appearance of difference. Second, the holographic film does not present the same subject–object dichotomies that appear in the images that it produces. When we try to understand, for example, some of the notions of emptiness (*śūnyatā*) associated with the *anātmavāda* position, this lack of subject–object characteristics in the implicate domain proves very helpful. Third, the notion that multiple explicate domains can be enfolded into one implicate domain allows us to conceptualize the relationship between God and the world in a way that the wheel and the hub do not do. This very sketchy outline of some of the advantages of the holographic model over the wheel model is developed more fully in the next section.

I also believe that the holographic model is a more effective model than the dominant models associated with some of the traditions I am exploring. In the following pages, I review the ideas of Gauḍapāda, the *ātmavādin*, Vasubandhu, the *anātmavādin*, and Richard of St. Victor, the theist. Each of these thinkers utilizes specific analogies to illustrate a position.[1] Gauḍapāda uses the analogy of the rope and the snake. Vasubandhu uses the analogy of the magician and the magically created elephant. Richard of St. Victor uses the analogy of the ark with two cherubs. A few brief comments begin to highlight the unusual characteristics of holography as well as illuminate why I believe that it is a more powerful analogy than those traditionally used. (It must be noted that the analogies that were used were the best that those individuals had available. Had each of these individuals been familiar with holography, I believe that they would have perceived the power of this analogy.)

The first analogy is the rope–snake analogy of the Advaita Vedānta tradition of Gauḍapāda. In this analogy, an individual walking through a forest sees a snake and reacts in fright to this experience. Upon reflection, the individual comes to realize that there was no snake; there was only a rope. By analogy, the snake is compared to the appearance of the phenomenal world—to all the experiences of the individual in a world of separate objects. The rope is compared to the real (Brahman), to the Being of the universe that is one without a second. As long as one experiences the snake (appearances), one does not know the rope (Being, Brahman).

This analogy has certainly served the Advaita tradition well in explaining how an appearance can mask the true nature of the real. However, the rope has no special characteristics and therefore it cannot illuminate the unusual characteristics of Brahman in the way that a hologram can. For example, each strand and piece of the rope is different from every other strand and piece of the rope. In addition, when the rope is seen, the snake is no longer seen. This may lead some to imagine that once Brahman is known, phenomenal existence is no longer experienced. Brahman is eternal; it does not come into existence when it is known; and the phenomenal world as *māyā* does not cease its phenomenal appearance once one has experienced Brahman. There is no before and after sequences between Brahman and the world as there is with the rope–snake analogy.[2] Holography with its simultaneous domains can be shown to illustrate how the nondual structure can exist simultaneously with the appearance of a holographic image, which does not really exist; it only appears to exist.

The second analogy is the Buddhist analogy of the elephant created by a magician. In this analogy, by means of a *mantra* (sacred formula), a magician can make an elephant appear in place of a piece of wood.[3] The audience experiences the former not the latter. Vasubandhu uses this example to illustrate the three-nature doctrine of Yogācāra Buddhism. The first nature (*parikalpita svabhāva*), the purely imagined nature, is associated with the elephant and the assumption that the elephant is real. The second nature is the relative nature (*paratantra svabhāva*)—the causes and conditions given which something can appear. This nature is associated with the form of the elephant and the conditions given which the elephant can appear. The third nature is the perfected nature (*parinispanna svabhāva*). This nature is associated with the nonexistence of the elephant, the existence of the wood, and it is associated with the realization of nirvana.

As in the case of the rope in the rope–snake analogy, the wood lacks the unusual characteristics of the *paratantra* and *parinispanna* natures. For example, the *paratantra* nature is said to be the causes and conditions by which all things appear. The wood is only part of the causes and certainly not the most active part in the example of the magician's elephant. In contrast, these natures can be illuminated more fully by the implicate domain of holography, which is the causes and conditions given which images can appear yet is itself without images and objects. Its nondualistic structure mirrors the nondualistic structure of the *paratantra* nature. Furthermore, in the case of holography, one can experience holography and analyze the component parts of holography simultaneously. In the magician's elephant, we need a magician to perform this feat of magic, and when the feat of magic is performed, we cannot be both subject of the experience and analyzer of the experience.

Richard of St. Victor uses the analogy of two cherubs sitting on top of the ark in order to discuss six levels of contemplation. The last two levels of contemplation entail mystical insights and are represented by two cherubs that stand facing each other. These two contemplations pertain to the two aspects of the divine nature—the oneness of God and the Trinity of God. One of the cherubs represents that aspect of divinity that is above reason, the Fifth Contemplation. This is the oneness of God. The other cherub represents that which is not only above reason, but beyond reason, the Sixth Contemplation. This is the Trinity. The Sixth Contemplation is above and beyond reason not because the Trinity is itself above and beyond reason, but because in light of the Fifth Contemplation, the unity of God, the Sixth appears to be above and beyond reason.

While the entire notion of the mystical ark with the two cherubs provides Richard with an enormous amount of latitude in developing his mystical theology, these final two contemplations represented by the two cherubs do not adequately portray the complexity of what Richard wants to convey. Richard himself informs us that he could find no similitude in the created world by which to envision these two aspects of divinity—namely, its Unity and its Trinity—or their relationship with creation.

Simultaneously explaining unity and multiplicity is a quandary. Furthermore, explaining how some of the diversity—namely, the Trinity—while not being different from the Unity, is different from the created world is an even greater quandary for Richard. I believe that holography provides us with a similitude within the created world by which we can envision how these diverse characteristics can be simultaneously existing—how the Fifth and Sixth Contemplations may be above and beyond reason, but not above nor beyond the analogy of holography. In the latter, we can illustrate how the implicate and explicate domains are simultaneously existing and mutually interpenetrating, yet not the same. Exploring that notion in conjunction with the possibilities that there can be more than one explicate domain enfolded into an implicate domain allows us to envision the enigmas that Richard of St. Victor sets before us. With more than one explicate domain enfolded into the unity of the implicate domain, one can envision how the Trinity can be one in substance with the unity of God, yet different from the created world, which would be an alternative explicate domain.

In closing this section, this holographic model should also be distinguished from the famous Jain story of the blind men and the elephant. In this story, a king assembles five blind men in front of an elephant. Each man touches a part of the elephant and each declares that the piece that they have touched is the nature of the whole object. For example, one man grabs the trunk of the elephant and declares that the object is a huge snake. Another blind man touches the leg of the elephant and declares that the object is a tree. Each man mistaking the part of the elephant for an object other than an elephant begins to argue with the other men about the nature of the object. They are obviously all wrong. The holographic model should not be conflated with this story. In the Jain story, each blind man experiences only one part of the elephant and that part is always only a part. The Jain analogy illustrates not only the partial nature of each of their perspectives, but the inadequate nature of each of their individual perceptions for an understanding of the whole. In this holographic model, while the perception of one of the holographic domains may not be a perception of all domains, the realization of one holographic domain is not inadequate—it will be correlated with that which is soteriologically effective.

## THREE PRESUPPOSITIONS

Underlying the development of this holographic model for pluralism are three presuppositions. Without these three presuppositions I could not develop this model for soteriological pluralism; a different model would be developed. These presuppositions allow us to look at holography in a particular manner and that manner allows us to conceptualize a pluralism of soteriological possibilities. For those who contend that such a procedure is circular reasoning, I agree. This model does not prove that there is a plurality of ultimate realities and it is not intended to prove that point. Instead, this model illuminates how a plurality of ultimate realities can be simultaneously existing and equal. The presuppositions that are being described presuppose a plurality of ultimate realities.

First, this holographic model presupposes that each of the holographic domains—namely, the implicate domain and the explicate domain—demand each other and that neither is ontologically more fundamental than the other. In the holographic situation, images are projected from an implicate domain in which these images do not exist. What exists on the holographic film are the interference patterns that in no way resemble the object that is recorded. These interference patterns are those that are created in the process of recording an image of an object. In this description, we see that there are objects, interference patterns and reproduced holographic images. The first and the third are explicate in nature; while the second corresponds to what Bohm has called the implicate domain. In this description, their relationship is symbiotic. There would be nothing enfolded in the implicate domain if there were no explicate entities. Equally so, as regards this holographic model, all explicate images/objects must be enfolded in an implicate domain. In light of this analysis, I am proposing that neither the implicate nor the explicate domain be viewed as more fundamental than the other.

Within this schema, it is legitimate to propose that there can be more than one implicate domain or more than one explicate domain. In such cases, it is conceivable that one implicate domain would be more fundamental than another implicate domain.[4] Equally so, it is conceivable that one explicate domain is more fundamental than another explicate domain. However, such a situation would not alter the basic relationship between that which is implicate and that which is explicate.

This presupposition that I am adopting here allows us to illuminate a greater variety of soteriological positions. Alternatively, if one envisions that one of these two domains is more fundamental, then we lessen the diversity of ultimate realities. For example, if we presuppose that an implicate domain is more fundamental than the explicate domains, then the characteristics of "undivided wholeness" take precedent over the characteristics of particularity and relationship. As such, by emphasizing the implicate domain, one ends up with some version of nondualism, and a theistic ultimate reality would be excluded. On the other hand, if we contend that the basic categories of reality refer to those things that can be identified, that is, explicit entities, then we lay our emphasis on the explicate domains. As such, one can develop some form of dualistic, possibly theistic, metaphysics, but nondualistic ultimate realities would be excluded. Therefore, in order to devise a model that includes dualistic and nondualistic traditions, we will assume that the implicate and the explicate domains logically demand each other.

As noted, the position that I am taking here is distinguished from the position of David Bohm. While Bohm acknowledges that the implicate and the explicate domains "are correlative categories, and that each implies the other,"[5] he proceeds to suggest that "these two categories are not completely symmetrical in their relationships. That is to say, *ultimately*, the wholeness of the whole and the parts is the major or dominant factor, while their partiality is a minor one."[6] As we have seen in the previous chapter, wholeness has been the underlying theme of Bohm's work. We saw it emerging in his early work reconciling quantum physics and relativity theory; and clearly, it was the major presupposition of his latter work. As a mathematical description of quantum physics, the notion of undivided wholeness may take precedent over the explicate entities. However, we will have to await the consensus of the scientific community to see if Bohm's interpretation is generally accepted. In addition, as Bohm himself notes, metaphysics needs to be distinguished from physics.[7] Therefore, even if we settled the scientific issue concerning which domain is mathematically more fundamental, we would still not have settled the metaphysical debates. We would still have to determine that that which is mathematically more fundamental is also metaphysically more fundamental. Furthermore, we would have to determine, somehow, that in addition to the alleged fundamental whole of the implicate domain, there was no agent, such as God, who put this all into play. Essentially, the assumption that that which is mathematically more fundamental is metaphysically more fundamental seems to me to be a form of reductionism. This would be a reductionism of parts to the whole, rather than a reductionism of wholes to parts.

The second presupposition of this proposal concerns the spatial relation between these different domains. As a metaphysical model, the implicate and explicate domains cannot be spatially separate. It should be acknowledged that in the optical holographic situation the implicate and the explicate domains *appear* separate. The explicate holographic image always appears projected away from the implicate holographic film since the film does not contain any images. The image may appear in front of the holographic film; it may appear behind the holographic film; but, since the film is two-dimensional and the holographic image appears as a three-dimensional image, they can never totally appear in the same place. How they appear and where they appear depend on the type of holographic images that are produced and whether those images are real or virtual images as described in the previous chapter. Nonetheless, in a metaphysical context, there would not be any separation between the implicate and the explicate domains. In this situation, we are presupposing that the implicate domain would be coextensive with the totality of existence; and therefore, any explicate domains could not be separate from the implicate domain. There would not be any place for an explicate domain to exist that was void of the implicate domain. Thus, because these domains are located in the same "space–time," however inappropriate that phrase may be, implicate and explicate domains would have to be mutually interpenetrating. In this light, it can now be said that one need not go anywhere to realize the implicate domain.

The third presupposition of this model is that the implicate and explicate domains are also simultaneously existing. Not only do these domains logically demand each other and not only do they exist in the same "space," but they exist at the same "time." They are not sequentially existent. An individual does not need to wait until some future time to uncover the implicate domain. In this model, it exists now. Likewise, an individual does not have to wait until some other time to experience another explicate domain. In this model, other explicate domains can also exist now. This is not to say that all explicate or implicate domains must exist at every given moment.[8] Their simultaneous coexistence would be like the coexistence of an implicate and explicate domain in the holographic situation. In the holographic situation, there must be an implicate domain and at the same time an explicate entity or explicate holographic image had to be simultaneously existing with that implicate domain. By saying that these domains can be simultaneously existing, we leave open the question of whether all domains are always simultaneously existing. Our only concern in this model is that human beings can experience both explicate and implicate domains simultaneously.

The simultaneous coexistence of the implicate and the explicate domains is an essential component in the formulation of this model; and therefore, for those unfamiliar with the viewing of a hologram, further elucidation may be helpful. As an example, we can use a hologram that is backed upon a piece of paper and illuminated by natural light. In this holographic situation, an individual can focus on the holographic image that appears on the film. Focusing on the holographic image, an individual experiences a three-dimensional image—an image that appears to be extended behind the paper or in front of the paper. Since the paper is opaque, we know that the image cannot extend out from the holographic film. At the same time, a second individual can focus on the film and experience the nonduality of the film. That individual can experience an entity without individuality or particularity. Both individuals are looking at the same geographical location at the same time; however, they are focusing in different ways and experiencing different things.

In line with this point, the notion of temporality and causality should be clarified. By saying that the implicate and the explicate domains exist simultaneously, I am not claiming that all explicate things are simultaneous. I am not claiming that there is no temporal sequence to explicate entities and therefore no past, present or future. At this point, all that I am saying is that whatever explicate entities exist, whether they exist just in the present or in some combination of past, present and future, a concomitant implicate domain simultaneously exists.[9]

In summation, these three presuppositions leave us with the notion that these different domains are ontologically equal, mutually interpenetrating and simultaneously existing. This scenario allows us to envision how different ultimate realities as professed by different religious traditions can be simultaneously existent and equal. It should now be obvious that this holographic model does not prove the existence of a plurality of ultimate realities. It does not prove the existence of even one ultimate reality. I do not believe that I, or anybody, could offer such proof. Instead, this proposal merely devises a way by which we could imagine that more than one religious truth claim could be simultaneously true, yet not the same, but nonetheless equal.

## RESTATING THE TYPOLOGY

The notion that within the major religious traditions of the world there are three allegedly mutually exclusive and contradictory views of ultimate reality is by no means an invention of this work. (Other views of ultimate reality, such as dualism, polytheism and materialism, can be added to this list of allegedly mutually exclusive and contradictory ultimate realities.) Specifically, the three positions that have been reviewed are (1) salvation is rooted in a personal relation between the self and the Other; (2) liberation is rooted in realizing that all is the one Self and there is no other; and (3) liberation is rooted in the realization that there is no self and no Self. The first position is theistic. While the name of God varies from tradition to tradition and while many of the theological details vary from religious group to religious group, there are certain aspects of divinity and the divine's relation to humanity that appear similar across theological and cultural boundaries. The second position presents a oneness of Being. This notion has reappeared in a number of different religious traditions each of which label the Being of the universe by a different name and explain in different ways how this one Being seems to manifest itself in such an apparent diversity of beings. The third position recognizes that there is no Self; there is no underlying substance; no unity of Being. This is a position of continuous flux.

The last two positions are those which John Hick associates with impersonal experiences of the Real. For both of these positions, there is no self that ultimately stands against an other, specifically no self that stands in relation to the Other. Both of these views posit forms of nondualism. With neither a self nor an Other, ultimate reality is impersonal—it lacks the characteristics of individuality and relationship. For both of these positions, the notion of an independent individuality is problematic. For those who envision ultimate reality in impersonal terms, individuality is a psychological/epistemological disease that makes us see the world in categories of subject and object—in self and other. The very structure of this form of thinking is problematic according to these positions. This must be distinguished from theistic positions in which the type of individuality that one expresses or manifests may be problematic, but individuality itself is not problematic. For the latter, individuality is an essential element in the structure of all things. For the theist, the individual's relation with God is paramount.

In the following pages, each of these positions is described. While a variety of individual thinkers and religious traditions may be associated with each position, one individual and that individual's school will serve as the primary source for the articulation of each position and its relationship to the holographic model. The nondualism of Being is modeled after the Advaita Vedānta tradition of Hinduism, specifically the work of Gauḍapāda. The description of the philosophy of becoming is drawn from Buddhist sources. As this position gets articulated into a notion of emptiness, the source for this material is Vasubandhu and the Yogācāra school that he helped form. Richard of St. Victor, twelfth-century Catholic mystic, informs the third position. As a consequence of this methodology, the following presentation is not beholden to defending any typological structure, although it may further illuminate this tripartite typology. Rather, the merits of this proposal for religious pluralism stand on its ability to relate each of these different religious thinkers to the holographic model.

## POSITION 1: GAUḌAPĀDA AND THE NONDUALISM OF BEING

The Advaita Vedānta tradition of Hinduism considers Gauḍapāda to be the *paramaguru* (the teacher's teacher) of Śaṅkara, the most famous Advaita Vedāntin. As such, Gauḍapāda is considered by some to be the most important individual after the Upaniṣadic sages to revive the monistic, nondualistic trends of the Upaniṣads.[10] Tradition maintains that he lived in the eighth century and authored the *Māṇḍūkya Kārikā*.[11] The latter, divided into four books, begins as a commentary on the *Māṇḍūkya Upaniṣad*, a very brief *upaniṣad* consisting of only twelve verses. The *upaniṣad* and the first book of Gauḍapāda's text focuses upon the four states of consciousness—waking, dreaming, dreamless sleep and *turīya*, the fourth and ultimate state of consciousness. About this state of consciousness, the *Māṇḍūkya Upaniṣad* says:

> They consider the fourth as perceiving neither what is inside nor what is outside, nor even both together, not as a mass of perception, neither as per-

ceiving nor as not perceiving; as unseen as beyond the reach of ordinary transaction; as ungraspable; as without distinguishing marks; as unthinkable; as indescribable; as one whose essence is the perception of itself alone; as the cessation of the visible world; as tranquil; as auspicious; as without a second. That is the self (*ātman*), and it is that which should be perceived.[12]

Gauḍapāda's commentary on this *śruti* (revealed) text reads as follows: "The fourth state (*turya*), all pervading, cessation of all suffering, is known as lord of all beings, non-dual, the imperishable, the shining one."[13] Gauḍapāda goes on to tell us that this state of consciousness is without perceiver and perceived, without object, and without mind.

The remaining three books of Gauḍapāda's *kārikās* develop into an exposition of the basic principles of Advaita Vedānta thought. According to the commentary, attributed to Śaṅkara, these other three books demonstrate by reasoning, respectively, (1) the falsity of duality, (2) the truth of nonduality, and (3) a refutation of the opponents' views on duality (and causality).[14]

Gauḍapāda's background and training led him to declare the reality of that which is nondual (*advaita*).[15] Brahman is this nondual ultimate reality. In the context of this model, Gauḍapāda's vision of reality as Brahman is shown to be a vision of the implicate domain as a oneness of being. Gauḍapāda describes Brahman as Being (*sat*), as that which lacks nothing, as that which is without birth (*ajāti*), as that which always is (*nitya*), as that which is the same throughout (*samatāṃ gatam*). It is therefore without distinguishing marks; it is without difference. Being without distinguishing marks and everywhere the same, ultimate reality is without relation. There is no part here that can be related to a part over there since there are no parts anywhere. To assume the reality of parts is to create marks of distinction. It is to separate this from that. Such an activity creates individuality; it creates subject and object, I and Thou. None of these characteristics are appropriate to this ultimate reality that is everywhere the same, Brahman. Gauḍapāda declares, "There is no disappearance (ceasing to be), nor origination (coming into being). There is no bondage, nor anyone who seeks liberation. There is no desire for liberation, nor anyone liberated. This is the highest truth."[16] Since the highest truth (*paramārtha*) is without individuality, there can be no one who suffers, seeks liberation, or is liberated.

For Gauḍapāda, Brahman is not bound by cause and effect; it is without anything earlier, anything external, anything subsequent, anything other.[17] Brahman is without beginning, middle and end; it is without measure and without end to measure.[18] This Being is not only everywhere the same, it is everywhere. It is infinite.

For Gauḍapāda, the real does not change; what appears to change cannot be real. Thus, creation is not ultimately real. Provisionally, one may say that things are created by *īśvara* (the lord) or by the *māyā* (illusory power) of *ātman* (true self).[19] But, even in that sense, individual objects are only *māyā*, only an illusion. Gauḍapāda compares them to a barren woman's son.

> Birth of that which is existent is reasonable through *māyā*, but not in reality. For whom the real is born, for them that which was born is indeed born.
>
> The birth through *māyā* of that which is not-existent (*asat*) is most certainly not reasonable in reality. Nor is the son of a barren woman born in reality or through *māyā*.[20]

Ultimately, all views concerning creation are false. As Karl Potter explains:

> Some false views are less misleading than others. By criticizing worse views one arrives by stages at better ones. . . .
>
> For example, the view that effects are different from their causes (*asatkāryavāda*) is worse than the view that the effect is essentially identical with its cause (*satkāryavāda*); within the latter, the view that the cause transforms itself into its effect (*pariṇāmavāda*) is worse than the view that it manifests its appearances as effect without itself changing in so doing (*vivartavāda*); still, all views that take causation seriously are inferior to non-origination (*ajātivāda*), since causal relations, as any relations, involve differences and are thus tinged with ignorance.[21]

From this perspective in which *ajātivāda* (nonorigination) is the highest truth, no individual (*jīva*) or object (*vastu*) can ever be born. Individuals do not come into existence or go out of existence. To predicate such origination is to imagine the reality of difference. From this perspective, truth means that there is no division—no division of one *jīva* from another *jīva*. Gauḍapāda employs the simile of space and the space of a pot (*akāśa* and *ghaṭākāśa*) to illustrate this point. With the destruction of the pot, the space of the pot dissolves into the totality of space. In that manner, the *jīva* is dissolved and there is *ātman*, Brahman, the nondual.[22] That is all there ever is.

In this view of ultimate reality, where sameness and not difference define the real, where individuality is only an appearance—an illusion (*māyā*)—there is only one *ātman* (true Self). Being is one and the Self is Being. It is this Self that must be known and this Self can be known because the nature of this Self/Being is consciousness (*cit*). This is not a particular consciousness; it is not one thought distinguished from another thought. This is not a particular mind. This consciousness is the nature of Being; Being and consciousness cannot be distinguished. Gauḍapāda declares that *ātman*/Brahman is known through meditation on *om*, through *asparśayoga*—the yoga of no touch, no relation. *Asparśayoga* is aimed at stopping the movement of the mind—making the mind no-mind. It is aimed at stopping the presentation of perceiver and perceived, the duality of subject and object.[23] *Asparśayoga* reveals nonduality; it reveals the nonduality of consciousness, which is the reality of Brahman. Gauḍapāda says:

> This duality whatsoever, comprised of the animate and the inanimate, is seen by the mind. When the mind is in the state of no-mind, duality is not perceived. (3:31)
>
> When one does not intend because of being connected with the truth of *ātman*, then one goes to no-mindedness. Without objects to be perceived, (there is) nothing perceived by that (mind). (3:32)
>
> It is said that the knowledge of that which is unborn and without imagination is not separate from the knowable. Knowledge of the unborn, eternal Brahman is awakened by the unborn. (3:33)
>
> There is nothing perceived, nor anything emitted where nothing is found. Abiding in *ātman* then, knowledge has become unborn and sameness. (3:38)
>
> That which is called *asparśayoga* is not accessible to all yogis. The yogis are afraid. From that which is without fear, fear is seen. (3:39)[24]

This Being/consciousness is said to be bliss, not as another thing, but as the nature of the one Self. It is the nondual awareness in which there is no subject looking at an object; it is the realization that overcomes the confines of individuality; it is the realization that frees one from the shackles of all human problems. The realization of that which is without measure and without end to measure, which is Being, consciousness, and bliss is the soteriological goal of this religious position. It is, for Gauḍapāda, the attainment of *ātman*/Brahman. This realization is *mokṣa*, liberation.

Gauḍapāda's presentation of *ātman*/Brahman, *asparśayoga* and *mokṣa* is epistemologically relative; however, that does not mean that it is ontologically irrelevant. From the perspective of this holographic model, Gauḍapāda looks for and uncovers a vision of the implicate domain as ultimately real, as soteriologically effective; and simultaneously, he understands the explicate domains to be that which obscures one's vision of this truth.

Unfolding this holographic analogy, we may say that the implicate domain may be seen as that which is the same throughout (*samatāṃ gatam*); each piece of the implicate domain contains the whole. Like Brahman, the implicate domain is not defined by individuality; it is not structured in the subject–object format that we experience; there is no self standing over and against another self in the implicate domain; rather, each piece is equal to every other piece. In this sense, there is only one self; this self is the being of the implicate domain in which the interference patterns are spread throughout the implicate domain, and the entirety of the implicate domain is, in this model, coextensive with all that exists. Viewing the implicate domain in this manner in which the interference patterns are spread across the entirety of the domain, in which each piece can reproduce the whole, difference is not the category by which this domain is being perceived. Here, the self of any part is the true self (*ātman*) of the totality. From this perception of the implicate domain, the *jīva* with its sense of individuality and particularity is not real; only the *ātman*, the self of the whole, is real.

Continuing with this analogy, the individual (*jīva*) is a category that is *only* appropriate to an explicate domain. In the implicate domain, the *jīva* is not existent; it is not even existent as an illusion in the implicate domain.[25] There is absolutely no object or subject in the implicate domain. From this perspective, the individual things of the explicate domains are projections from the implicate domain. They are the projections of subject and object from that which is the undivided wholeness, from that which is without subject and object. These projections are, for Gauḍapāda, *māyā*. In order to appear as explicate entities, these projections must appear as subjects and objects. Thus, these projections obscure one's knowledge of the nonduality and the undivided wholeness of the implicate domain/Brahman. It is here that we can see the two characteristics that Śaṅkara attributes to *māyā*—the nonperception of the real and the misapprehension of reality.[26]

Just as the Advaitin tells us that Brahman is unaffected by the world of *māyā*, so also the undivided wholeness of the implicate domain is unaffected by the transformations of the explicate domain. The implicate domain remains a domain of undivided wholeness in spite of the appearance and/or disappearance of explicate entities. The interference patterns that enfolds space (and time) may be changing, but the undivided wholeness of the implicate domain does not change. This appears to be the aspect of reality upon which the monistic nondualist focuses. From this perspective, we can see how Gauḍapāda declares

Brahman unchanged, constantly nondual, without subject and object dichotomies and thus unaffected by birth and causation.

Using this perception of the implicate domain, we can envision the notion of liberation that is described by the *ātmavāda* position. Here, ultimate reality is realized when one knows that "thou art that" (*tat tvam asi*). From this perspective, one needs to realize that the true nature of the individual self is not to be identified with the dualistic projections of subject and object. The true nature of the individual is not uncovered in explicate relations. Rather, the monistic nondualist, the Advaitin, seeks to transcend explicate relations and to uncover the deepest part of the self—specifically, its fundamental implicate nature—which turns out to be the undivided wholeness of the implicate domain. Gauḍapāda was looking to transcend explicate relations and to uncover the being of the self which is the Being of all. In holographic language, to know the nature of any piece would be to know the whole. The recognition of the whole would liberate one from the confines of particularity; it would destroy the illusion that the only reality is that of subject and object; it would present a being that is everywhere the same. "One" would realize "one's" oneness with all that is. Or, from this perspective, it can be said that there is no thing (*jīva*) to be absorbed into anything else since the notion of separate things (*jīvas*) is a category inappropriate to the implicate domain as it is to Brahman. This would be a "unitive experience," an experience of the nonduality of all Being; and as such, it would be the attainment of nonduality. This would be liberation from the confines of particularity. It would be freedom (*mokṣa*) from the false view that any part of the implicate domain, any part of Brahman, is different from any other part.

## POSITION 2: VASUBANDHU AND THE NONDUALISM OF BECOMING

The second position embodies a philosophy of becoming. From this perspective, it is change and flux that constitute the primary categories of ultimate reality. That which appears to be an object, to be an enduring entity, is actually an aggregate of parts, each of which is itself in constant change. Nothing endures; each thing is momentary. "It" arises, exists and perishes in a momentary cacophony of cause-and-effect relations. Here the constitutive events (*dharmas*) of one moment give rise to the constituent events of the next moment in an endless stream of succession (*pratitya-samutpāda*). It is these events that define existence, not objects.

Individuals are likewise constituted by this endless stream of change. Individuals are not enduring objects; they are not enduring subjects. They are aggregates of different elements ranging from a material element (form) to sensations, perceptions, volitions, and conscious elements. Each of these aggregates (*skandas*) is momentary. None of these elements persist; none of these constitute an enduring self. From this perspective, there is no self (*anatta*). To believe that there is a self is ignorance (*avidyā*). It is the root of egoism and the endless problems and anxieties that make the human condition problematic. This ignorance and the thirst (*taṇhā*) for those things that affirm one's belief in a self propel one's sorrowful condition into the future. Such is the Theravāda Buddhist analysis of the human condition and its need to blow out all notions of self in order to achieve nirvana.

Building upon the fundamental notions of impermanence and no-self, Mahāyāna Buddhism arrives at the notion that "everything" is without a self-nature. All things are empty of a self-nature. The *Madhyāntavibhāga Sūtra* states: "The non-existence of persons (*pudgalas*) and events (*dharmas*) is emptiness (*śūnyatā*)."[27] This emptiness of self-nature is that which allows for the constant change. Since no thing has a fixed nature, each event can influence other events in an endless web of interactions.

Emptiness also indicates the nonexistence of the duality of subject and object.[28] Subject and object imply a self-nature that stands over and against another subject/object. Since all is without a self-nature and since all is interconnected in a web of dynamic relationships, the notion of subject and object does not correspond to this ultimate reality. There is no subject independent of all the interrelated factors that give rise to the appearance of any one subject or object. The notion of subject and object is a psychological and epistemological imposition upon an ultimate reality that is empty of self-nature. It is a psychological attempt to reify experience into permanent objects—to fabricate a self and a world of objects. Here again, we see that the cause of human suffering is the imposition of a notion of self upon that which is empty of self.

In this view of reality, where there is no self and all is empty of self-nature, emptiness is the nature of all. Emptiness is not other than those things that appear to have a self-nature, but do not have a self-nature. It is not other than what appears to be subjects and objects, but is without subject and object. From this perspective, form (what appears as an object) is emptiness and emptiness is form. Form is empty of self-nature and emptiness is not other than form that has no self-nature.

Vasubandhu, an Indian monk of the fifth century C.E., was trained in the Theravāda tradition sketched previously and was subsequently converted by his half brother, Asaṅga, to Mahāyāna Buddhism. In line with the former, Vasubandhu wrote the classic *Abhidharmakośa* of the Sarvāstavādin school and a commentary on that text from the perspective of the Sautrāntika school. From the Mahāyāna perspective, he wrote some of the classic Yogācāra texts—*Viṃśatikā, Viṃśatikāvṛtti, Triṃśikā, Madhyāntavibhāgabhāṣya* and *Trisvabhāvanirdeśa*. In spite of the twofold fact that a great deal of the historical information surrounding his life and his compositions is uncertain and that there is a great deal of debate about the idealistic tendencies within his thought, there is little debate that Vasubandhu is one of the great figures within Indian Buddhism.[29]

Vasubandhu presents the notion of *śūnyatā* (emptiness) in the context of the theory of the three natures (*svabhāvas*). As mentioned in the discussion of the traditional similes, these three natures are (1) *parikalpita svabhāva*, the purely imagined nature, (2) *paratantra svabhāva*, the relative nature and (3) the *pariniṣpanna svabhāva*, the perfected or consummated nature. His *Trisvabhāvanirdeśa* puts forth the basic definitions of these natures.

> *Paratantra* is that which appears; its transformations are dependent on causes. How it appears is *parikalpita*; its nature is only a construction.
>
> The way that which appears appears is never existent. It is to be known as *pariniṣpanna* nature for it is not other (than that).[30]

What appears or manifests is said to be the *paratantra* nature; however, how it appears is not the *paratantra* nature. How it appears is the *parikalpita* (imagined) nature. The latter appears with duality; the former is without duality. We experience the dual, not the nondual; yet somehow, according to the Yogācāra tradition, it is the nondual that is the causes and the conditions for our experience.

The Yogācāra tradition refers to the *paratantra svabhāva* as the unreal construction (*abhūtaparikalpa*). It is the form (*ākāra*) of that which manifests. However, it is *ākāra* (form) without the duality of that which we experience. The nature of this form that has no duality and is said to be that which manifests must be understood. Somehow for the Yogācārin, while the form is considered to be an unreal construction and without duality, it is understood to be the causes and conditions for that which manifests. This *paratantra* nature is associated with the Yogācāra concepts of the *ālayavijñāna* and *pravṛttivijñana*—the store consciousness and the functioning consciousness. About the latter it can be said that "the 'objects' of the store-consciousness are not such that an agent can be consciously aware of them, that they are extremely subtle and that conscious experience does not therefore occur in the store-consciousness."[31] Thus, it can be said that the unreal constructions *(abhūtaparikalpa)* of the *paratantra* nature are (1) the causes and condition for that which manifests, (2) they are themselves without duality of subject and object, and (3) they are so subtle that their nature cannot be perceived as "objects."

On the other hand, when the *paratantra* nature appears as subjects and objects, it is the *parikalpita* nature (the purely imagined nature). The *parikalpita* nature is not a denial of the world as experienced; but rather, it is a denial of the dualistic structure that we impose upon experience. Finally, the perfected nature (*pariniṣpanna*) is that which never appears dualistically—never appears as subject and object; it is without discrimination; it is *paratantra* without *parikalpita*.

This three-nature theory of the Yogācāra school is not intended to divide the world into three separate ontological domains. Rather, there is only one world, which can be experienced in three ways.[32] Gadjin Nagao expresses this point and its significance as follows:

> The principle of "convertibility" (expressed by words such as "change," "transformation," or "conversion" in the previous discussion) is a remarkable and important feature of the three nature theory. It prevails in all three natures and enables them to constitute one and the same world. Through "convertibility," it is possible for the world to be one and at the same time to possess the three natures. These changes, conversions, or transformations are possible only on the "basis" of the other-dependent nature.[33]

This one world whose basis is understood to be the *paratantra svabhāva* can appear in three natures because each nature lacks a self-nature (*niḥsvabhāva);* emptiness is the nature of each nature.[34]

The emptiness that Vasubandhu and his Yogācāra tradition talk about is not nonbeing. It is not negative in character.[35] "Indeed, the characteristics of emptiness are the non-existence of duality and the existence of the non-existence."[36] Along these lines, the tradition also tells us that "*śūnyatā* is the removal of the perceiver and the perceived from the *abhūtaparikapa* (the non-existent construction)."[37] This is the removal of duality—subject and object—from *paratantra svabhāva*. This statement is amplified by the following: "The construction of the unreal exists; duality is not found there. However, emptiness (*śūnyatā*) is found there. In that (emptiness/*śūnyatā*), it (the construction of the unreal) is found."[38] From these statements, we see that the *paratantra* nature, which is identified with the construction of the unreal, is without the duality of subject and object, but not without that which are the causes and conditions given which duality can appear. This is what remains—the causes and conditions. This *paratantra* nature, which is the causes and conditions, is emptiness/*śūnyatā*; it is *parinişpanna*. From a list of synonyms for *śūnyatā*, we see that emptiness is suchness (*tathatā*), signless (*animittam*) and ultimate (*paramārtha*);[39] and from the previous quotes, we see that it is without duality, but it is the causes and conditions given which duality can manifest.

The realization of emptiness, of the *paratantra* nature—breaks one's entrapment to duality and presents the other natures. Vasubandhu says:

> First, the nature of the non-being of duality, the *paratantra*—the relative nature—is penetrated. Then, the non-existent duality which is only a construction is penetrated.
>
> Then, the perfected nature—*niṣpanna*—having the nature of the non-being duality is penetrated there. Therefore, it is said that it is and it is not.[40]

It seems that the realization of the *paratantra* nature—namely, the causes and conditions for duality which is itself without duality—is that which allows one to penetrate the other two natures. Vasubandhu also tells us that the realization of these three natures allows one "to attain liberation without effort."[41]

For Vasubandhu and the Yogācāra tradition this realization is seeing/knowing the way "things" are. It is freedom from the confines of subject and object as independent entities existing in separation from each other. This knowledge frees one from the confines of the notion of a self. It is the realization that form is empty of self. The realization that any form is emptiness is the realization that all form is emptiness. Thus, the true knowledge of any object or the emptiness from which it arises frees one from all conditions of bondage and self. This realization that emptiness is form frees one from the notion that liberation is somewhere else; it frees one from the notion that liberation is separated from what appears in one's world. This is the realization of the *dharmadhātu* (nature of reality). Vasubandhu says: "By the non-perception of duality, there is the perception of the *dharmadhātu*;

by the perception of the *dharmadhātu*, there is the perception of *vibhutva* (unlimitedness)."[42]

In the holographic model that I am presenting, this vision of ultimate reality, like the preceding one, would be understood in terms of the implicate domain. I am comparing the implicate domain with its interference patterns to the notion of emptiness and to the enfoldment and unfoldment of the three *svabhāvas*. Interference patterns are not static objects; they are wave patterns. The implicate domain is not constituted by entities that stand in subject–object relation to each other. It is empty of duality. In fact, the implicate domain is empty of all particularity—there are no images/objects in the implicate domain. However, the implicate domain is constituted by interference patterns, which are the causes and conditions for that which appears. In this light, the implicate domain seems to mirror the *paratantra svabhāva*.

The interference patterns are by nature dynamic, continuously flowing. They are constantly flowing wave formations converging with other wave formations. Like the seeds (*bījas*) of the *paratantra* nature, these wave formations cannot be perceived as individual objects until they are projected into a dualistic form. What appear are the interference patterns—the causes and conditions, the *paratantra* nature; however, how they appear is dualistic. These nondual interference patterns appear like the *parikalpita* nature. Like the latter, the projections from the implicate domain always appear as subjects and objects. The distinction in the three-*svabhāva* doctrine between what appears and how it appears seems to be mirrored in the holographic model. From this perspective, duality is not real. Here, the implicate domain, the grounds from which all form manifests, is seen as the fundamental nature and all duality is that which obscures knowledge of that domain.

As indicated, the conditions given which something can appear in a holographic situation are enfolded in the implicate domain, which is itself nothing but those conditions and also not itself a being. There is no particular thing in the implicate domain. In this sense, the implicate domain is empty of being (*śūnyatā*)—empty of duality—yet with its interference patterns, something remains. It is not a nothingness, but there is no subject and object. From this perspective on the implicate domain as interference patterns, one can imagine that which the Yogācārins had in mind when they talked about *paratantra* and *śūnyatā*. Likewise, from the perspective of *paratantra* as the fundamental reality, all duality is only a projection. From this perspective, duality is not real (*parikalpita*); and furthermore, attachment to such duality conceals that which is always without duality (*parinispanna*). By analogy, the Yogācārin, having penetrated the implicate domain and overcome the problems associated with duality, has come to see that intoxication with that which unfolds from the implicate domain (the *parikalpita svabhāva*) does not lead to liberation but to bondage.

It must be noted that in the reified situation of a holographic piece of film, the implicate domain appears to be other than the interference patterns. In our use of this analogy, such reification would be inappropriate; it would constitute a negative analogy. It would lead us to assume there can be an object—namely, the film—that is separate from the interference patterns and separate from the rest of the world. Insofar as we have presupposed that in a metaphysical situation the implicate domain is coextensive with all that exists, there cannot be a separation between the implicate domain and the interference patterns. There may be multiple sets of interference patterns, but the totality of interference patterns would constitute the implicate domain to which we are referring.

I believe that these descriptions of the implicate domain mirror the description of the Buddhist notion of emptiness and the three *svabhāvas* described previously. From the perspective of this holographic model, this type of perception of the implicate domain would be the realization that all notions of self are not ultimately real. The realization that any particular object is grounded in an implicate domain, which is empty of all objects, would be the realization that all objects are equally empty. This would be the realization that emptiness is the nature of all and such a realization is complete liberation from all the conditions that bind human existence to suffering. A realization, at any given "place" and "time," of the emptiness of the implicate domain would be a realization of the entirety of the implicate domain. Thus, it would constitute complete liberation—a complete knowledge of the nature of emptiness and a complete overcoming of all defiling conditions. Such knowledge would be coextensive with all that is empty of particularity. Furthermore, as we have seen, it would not be the only knowledge of all that exists; there is the *ātmavāda* perception of the oneness of being.

## REFLECTIONS ON THE IMPLICATE DOMAIN

At this point, I need to reflect upon the previous two sections. Drawing upon two different religious traditions, I have described two views of "self" and their concomitant ultimate realities—an ultimate reality of Being/Self and an ultimate reality of becoming/emptiness. I have also related each of these ultimate realities to the implicate domain of this holographic model. Three related questions arise.

First, how can this model simultaneously accommodate the Buddhist notion of no-self at the same time that it accommodates the Advaitin notion that all is the Self? Because this question is further complicated by the presentation of Richard of St. Victor's notion that each individual has an immortal soul, it will be reviewed after the presentation of Richard's views.

Second, are these really different ultimate realities? Is the experience of nondual Being different than the experience of emptiness? Perennialists, for example, would equate these two experiences. Scholars of these two traditions have debated the historical relationship between these two traditions and the relationship between their notions of the "absolute."[43] However, these traditions, in this case Advaita Vedānta and Yogācāra Buddhism, have maintained that these ultimate realities are different. Consistent with that approach, I have related each view of ultimate reality to a different perception of the implicate domain. While both seem to overcome a problematic identification with the individual self, neither is willing to accept the solution that the other uncovered. As such, I leave these positions to stand as they are.

The third question, which is related to the first and is the inverse of the second, is: How can the implicate domain simultaneously be used as an analogy for two different views of ultimate reality? Can the ceaseless converging patterns of energy simultaneously be viewed as changeless being? Can we imagine this implicate domain as Being, as the One, and simultaneously imagine this implicate domain as emptiness?[44]

To illuminate this issue, we return to the insights of David Bohm and some of the controversy surrounding his work. As already stated, Bohm sees his position as one of "undivided wholeness." Bohm says:

> Throughout this book the central underlying theme has been the unbroken wholeness of the totality of existence as an undivided flowing movement without borders.
>
> It seems clear from the discussion in the previous chapter that the implicate order is particularly suitable for the understanding of such unbroken wholeness in flowing movement, for in the implicate order the totality of existence is enfolded within each region of space (and time). So, whatever part, element, or aspect we may abstract in thought, this still enfolds the

> whole and is therefore intrinsically related to the totality from which it has been abstracted. Thus, wholeness permeates all that is being discussed, from the very outset.[45]

In this passage, Bohm makes two points that need to be highlighted. First, he tells us that this is a view of unbroken wholeness. Second, this wholeness is one of flowing movement. We have already indicated that Bohm maintains that one of the limitations of the hologram analogy is the static nature of the film. In its place, he develops the notion of holomovement that is structurally more akin to the process by which holograms are made—the convergence of wave patterns.

Returning to the basic understanding of the process of holography, we can see both its dynamic and its unitive natures. Holography is a process by which dynamic wave formations converge with each other to form patterns of superimposition in which information is spread throughout the entire pattern. The first part of this description—the dynamic wave formations—is consistent with our understanding of the implicate domain as everywhere a changing reality without subject and object. It is also consistent with the presentation of the second ultimate reality of emptiness. The second part of this description—a superimposition in which space and time are spread throughout the totality—corresponds to our first view of ultimate reality in which there is only one Self. Each view of the holographic process is descriptive of the totality of the implicate domain; and therefore, analogously, each view can not only serve as a model for an ultimate reality but can also explain the soteriological effectiveness of that ultimate reality. However, each view of the holographic process, while describing the totality of the implicate domain, does not describe all the natures of the implicate domain; and therefore, analogously, this domain can serve as a model by which two ultimate realities can exist simultaneously. In light of this, I proceed with both views of ultimate reality.

This issue brings us very close to a discussion of time. Are all moments—past, present and future—enfolded in the implicate domain? Is only the present enfolded? Is there some combination of past, present and future enfolded?

Bohm's view of time entails the notion that all times are enfolded. He says:

> "All implicates all," even to the extent that "we ourselves" are implicated together with "all that we see and think about." So we are present everywhere and at all times, though only implicately (that is, implicitly). . . .

> The general law, i.e., holonomy, has to be expressed in all orders, in which all objects and all times are "folded together."[46]

First, it must be noted that although Bohm seems to emphasize the dynamic aspect of the interference patterns in the previous quote, this passage leads us to a more static, Being-like description of the implicate domain. If past, present and future are enfolded in the implicate domain, then temporality is enfolded and all is one. This latter position of Bohm's has been criticized by a number of scholars who believe that the reality of causality, creativity and freedom is undermined in his view of time. For example, David Griffin says:

> Another set of problems could be created by Bohm's suggestion that all *times* (as well as places) interpenetrate in the implicate order . . . which implies that the implicate order would be beyond time . . . in the sense that the *distinction between past, present, and future would not be real* in that order. In the first place, there is the problem of the compatibility of the belief in genuine freedom and creativity, which Bohm wants to affirm, with the belief that in the "really real" order the totality of what *we* regard as future is already settled. If those events which are still future for us are, in some more real realm, as fully settled as those which we regard as past, that is, *if the present implies the details of the future as fully as it implies the details of the past, then each present event really has no power of self-determination.*[47]

John Cobb also offers us an analysis of Bohm's understanding of time. Cobb posits two Bohms—a Bohm I and a Bohm II. The former Bohm conflates past, present and future in the implicate domain. Bohm II envisions a reciprocity between enfolding and unfolding.[48] Bohm responds to Cobb's comment by proposing a Bohm III, which contends that "the 'particles' of physics would be recurrent moments, unfolding from an implicate order and folding back to it."[49] Bohm's response shows that he envisions this holographic model allowing for both a dynamism related to the holomovement and a timeless nature in which all is enfolded.[50]

Having briefly sketched this issue, I am not going to enter the debate over the nature of past, present and future and the merits of the different views. On the one hand, this project is not a project in physics. I am not trying to uncover which notion of temporality corresponds to the world; and therefore, it would be inappropriate for me to defend one view over another. On the other hand, different religious traditions have different views of time. The pertinent issue is whether this holographic model can accommodate such a variety of views. The preceding discussion established the flexibility of this model for accommodating both a dynamic and a static view of ultimate reality. In addition, this holographic model could accommodate a number of different views on the nature of time, specifically different views on the nature of past, present and future.

This model has posited that more than one explicate domain can be enfolded into the implicate domain. Such a notion allows us to imagine how one could conceive at least three views of time and temporal relations. First, we can use this model to understand that just the present is enfolded in the implicate domain and explicated from the implicate domain, although more than one explicate domain may be simultaneously present. Second, we can use this model to imagine that all times—past, present and future—are enfolded in the implicate domain, just as multiple explicate domains can be enfolded into one implicate domain, but that only the present becomes unfolded, explicate. Third, we can imagine that the past and present are enfolded and that only the present is unfolded. The question of which view of time is true or which view of time best accommodates my personal beliefs on this subject is not the issue. The more pertinent issue would be to explain the different views of time that are found in the religious traditions that we are examining and relate them to this model. As indicated, I believe that this model can accommodate a number of views.

The notion of time in each of the traditions is a legitimate but complex subject that would demand at least another chapter to review and would take us beyond the scope of this work. How, for example, do we understand Gauḍapāda's view of time? On the one hand, Gauḍapāda proclaims the doctrine of *ajāti*—no birth, no origination. In such a view, there are no objects, no causation, no change and therefore no time at all. All is Brahman and there is only Brahman. On the other hand, there is the world of appearance with its *karma*, rebirth, creation, and so forth. How we put these ideas together and relate them to the problem at hand demands more than a facile response. Similarly, how do we deal with Vasubandhu and the Buddhist tradition? Vasubandhu, as a Yogācārin, is critical of the Vaibhāṣika school of Buddhism with its notion of the continued existence of past *dharmas*. In its place, the Yogācāra tradition offers us the notion of the storehouse consciousness (*ālayavijñāna*) in which there are seeds of experience as an ever changing series of tendencies. Here, the past is not existent as an object, but it never was really existent as an object according to the Yogācārin. To say that the past remains as a changing series of tendencies does not resolve all questions about the relation of past, present and future, especially with regard to this holographic model; but rather, it seems to me that it opens up fertile ground for future comparisons.[51] Finally, what are we to say about Richard of St. Victor who talks about predestination and God's foreknowledge and sits within a tradition that places paramount significance on creation, free will and human responsibility? After reviewing the position of Richard of St. Victor, we shall return to the first question raised concerning the different views of "self."

## POSITION 3: RICHARD OF ST. VICTOR AND THEISM

Before turning to Richard of St. Victor, a description of the general characteristics of theism will allow us to contrast this view with those that have preceded. The theistic ultimate reality denies the nondualistic claims that individuality and particularity are not real. Distinctions are not to be overcome in some amorphous realization of nonduality. Rather, the theistic ultimate reality is grounded upon the notion of particulars and the fulfillment of one's particularity in relationship. It is in relationship that one attains meaning. One's identity is defined in relationship to that which is other, never in isolation or in an otherless nonduality. Human identity is defined in relationship to the Other, to the Numinous, to the Holy, to God. Individual selves are real, but their reality cannot be understood apart from God. God is the support for the meaningfulness of individuality. God is that being which does not let ephemerality define existence. In this view, individuality is not a passing phenomenon, but a reality guaranteed by God. It is a loving, gracious God who guarantees the individual's existence. Thus, God defines and creates the nature of personal existence and this existence is marked by personality, difference and relationship. God as creator and guarantor of individuality is therefore also personal. It is a personal, loving God who guarantees that ephemerality is not the defining characteristic of the individual. God is that being which can ensure that each individual can not only continue to be, but whose continuation achieves an end that transcends the particularity of any given event. God provides a telos that transcends the ephemerality of our present existence.

Insofar as God allows for the creation and sustenance of one's individuality, the highest fulfillment of one's individuality—one's ultimate end—is achieved in relationship to that being who guarantees one's own being. As such, God is worthy of adoration, of love, of sacrifice, of devotion. Without God, ephemerality would define existence and there would be no telos to personal existence beyond the ephemeral. The relationship between God and the individual is to be sought by the person. It is to be cultured in one's love and devotion to God. This relationship is also presented as an act of God's grace. It is God's grace which sustains and nurtures the relationship between the individual and God. The theistic ultimate reality finds joy and salvation in the difference between God and the individual. It is a difference that is not to be eradicated in some form of nondualism, nor to be forgotten and forsaken by the beguilements of life.

Theists have conceived of God's relation to the world in several broad ways. First, God may be conceived as separate from the world although active within the world; here God and the world are radically other. This is the view of Western classical theism. There are, on the other hand, theists who maintain that after having set the world in motion, God is inactive in the world. This view is referred to as deism. In addition, there are theists for whom the world and the individuals within the world may be conceived to be part of the body of God. Here, all things are not other than God, yet God is not limited to all things; nor is God identified with all things. This is a panentheistic view. Each form of the theistic ultimate reality maintains that one's ultimate goal lies in a relationship or fellowship with God.

A glimpse at one theist—Richard of St. Victor—helps to illuminate the specifics of my proposal. Richard of St. Victor (d. 1173) was a Christian mystic living in a Paris abbey in medieval Europe. He proclaimed the oneness of God and the Trinity of Persons with faith that the Trinity finds its incarnation in Jesus Christ.[52] Separated by centuries, by cultures, by religious traditions, by literary styles, by soteriological goals and by views of ultimate reality, Richard of St. Victor is a far cry from Gauḍapāda and Vasubandhu. Yet, I believe it is possible to listen to that which Richard and other theists have to say and to conceive of it within the same holographic model for ultimate realities that has been presented thus far.

Richard did not seek a oneness with God. Rather, he sought through various activities, such as devoted prayer, scripture reading and contemplation, as well as through the grace of God, "some pledges of that future fullness when we shall engage forever in eternal contemplation."[53] Such future contemplation is not solitary, but communal—it "will be that consonant concord and concordant consonance of supercelestial souls in so great a multitude of so many thousands of angels and so many holy souls exulting and praising

Him who lives world without end."[54] Richard sees persons and their relationships as paramount. In fact, for Richard, a defining characteristic of divinity is its relational characteristic, in particular the relationship of charity/love. Ewert Cousins describes Richard's position as follows:

> He examines experience and makes the affirmation that nothing is better than charity. In view of his exemplaristic metaphysics, then, God must possess charity in the highest degree. But the highest degree of charity, as is seen from human experience, is not self-love, but self-transcending love for another person. Hence, within God there must be self-transcending love for another person of equal dignity. But no creature has such dignity itself, there must be a self-transcending love of one divine person for another divine person.[55]

For Richard, this relationship must be trinitarian since "in mutual and very fervent love nothing is rarer or more magnificent than to wish that another be loved equally by the one whom you love supremely and by whom you are supremely loved."[56]

Richard presents his vision of ultimate reality within the context of six levels of contemplation. The first four contemplations refer to contemplations on created things, either visible or invisible. The last two contemplations are directed toward that which is uncreated; they are contemplations on divinity. In the context of his treatment of the mystical ark as representing the ascent of the soul, the last two contemplations—the Fifth and the Sixth Contemplations—are represented by two cherubs that stand facing each other. These cherubs represent the different aspects of divinity—namely, the unity of God and the Trinity. Neither the Fifth nor the Sixth Contemplation is superior to the other; they are equal.

In the Fifth Contemplation, which reveals the unity of God, Richard stresses that God is absolutely simple and truly One. Divinity is described here as being without division, as unchangeable, as infinite and boundless, as being present everywhere yet as most absent, as supreme goodness and supreme happiness, as supreme power and supreme wisdom. In Richard's words:

> Therefore, essentially He is within all things and outside all things, below all things and above all things . . . if He is in every place, nothing is more present than He is. If He is outside every place, nothing is more absent than He is. But is anything more absent than that very One who is the most present of all, and is anything more present than that very one who is the most

absent of all, who does not have to be one thing and another in order to be everything that exists?[57]

In this aspect of divinity, the notions of simplicity, unity and infinity are the relevant categories. The notion of particularity and the relationships that develop within the contexts of particulars are not relevant categories. God's nature as present everywhere is not the presence of particularity and its accompanying relationships. As such, Richard notes that God is most absent—absent as a particular entity in relationship to other entities. This aspect of divinity which is both present everywhere and absent, which is a oneness and a boundlessness and thus not a particular entity nor a relational entity, is illuminated later by the implicate domain of this holographic model.

It is the Sixth Contemplation in which particularity and relationship are preeminent. This contemplation represents divinity as the Trinity of persons. God is here Father, Son and Holy Spirit. Each is one person yet all have one substance. Richard confirms Church teaching that the Trinity of persons is such that "the Father from nothing, the Son from the Father only, the Holy Spirit from the Father and the Son; the Son by having been begotten, the Holy Spirit by having proceeded."[58] Richard finds that the Trinity of persons is above and beyond reason as distinguished from the Fifth Contemplation, which is above reason but not beyond reason. The Sixth Contemplation is both above and beyond reason because it is looked at in light of the unity of God. To simultaneously hold the characteristics of both the Fifth and the Sixth—of oneness and particularity, of changelessness and relationship—equally and at the same time seems to press reason beyond itself.

If the Father is unbegotten and the Son is only-begotten, will not the substance of the Father be unbegotten and that of the Son be begotten? And since both have one and the same substance, will not the same substance be begotten and unbegotten, that is begotten and not begotten? Can the same substance beget itself and be born from itself? Can the same substance be born and not be born; can it experience birth and not experience birth?[59]

Describing the notion that divinity is both above and beyond reason, Richard says:

What would imagination do there, where there is no changing and no shadow of vicissitude; where the part is not less than the whole, nor the whole is more universal than its parts; indeed, where the part is not lessening the whole, and the whole is not made up of parts, since that is simple

> which is set forth universally, and that is universal which is brought forth in the particular as it were; where the whole is single; where all is one and one is all? Certainly without doubt human reason fails in these things?[60]

Richard's description of the relationship between the unity of God and the Trinity of God as well as his corresponding description of the relation between the whole and the parts pushes reason above and beyond itself. Richard could find no similitude within the created world for these relationships. But, can we not apply all that we have uncovered about holography to these theological enigmas? How far would one have to go to compare Richard's description of the relation of part to whole to a holographic description of the relation of part to whole and whole to part? In light of all we have said, the comparisons seem obvious.

It seems to me that one could also illuminate Richard's description of the enigmas surrounding the unity and Trinity of God with holography. Here Richard was concerned with how one substance could be begotten and unbegotten. The substance of God—its unity—refers to the Fifth Contemplation and in the holographic model corresponds to the implicate domain. The Father, Son and Spirit refer to the Sixth Contemplation and thus are illuminated in terms of explicate domains. In an explicate domain, explicate relations are essential. Here persons are defined in relation to other persons. Thus, the Son can be distinguished and defined in relation to the Father. The Son can be said to be begotten from the Father as regards their explicate nature, but as regards the implicate nature of divinity (the Fifth Contemplation), there is no Trinity of persons—no particularity, no change. Richard tells us there is only one substance, which is a oneness without change and without shadow of vicissitude. Nonetheless, the Trinity of Persons is explicated from the Oneness without denying, destroying or changing the Oneness. In the holographic model, the appearance of an explicate image does not affect the simultaneously existing oneness of the implicate domain. One substance—the implicate domain—can implicate qualities which, on an explicate level, contradict the implicate oneness. The explicate relations of the Trinity—their separate personas and their begetting and begottenness—do not affect the unity of the implicate domain. With this model, we can see how the oneness of God and the Trinity of Persons can face each other, like two cherubs of the mystical ark, as equals.

In addition, the intersecting relationship between the implicate domain and the explicate domains can be utilized as a means of conceptualizing the relationship that Richard envisions between God as One, God as Trinity and the created world. The Fifth Contemplation is one, everywhere, infinite. The Sixth is the Trinity. For Richard, God is both One and Three, but the created world is explicitly different from the Trinity. The explicateness of the created world is other than the explicateness of the Trinity; while the latter is one with the Oneness of God. In terms of this holographic model, we may say that the implicate domain is one with all explicate domains—namely, the Trinity and the created world. However, each explicate domain is explicitly different from all other explicate domains; and as such, the explicateness of God is different from the explicateness of the created world. This model allows us to envision how God can simultaneously be one with all that is and yet, in another sense, God's explicateness or Trinitarian nature can be explicately different from all created things.

Richard in particular and theists in general do not focus their soteriological hopes on the implicate domain. They are not looking for a form of nonduality. Rather, they focus their attention on the explicate domains and the relationship between the different explicate domains. In this model, we are envisioning that just as the implicate domain is ultimate—not reducible to another—so also, at least some explicate domain or domains are ultimate. In this model, I have said that both domains logically demand each other, are simultaneously existing and mutually interpenetrating. As such, the existence of an implicate domain demands an explicate domain to enfold and hence unfold. These domains would be distinct, but not separate. It has also been said that there may be more than one explicate domain enfolded into an implicate domain.

Utilizing this information, one may hypothesize that God's explicateness, God's personality, need not be concentrated within our spatial-temporal explicate domain. God as particular and the world as particular are the presentations of different explicate domains. In this model, not only can one imagine explicate domains that are no longer explicate—explicate domains which are past—but one can imagine more than one explicate domain manifest at the "same time." Here, Richard and other theists discover that God and the world are other; the locus of their separate existences are in different explicate domains. Nonetheless, there is a relationship between these explicate domains. The relationship between these domains is secured by the fact that the explicate domains are implicated within the one implicate domain. This structure of implicate and explicate domains allows us to envision how God and the world can be other, yet God can also be said to interact with the world. These distinct explicate domains share an implicate domain.

This theistic view of ultimate reality incorporates the distinctiveness of the different explicate domains with an understanding of the oneness provided by the implicate domain. Utilizing this holographic model, we may say that the implicate domain can be envisioned as the oneness of God—the body of God in which all things exist. While theists such as Richard recognize the oneness of God's being—a oneness now represented by the implicate domain—this oneness does not take precedence over the individuality of God and God's relationship to individuals. Here the theist celebrates personality and difference as represented by the explicate domains of the holographic model. Thus, the theist looks for salvation in a personal relationship in which God's power, love, and grace call forth the essence of the individual. This relationship allows the individual to unfold and fulfill its individuality in this explicate domain or any other explicate domain in which God ensures individuality. This relationship, which constantly calls forth one's individuality, guarantees that individuality. The theist may now state that one's individuality is guaranteed in alternative explicate domains all of which have a relationship to God as that power which calls forth individuality—explicateness. Salvation is therefore found in this relationship which ensures the nature of individuality and which nurtures individuality through the powers of love and grace.

## ONE MODEL FOR DIFFERENT ULTIMATE REALITIES AND DIFFERENT "SELVES"?

This chapter has reviewed three views of ultimate reality consistently considered to be mutually exclusive by the proponents of those positions and by individuals engaged in comparative analysis. Each of these positions has been related to the same holographic model. This proposal for religious pluralism illuminates how all three of these positions can be simultaneously possible and simultaneously ultimate, but not the same. Simply stated, first with regard to the two impersonal ultimate realities, one can realize the emptiness of existence or the nonduality of Being. Either realization would be soteriologically effective. Each realization liberates one from the shackles of ignorance and provides an insight into one of the *natures of Reality*, but not *all the natures of Reality*. (I am using the term *Reality* here as we did in the discussion of Professor Panikkar in chapter 2. It correlates with the metaphysical Reality that encompasses these three ultimate realities, but need not be limited to these ultimate realities.) In addition, the theist uncovers (or finds revealed) that the problems of human existence can be overcome and that one can find ultimate fulfillment in an I–Thou relation with that Being whose explicate nature can ensure the continued existence of the individual. In this model, such fulfillment providing the completeness of divine bliss can be simultaneous with each of the other two ultimate realities—none adding to or subtracting from the others. Here, too, this divine nature in its oneness would be coextensive with all that exists and thus revelatory of *the nature of all Reality*, but not revelatory of *all the natures of Reality*.

This last distinction, highlighted in the preceding italicized phrases, is very significant for this project and warrants further attention. The realization of the nonduality of Being is, analogously, an insight into the nature of the entirety of the implicate domain and as such would allow one to realize the oneness of Being. However, it is not an insight into all the natures of the implicate domain—into all the ways that the implicate domain can be perceived. The implicate domain can also be seen as emptiness. Specifically, the realization of the emptiness of any form is the realization of the emptiness of all form and the emptiness of the entirety of the implicate domain. As such, it is the realization of all "existence"—both being and nonbeing—but it is not the realization of all the natures of Reality.[61] Likewise, a realization of the oneness of God and the explicateness of God would reveal the nature of all, but not all the natures of all.

As the final point in this chapter, one may argue that the preceding reviews of the three views of ultimate reality did not sufficiently examine the nature of the "self" in each of these positions. Furthermore, one might be inclined to declare that an examination of the different views of "self" would render this proposal untenable. Therefore, each of the three views of "self" must be contrasted again and their allegedly contradictory natures confronted.

Fundamental to Buddhism is the notion of no-self (*anatta*). Fundamental to Christianity, and theism in general, is the notion of a soul—an immortal soul. Fundamental to Advaita Vedānta is the notion of only one Self, one *ātman*. And fundamental to this project is the notion that all three are simultaneously possible. But how? If everything is changing and there is no unchanging, uncompounded entity (*dharma*), how can there be such a thing as an immortal soul in the Christian (or theistic) sense? Conversely, if there is an immortal soul, how can all things be changing? And finally, how can there be an individual soul or there be "no-soul" (*anatta*) if all is the one *ātman*?

The last question has already been analyzed at least with regard to the Buddhist-Advaitin part of the question. We have seen how one can simultaneously understand the implicate domain as Being at the same time as one sees it as continuous flux in which there is no enduring object—no *dharma* that is uncompounded and that lasts. While Advaita Vedānta does not stress the notion of constant change, it very clearly understands that the *jīva* (mind and body) and the material world undergo regular change. It is subject to the laws of cause and effect to the extent that such laws and those objects are only relatively true (*saṃvṛtti satya*). Advaita Vedānta would agree that there is no individual self that is an unchanging substance. In this sense, Advaita agrees with Buddhism that there is no *unchanging, individual* soul. Actually, Christians would also agree. The Christian notion of an immortal soul does not mean that the soul is an unchanging, uncompounded substance or element. Its immortality means that the soul does not cease to exist at death, but continues to exist as a vital, relational spiritual substance.[62] The Buddhist no-*ātman* is not a rejection of the Christian notion of an immortal soul. The Buddhists were interested in rejecting the Advaitin (Upaniṣadic) notion of *ātman*. The Advaitin rejection of Buddhism is not a rejection of the notion that individuals—their minds and bodies—are compounded and constantly changing. The Advaitin rejection of Buddhism is a rejection of the Buddhist notion that there is no *ātman*/brahman sublating the phenomenal world.

In light of this distinction, we have already seen how the realization of no soul and emptiness can be ultimate at the same time as one realizes that *ātman* is ultimate. A Christian theist's rejection of the no-soul theory and the one-soul theory would not be a rejection of the notion that change is vital to the nature of the individual, nor would it be a rejection of the notion that the oneness of God pervades all. Rather, the Christian rejection of these positions would be an affirmation that salvation is attained in relationship—in the soul's dynamic relationship with God, who ensures the continuation of the soul. This "immortal soul" can continue to exist at the same time as one realizes the oneness of Being and at the same time as another realizes that all form is emptiness and that there is no self. In this model, these three views of self and their corresponding views of ultimate reality can simultaneously "exist."

## NOTES

1. The analogies cited here are dominant analogies that each of these thinkers use. It is not to say that these are the only analogies that each thinker uses. For example, Gauḍapāda also uses the analogy of a whirling firebrand and the relationship between waking and dreaming. Vasubandhu employs other analogies such as the iron ore–gold analogy and waking–dreaming analogy. (See Gadjin Nagao, "The Buddhist World-View as Elucidated in the Three-Nature Theory and Its Similes," *Eastern Buddhist* 16 [1983]: 1–18.) Richard of St. Victor employs the entire notion of the twelve patriarchs to lay out his mystical vision. See Grover Zinn, introduction to *Richard of St. Victor* (New York: Paulist Press, 1979), 10 ff.

2. There is certainly diversity of opinion with the Advaita school on this point. I believe that this is the position of Śaṅkara and Gauḍapāda. Some might disagree with the assessment of the latter in light of his *ajātivāda*. For a discussion of this issue, see Karl H. Potter, *Presuppositions of Indian Philosophy* (Englewood Cliffs: Prentice Hall, Inc., 1962), 236 ff.

3. This analogy is found in Vasubandhu's Trisvabhāvanirdeśa. For an analysis of this material, see by this author, "A Holographic Alternative to a Traditional Yogācāra Simile," *Eastern Buddhist* 23 (1990): 56–78.

4. Bohm describes this possibility. See the previous chapter for a description of this.

5. David Bohm, *Wholeness and the Implicate Order* (London: Routledge and Kegan Paul, 1980), 33.

6. Bohm, "The Implicate Order: A New Approach to the Nature of Reality," in *Beyond Mechanism: The Universe in Recent Physics and Catholic Thought*, David L. Schindler ed. (Lanham, Md.: University Press of America, 1986), 34. In the same volume, John Cobb ("Bohm's Contribution to Faith in Our Time," 38–50) is critical of Bohm for overstating the priority of the whole over the parts.

7. Bohm distinguishes metaphysics from physics; see David Bohm and Sean Kelly, "Dialogue on Science, Society and the Generative Order," *Zygon* 25 (1990): 456–457.

8. The issue of time and causality in the implicate domain is reviewed later. At this point, it should be noted that the notion of time in the implicate domain may appear to be out of place. Since there are no objects, how can there be time?

9. This point is being mentioned here so as to not conflate it with one of the criticisms that has been leveled against David Bohm. As we will see, Bohm has been criticized by some, most notably by David Griffin and John Cobb, for his views on temporality and causality. See notes 46–50.

10. Surendranath Dasgupta, *A History of Indian Philosophy*, Volume I (Delhi: Motilal Banarsidass, 1975), 422.

11. There is a great deal of historical uncertainty regarding the identity, the date and the works attributed to Gauḍapāda. While tradition claims that Gauḍapāda was Śaṅkara's teacher's teacher and thus relatively close to Śaṅkara, some historians place him closer to the sixth century C.E. There is also an enormous debate about the authorship of the *Māṇḍākya Kārikā* and whether this work was the work of a single author or a composition by a group of authors. Furthermore,

there is a great deal of debate concerning the integrity of the *Māṇḍākya Kārikā* and whether its four sections (*prakaraṇas*) are really one book, two books or even more. For a review of this literature, see by this author "Culture, Genre and the Māṇḍākya Kārikā: Philosophical Inconsistency, Historical Uncertainty, or Textual Discontinuity," *Asian Philosophy* 6 (1996): 131 ff. Furthermore, there is a great debate over the influence of Mahāyāna Buddhist thought on Gauḍapāda. There is no doubt that Gauḍapāda was aware of and influenced by Buddhism. There is also no doubt that the Advaita tradition aligns itself behind Gauḍapāda and against Buddhism and any charges of crypto-Buddhism. For a recent discussion of these issues see Richard King, *Early Advaita Vedānta and Buddhism: The Mahāyāna Context of the Gauḍapādīya-kārikā* (New York: State University of New York Press, 1995). In all that follows, I treat Gauḍapāda as an Advaitin whose tradition is different than, but certainly related to, Yogācāra Buddhism.

12. *The Māṇḍūkya Upaniṣad* 7, quoted from Patrick Olivelle trans., *Upaniṣads* (Oxford: Oxford University Press, 1996), 297.

13. *Gauḍapāda, Māṇḍūkya Kārikā,* 1:10. All Sanskrit references from Gauḍapāda and for Śaṅkara's commentary (*bhāṣya*) on the *Māṇḍūkya Kārikā* are quoted from Gauḍapāda, *Māṇḍūkyopaniṣad, Gauḍapādīya Kārikā, Śaṅkarabhāṣya* (Gorakhapur, Uttar Pradesh: Gita Press, Samvat 2026) and all translations are by this author unless otherwise noted. Each text will be listed by name of text only. *nivṛtteḥ sarvaduḥkhānāmīśānaḥ prabhuravyayaḥ/ advaitaḥ sarvabhāvānaṃ devasturyo vibhuḥ smṛtaḥ//*

14. *Māṇḍūkya Kārikā Bhāśya,* 1:1.

15. This section on Gauḍapāda and the subsequent section on Richard of St. Victor are substantially revised from an earlier publication—"A Holographic Analysis of Religious Diversity—A Case Study of Hinduism and Christianity," *Journal of Religious Pluralism* 2 (1993): 29–59.

16. *Māṇḍūkya Kārikā,* 2:32. *na nirodho na cotpattirna baddho na ca sādhakaḥ/ na mumukṣurna vai mukta ityeṣā paramārthatā//*

17. *Māṇḍūkya Kārikā* 4:55–56 read as follows: "As long as one maintains a conviction that there is cause and effect, to that extent there will be that which arises from cause and effect. With the destruction of cause and effect, saṃsāra is not indulged. As long as there is a conviction in cause and effect, to that extent saṃsāra is maintained. With the destruction of cause and effect, saṃsāra is not indulged."

18. *Māṇḍūkya Kārikā,* 1:29.

19. *Māṇḍūkya Kārikā,* 2:13, 2:19, 3:28.

20. *Māṇḍūkya Kārikā,* 3:27–28.

21. Karl Potter, *Encyclopedia of Indian Philosophies: Advaita Vedānta up to Śaṁkara and His Pupils,* Volume III (Delhi: Motilal Banarsidass, 1981), 7.

22. *Māṇḍūkya Kārikā,* 3:3–7.

23. In other publications (Kaplan, *Hermeneutics, Holography and Indian Idealism* [Delhi: Motilal Banarsidass, 1987]), I have argued that Gauḍapāda is not an idealist. He does not claim that mind creates objects. This presentation of Gauḍapāda is consistent with my earlier publications. According to Gauḍapāda, when one realizes the nonduality and oneness of Brahman, the implicate domain, then one

realizes that the explicate entities are not truly real. The latter distracts an individual from that which is ultimately real. This is not to say that Gauḍapāda believes that the mind creates objects as many have assumed. It seems to me that Gauḍapāda holds a holographic-like theory of perception in which the mind's perception of objects entails the mind going out and taking the form of the object, much like in a holographic presentation of images. These holographic-like images perceived by the mind are created by the mind; the objects are not created by the mind.

24. *Māṇḍūkya Kārikā*, 3:31. *manodṛśyamidaṃ dvaitaṃ yatkiṃcit sacarācaram/ manaso hyamanībhāve dvaitaṃ naivopalabhyate// 3:32 ātmasatyānubodhena na saṇkalpayate yadā/amanastāṃ tadā yāti grāhyābhave tadagraham// 3:33 akalpakamanajaṃ jñānaṃ jñeyābhinnaṃ pracakṣate/brahmajñeyamajaṃ nityamajenājaṃ vibudhyate// 3:38 graho na tatra notsargaścintā yatra na vidyate/ ātmasaṃsthaṃ tadā jñānamajāti samatāṃ gatam// 3:39 asparśayoga vai nāma durdarśaḥ sarvayogibhiḥ/ yogino bibhyati hyasmādabhaye bhayadarśinaḥ//*

25. One may compare this notion to Krishnachandra Bhattacharyya's analysis of *tucchamāyā*, "Śaṅkara's Doctrine of Maya," in *Studies in Philosophy*, Volume I, Gopinath Bhatacharyya ed. (Calcutta: Progressive Publishers, 1958), 95–106.

26. *Māṇḍūkya Kārikā Bhāṣya*, 1:16: "*ubhayalakśanena tatvāpratibodeharūpena bījātmanānyathāgrahaṇalakśaṇena.*" One can see also Sarvajñātman, *Saṁkṣepaśārīraka*, N. Veezhinathan trans. and ed. (Madras: Centre for the Advanced Study in Philosophy, 1972), 10. "Avidyā, owing to the strength of having the pure consciousness as its locus and content, comes to have a veiling and a transfiguring faculty. It veils the ever-luminous Brahman-Atman, and (then) projects it illusorily in the form of embodied souls, God and the phenomenal world."

27. Vasubandhu, *Madhyāntavibhāga Bhāṣya*, 1:20: "*pudgalasyātha dharmāṇāmabhāvaḥ śūnyatātra hi.*" All Sanskrit verses of the *Madhyāntavibhāga* and the *Madhyāntavibhāga Bhāṣya* are quoted from Stefan Anacker, *Seven Works of Vasubandhu: The Buddhist Psychological Doctor* (Delhi: Motilal Banarsidass, 1984) and, while indebted to other translations, are the responsibility of this author unless otherwise noted. It should also be recognized that there is a debate over the author of the *Madhyāntavibhāga*—being either Maitreya or Asaṅga. For sake of consistency with Anacker's volume, I refer to the author of the latter as Maitreya, but hereafter list them by the name of the text only.

28. See note 38 for the textual reference.

29. The literature on these issues is extensive. For an overview of the debate on idealism, one can see by this author "The Yogācāra Roots of Advaita Idealism? Noting a Similarity between Vasubandhu and Gauḍapāda," *Journal of Indian Philosophy* 20 (1992): 191–218. For the debate on the identity of Vasubandhu, see: E. Frauwallner, "On the Date of the Buddhist Master of the Law Vasubandhu," *Serie Orientale Roma*, III, 1951; P. S. Jaini, "On the Theory of Two Vasubandhu's," *Bulletin of the School of Oriental and African Studies* 21 (1958): 48–53; and Alex Wayman, "Vasubandhu—Teacher Extraordinary," *Studia Missionalia* 37 (1988): 245–281.

30. Vasubandhu, *Trisvabhāvanirdeśa*, 2 and 3: *yat khyāti paratantro 'sau yathā khyāti sa kalpitaḥ/ pratyayādhīnavṛttitvāt kalpanāmātrabhāvataḥ// tasya khyātur yathāk-*

*hyānaṃ yā sadā 'vidyamānatā/jñeyaḥ sa pariniṣpannaḥ svabhāvo 'nanyathātvataḥ//* Sanskrit text quoted from Fernando Tola and Carmen Dragonetti, "The Trisvabhavakārikā of Vasubandhu," *Journal of Indian Philosophy* 11 (1983): 225–266. All translations, while indebted to other translations of this text, are the responsibility of this author.

31. Paul J. Griffiths, *On Being Mindless: Buddhist Meditation and the Mind-Body Problem* (LaSalle, Ill.: Open Court, 1986), 96.

32. Nagao, "The Buddhist World-View," 6.

33. Nagao, "The Buddhist World-View," 6.

34. See Vasubandhu's *Triṃśikā*, 20–24, and the *Madhyāntavibhāga Bhāṣya*, 3:7.

35. Gadjin Nagao brings this to our attention:

> The expression, "something remains" (avaśiṣṭa), however, is enigmatic indeed, for sunyata is generally accepted as non-being, negative in character, while "something remains" positively assets the existence of something. Perhaps one should understand this as an ultimate reality which is never denied, not even at the extremity of radical negation; it is, for instance, similar to the situation in which one cannot negate the fact that he is negating. ("What Remains in Sunyata: A Yogacara Interpretation of Emptiness," in *Mahāyāna Buddhist Meditation: Theory and Practice*, Minoru Kiyota ed. [Honolulu: University of Hawaii Press, 1978], 70)

36. *Madhyāntavibhāga*, 1:13. *dvayābhāvo hyabhāvasya bhāvaḥ śūnyasya lakṣaṇam/*

37. *Madhyāntavibhāga Bhāṣya*, 1:1. *śūnyatā tasyābhūtaparikalpasya grāhyagrāhakabhāvena virahītatā/*

38. *Madhyāntavibhāga*, 1.1. *abhūtaparikalpo 'sti dvayaṃ tatra na vidyate/ śūnyatā vidyate tvatra tasyāmapi sa vidyate//*

39. *Madhyāntavibhāga*, 1.14.

40. *Trisvabhāvanirdeśa*, 24–25. *dvayābhāvātmakaḥ purvaṃ paratantraḥ praviṣyate/ tataḥ praviṣyate tatra kalpamātramasaddvayam// tato dvayābhāvabhāvo niṣpanno 'tra praviṣyate/ tathā hyasāveva tadāstināstīti cocyate//* On this point, see also: Vasubandhu's *Viṃśatikā Vṛtti*, 10.

41. *Trisvabhāvanirdeśa*, 35. "*mokṣāpattirayatnataḥ*"

42. *Trisvabhāvanirdeśa*, 37. *dvayoranupalambhena dharmadhātūpalambhatā/ dharmadhātūpalambhena syādvibhutvopalambhatā//*

43. The arguments over whether Gauḍapāda and Vasubandhu hold the same view of ultimate reality have, at points in the history of this debate, been intertwined with the individual's view of the independence of Gauḍapāda from Yogācāra. Those who saw Gauḍapāda as a Buddhist, saw him holding the same view as Vasubandhu or other Buddhists. Those who denied significant Buddhist influence on Gauḍapāda obviously took a different position. Two current works have reviewed not only the history of this debate, but have clearly argued that Mahāyāna Buddhism, specifically Madhyamika and Yogācāra, holds different views of ultimate reality than Advaita. See Richard King, *Early Advaita and Buddhism*, and Michael Comans, *The Method of Early Advaita Vedanta: A Study of Gauḍapāda, Śaṅkara, Sureśvara and Padmāpada* (Delhi: Motilal Banarsidass, 2000).

44. Illustrating the point that Advaita does not see its position as consistent

with the Buddhist position, specifically with regard to the issue at hand, Śaṅkara says: "We say, no, since Brahman is known to be changeless from the Upaniṣadic texts denying all kinds of change, such as, 'That great birthless Self is undecaying, immortal, undying, fearless, and Brahman' (Br. IV. Iv. 25). . . . For one cannot comprehend that the same Brahman can be possessed of the attributes of change and changelessness" (Swami Gambhirananda trans., *Brahma-Sutra-Bhasya of Sri Śaṅkaracarya*, II.i.14, 332).

45. Bohm, *Wholeness and the Implicate Order*, 172.

46. Bohm, *Wholeness and the Implicate Order*, 167.

47. See David Griffin ed., "Bohm and Whitehead on Wholeness, Freedom, Causality and Time," in *Physics and the Ultimate Significance of Time* (Albany: State University of New York Press, 1986), 134. See also John B. Cobb Jr., "Bohm and Time," in same volume, 156 ff.

48. Cobb, "Bohm and Time," 156.

49. Bohm, "Reply to Comments of John Cobb and David Griffin," in *Physics and the Ultimate Significance of Time*, Griffin ed., 172.

50. My intention here is not to enter a debate about the physics of time. This is not a proposal in physics. Nonetheless, it may be worth citing F. A. M. Frescura and B. J. Hiley, "The Implicate Order, Algebras, and the Spinor," *Foundations of Physics* 10 (1980): 20:

> Subject to the above-mentioned restrictions, the marriage of two operations into a single system by the algebra provides a powerful tool for the simultaneous discussion of both the static and the dynamic properties of a geometry. Exploitation of the vector space structure, which is governed by the operation of addition, highlights the static features, while the multiplicative structure serves at least for the partial discussion, or sometimes even for the full discussion (as is the case with norm simple algebras), of the dynamic properties.

51. Along these lines, Robert Thurman's comment on the *Gaṇḍavyūha* is worth citing: "They thus visionarily saw how every moment of time was contained in that very moment, and yet each moment was itself intact" (Robert A. Thurman, "Transcendence and the Sacred in the Mahāyāna Middle Way," in *Transcendence and the Sacred*, Alan M. Olson and Leroy S. Rouner eds. [Notre Dame: University of Notre Dame Press, 1981], 112).

52. Richard of St. Victor wrote *The Trinity* in which he attempts to prove that God must be trinitarian. About this work and Richard's place in the history of Christian theology, Richard Swinburne writes:

> But for explicit a priori argument of the kind which I have given as to why there need to be three and only three divine individuals, we have to wait for Richard of St. Victor in the twelfth century. In *De Trinitate* he developed the points both that perfect love involves there being someone else to whom to be generous; and also that perfect loving involves a third individual, the loving of whom could be shared with the second. (Richard Swinburne, *The Christian God* [Oxford: Clarendon Press, 1994], 190)

In light of Swinburne's analysis, it is interesting to note that *The Mystical Ark*, which is discussed later as articulating Richard's view of ultimate reality as simultaneously the Oneness of God and the Trinity of God, can be characterized by the lack of Christological references. For a discussion of this issue referred to as "apophatic Christology," see Steven Chase, *Angelic Wisdom: The Cherubim and the Grace of Contemplation in Richard of St. Victor* (Notre Dame: University of Notre Dame Press, 1995), 18, 104.

53. Richard of St. Victor, *Mystical Ark*, Book 1:2, 153 ff. All translations of Richard of St. Victor are from Grover A. Zinn trans., *The Twelve Patriarchs, the Mystical Ark, the Book of the Trinity* (New York: Paulist Press, 1979). Future references are to this volume by the particular work.

54. Richard of St. Victor, *Mystical Ark*, Book 3:24, 257 ff.

55. Ewert Cousins, "A Theology of Interpersonal Relations," *Thought* 45 (1970): 65–66.

56. Richard of St. Victor, *Trinity*, Book 3:11, 384.

57. Richard of St. Victor, *Mystical Ark*, Book 4:17, 291–292.

58. Richard of St. Victor, *Mystical Ark*, Book 4:18, 292.

59. Richard of St. Victor, *Mystical Ark*, Book 4:18, 293.

60. Richard of St. Victor, *Mystical Ark*, Book 4:4, 263–264.

61. One can see how the realization of such emptiness would not allow one to discuss whether the realizer, that is, the buddha, exists, does not exist, both exists and does not exist, neither exists nor not exists. All such categories do not apply to the implicate domain as emptiness, whereas different categories arise when the implicate domain is perceived as the unity of Being.

62. In light of this discussion, it should be noted that this proposal appears to have a greater problem with Samkhya and Jain notions of the individual soul than with the Christian notion of soul. Since these two views have not been discussed, I leave that issue to a future work.

*Chapter Six*

# Conclusion: Problems and Possibilities

## FINAL OVERVIEW

In this book, I have tried to illuminate how three different ultimate realities could be simultaneously existing, equally real and mutually interpenetrating. I have shown how, individually, each of these views of ultimate reality can be related to this holographic model; and how, simultaneously, all three of these views can be related to this holographic model. These three views of ultimate reality are consistently thought to be mutually exclusive. Allegedly, the world can be structured in manner A, manner B or manner C, but certainly, it is said, that it cannot be structured in all three ways. Contrary to that position, I have shown how salvation/liberation can be envisioned as Being, as Emptiness and as rooted in an I–Thou relation. Each of these ultimate realities could be simultaneously existing within one holographic-like metaphysical structure. Each nature is equally as real; each nature would be as soteriologically effective as any other nature. An individual who realizes the nature of one of these ultimate realities would have realized a soteriological conclusion to human existence as described by one or more of the world's major religious traditions. In this model, none of these ultimate realities are higher than another; each is equally effective.

In describing three ultimate realities and three corresponding soteriological experiences, I believe that we have also moved one step closer to understanding the diversity of mystical experience. This diversity is rooted in the diversity of ultimate realities. Different individuals with different expectations, beliefs, practices and so forth have different experiences, in part, because there are different realities to experience. Different paths lead to different mountaintops. This model does not demand that we see all mystical experiences as the same, nor does it demand that we rank the experiences in some hierarchical fashion. Furthermore, this model accommodates the constructivist epistemological view. This is not to say that any two people experience the same ultimate reality in the same way. Each experience of each ultimate reality may be constructed, at least with regard to how the individual knows/interprets that experience to oneself and with regard to how one retells that experience to others.

The mystical experience that appeared to be most endangered by a constructivist position was the pure consciousness experience. My analysis revealed that the claim that such an experience was mediated or unmediated rested upon ontological presuppositions. If consciousness is ontologically independent of mind/body, as many within the Hindu traditions claim, then the "experience" of pure consciousness is epistemologically feasible. However, such a position would not invalidate the notion that when an individual returns to a state of mind, from no-mindedness, then that state of mind would be mediated. Therefore, one's own mental—mind—knowledge of that state would be mediated in the way that the constructivists have suggested. In addition, one's interpretation of that experience—whether it is Brahman or the One of Plotinus—and one's explanation of that experience to others would be mediated by one's cultural and philosophical background.

In developing a constructivist epistemology rooted in ontological pluralism, the chasm that Hick highlighted between the different views of ultimate reality can be overcome. Hick explained that a singular Real cannot be both personal and impersonal. It cannot be both Being and Emptiness. Therefore, either only one of the traditions is right or these different types of experiences must refer to the Real as experienced, not the Real *an sich*. From the latter perspective, Reality is not a personal divinity; it is not Being; it is not emptiness. It is none of the above. Each tradition that claims it is one of the above must be wrong.

In contrast, in this holographic model, the chasm between the diversity of reported experiences of ultimate reality and the variety of ultimate realities to support such experiences is narrowed. The diversity of experiences is concomitant with a diversity of ultimate realities. Needless to say, each of these ultimate realities will be understood and described in culturally specific ways. But in this model, we need not tell a religious tradition that that which it has experienced as ultimate reality is not ultimate reality.

In this model, I am trying to affirm that which a religious tradition says is true, but not affirm that which it says is false. As we have seen, Gauḍapāda's claim, Vasubandhu's claim and Richard of St. Victor's claim about ultimate truth can each be understood in light of this holographic model. Each of these visions of ultimate reality, along with its soteriological experience, may be true without demanding that the others are false. Here each tradition can have its own cake, not some generic cake that no one wants, knows or experiences. In this model, having one's own cake does not entitle one to belligerence. It does not entitle one to shove that cake in someone else's face. Each can have its cake and eat it, too.

This model calls for individuals to choose. Without making a commitment to a particular path and a particular practice, one goes nowhere and discovers nothing. Choice is necessary; action is essential. That which one can uncover is dependent upon that to which one is committed. Different practices have different consequences. Each practice engages the individual in distinct ways and as such leads the individual in a specific direction. Reversing the notion that different paths lead to the same summit, this model leads us to the conclusion that different paths terminate in different summits.

This is a proposal for metaphysical democracy. Democracy, understood here as the ability and freedom to choose, is enshrined in the ontological structure of the universe. One has freedom of "Being"—that is, the freedom to choose the type of "Being" that one wants to be. This is not, however, metaphysical idealism. One does not create a metaphysical world of one's own choosing. Rather, one can come to know and experience that which one intends to know. If successful, one becomes that which one intends to become. Intentionality becomes ontology, but this does not mean that the ontological reality is created by the mind. If one seeks the nonduality of Being and one comes to realize the nonduality of Being, "one" can be the nondual Being. Likewise, if one searches for emptiness, one may realize the emptiness of the "one" who was searching and the emptiness of all. Simultaneously, one could place one's faith in that Other whose grace ensures that individuality is not a passing phenomenon and marvel in that relationship of the individual to the Other. In this model, oneness, emptiness and individuality are ways of "being" that one chooses;

they are not metaphysical impositions from a monolithically structured universe.

## CONFRONTING THE PROBLEMS AND THE POSSIBILITIES

Throughout this book, I have tried to address some of the problems that religious pluralists in general must face, and I have also tried to address some of the major issues that face this particular proposal. It was these concerns that led us to the discussions of Hick, Panikkar, Katz and their respective critics. I believe that this proposal has adequately responded to the issues that each has raised. However, these responses did not resolve all the problems that arise in relation to this model for religious pluralism. Some of the issues arise from the fact that proposing a plurality of ultimate realities affects the way in which we conceive of each of the individual ultimate realities. In other words, it must be acknowledged that proposing a pluralism of ultimate realities alters some of the philosophical and theological issues surrounding our understanding of a given ultimate reality. Second, other issues arise from the fact that the different ultimate realities reviewed as simultaneously existing appear in different cultural worldviews with very different presuppositions. Finally, there remains a quandary internal to this proposal—namely, if the ultimate realities are mutually interpenetrating, in what sense are the different soteriological conclusions mutually exclusive?

## CROSS-CULTURAL ISSUES

I believe that the best way to illuminate the problems that arise when traversing different cultural boundaries is to examine concrete examples. For example, different religious cultures have different ways of conceptualizing the issue of moral judgment and retribution. In some of the religious traditions to which we have been referring, God is the judge of all moral actions. God "watches" what each of us does and rewards or punishes us appropriately. In other systems, for example, the Indian religious systems, there is a belief in *karma*—an impersonal system in which for every action there is a reaction. Thus, one may ask at this point whether morality is under the watchful eye of God or whether morality is ensured by the impersonal cosmic forces of *karma*? This question is pertinent to many projects in comparative religions; however, I do not believe that it pertains to this project. This point needs to be elucidated.

The soteriological diversity that we have reviewed is not confined to a particular religion or geographical region. I am not comparing Indian religions with their doctrine of *karma* to Western theological systems with their notions of divine oversight. (That would be a completely different project.) Rather, I am examining how a theistic form of salvation, whether in India or in the West, can simultaneously exist with a nontheistic form of liberation, whether in India or the West. As such, this proposal could have been confined to the different forms of ultimate reality in Western religions or to the different forms of ultimate reality in Indian religions. If we took either track, we would still be confronted with the diversity of ultimate realities discussed throughout this work and still could develop a model for soteriological diversity without having to debate whether morality is under the watchful eye of God or *karma*.

The question of a single birth or many rebirths presents us with another, and for our purposes, final example of this type of issue. Western religions generally believe that human beings are born once. At the end of that one life, each individual is judged. Indian religions, on the other hand, believe in the notion of rebirth—an individual is born and reborn until he/she finally achieves liberation. The liberation that is sought could be in a theistic I–Thou relationship such as described by Rāmānuja's Viśiṣṭādvaita Vedānta or it could be in a nondualistic awareness as described by Gauḍapāda's Advaita Vedānta. Once again, we could discuss a plethora of ultimate realities and a model for religious pluralism merely by discussing the different theological positions that populate the Indian landscape or the landscape of the Western religious traditions. Therefore, this model for ontological pluralism is independent of this question of one birth or many births. This model can be presented without resolving the cross-cultural issues that still divide the religious traditions within each culture. These are all important questions in comparative religions, but different from the issues with which I am dealing.[1]

## THEOLOGICAL ISSUES

The second issue that needs to be examined concerns the impact of this pluralistic model on specific theological positions. First, I examine the impact of this pluralistic model on the understanding of God as Lord of all individuals within the universe. In this model, all individuals are not beholden to the Lord for their salvation. There are other forms of liberation. Therefore, I must ask if theism can remain theism if the Lord is not responsible for the salvation of all individuals? Could one have a theism in which the Lord was only responsible for those who wanted salvation?

These questions may bring to mind the notion that the Lord is the Lord of only a certain group of people. While henotheistic religions entertained such notions, postaxial religions seem to reject this concept. For example, this notion was rejected by Judaism when it realized that its covenant with God did not exclude the fact that all living creatures also had a covenant with God, the covenant of Noah (Genesis 9). Christianity, in its most exclusivistic bent, has held to the doctrine that there is no salvation outside the church. This doctrine has the practical effect of excluding whole hosts of people; however, such a restriction would be the Lord's doing. In that case, God would be setting the rule that no one can achieve salvation unless one does it in "this" way. Such an exclusionary notion of salvation is very different from what I am presenting. In this model, the individual can choose to seek salvation or to realize an impersonal form of liberation. Thus, it is not only God who can choose whom to save, but individuals can choose whether they seek an I–Thou salvation or a different type of liberation.

Is it conceivable that God would not demand or could not demand that all people try to achieve one type of salvation—a theistic salvation? Admittedly, the notion that some people can opt out of a theistic salvation sounds strange.[2] But why? We are not talking about individuals getting away with rape or murder. (Please note that I am not implying that people could choose not to be morally judged. As noted previously, that discussion raises different issues.) Here, I am talking about individuals who have achieved a means of overcoming all human suffering, all egoistic problems, who, for example, have realized the identity of all Being. Would an alternative form of salvation be an infringement on God's being, power or grace? Rather than find this notion so strange, one might want to think that an all-loving, gracious God would want individuals to overcome the limitations of existence in any way possible. Such a loving God may grant some individuals a personal relation with that Being who can guarantee one's existence while other individuals may uncover the nonduality of Being or the emptiness of all existence.[3]

The notion that some individuals can realize a form of liberation different from that attained by being saved in an I–Thou relationship raises another issue. This model implies that an individual immortal soul would not necessarily remain individual and thus not remain immortal. On the one hand, according to this model, we have seen that that which can be conceived as a particular, relational entity can simultaneously be viewed, from its implicate nature, as empty of particularity. Both exist at the same time. However, as we see in the last section of this chapter, to realize the emptiness of all existence demands that an "individual" not be dependent upon God. It necessitates that an "individual" overcome all I–Thou relations and the particularity associated with an immortal soul. Therefore, it must be asked, is it conceivable to imagine that immortal souls would not remain immortal?

As we have seen, the Christian tradition affirms the immortality of the soul.[4] However, it should be noted that within Roman Catholicism, for example, the question arises whether this immortality is an attribute of the soul or a product of grace.

> The Catholic Church affirms that each human being has only one soul; that the human soul is spiritual, for, as Aquinas explained, its higher-order activities are neither material nor intrinsically dependent upon matter; that it is created directly by God and simultaneously with the body; and that it is immortal, although whether this attribute is natural or a gift of grace has never been defined.[5]

In one sense, even if the immortality of the soul were natural, its nature is itself a gift of God, according to the tradition. Thus, for those traditions that maintain that God creates immortal souls as an act of grace, we can once again ponder whether God's grace would allow an individual to transcend the particularity associated with an immortal soul and realize a nondualistic ultimate reality? This question thus returns us to the idea presented previously that a truly gracious God might allow individuals to overcome the limitations of human existence in a variety of ways.

I certainly do not know whether a loving God would find alternative soteriologies an infringement. I am only trying to develop a model in which more than one of the soteriological possibilities found in the world's religions could be simultaneously true and to examine the consequences of such a proposal. Once again, the truth of any of these positions is absolutely beyond my knowledge.

The theistic position that was described in the preceding chapter encompasses both a generic account of theism as well as Richard of St. Victor's account of the different levels of divinity. At this point, one may ask about the specific natures and qualities of God found in different traditions. Is God to be understood as Yahweh, as the Trinity, as Allah, as Vishnu, as Siva, and so forth? Each tradition holds one of these Gods to be supreme and ultimate. Each God is the Lord of the universe—the one to whom they look for salvation. While these Gods have overlapping functions, each one has a different history, a different personality and so on. Herein begins the problem of deciding who exactly is God, what does the one God do, and what are the characteristics of this God?

My resolution to these questions is generally consistent with John Hick's and indebted to his work. However, given my premise of a plurality of ultimate realities, my perspective differs from his. Basically, Hick proposes that the different Gods are the manifestation of different personalities of the Real *an sich* developed in a relationship between a community of believers and the Real.[6] For example, in reference to Judaism, Hick says:

> The Adonai of Judaism exists at the interface between the ultimate transcendent Reality and the Hebrew people. He is the Transcendent as seen through Hebrew eyes and as given form by the Hebraic religious imagination. And his laws are the particular way in which the practical difference that the presence of the Transcendent makes for human life has come to consciousness in Hebrew experience. But this particular concrete divine *persona* did not exist prior to and independently of the strand of history of which he is an integral part. What existed prior to and independently of that history is the transcendent Reality itself, whose impact upon the stream of Hebrew consciousness has taken this particular experienceable shape. The concrete figure of Jahweh is thus not identical with the ultimate divine Reality as it is in itself but is an authentic face or mask or persona of the Transcendent in relation to one particular human community.[7]

Such a view of God and God's relation to different communities could be illustrated easily using this holographic model. Holography allows us to envision how different people looking at the same location, but from different perspectives, can see different images. While agreeing with much that Hick proposes, my perspective differs slightly from his. Following the theistic traditions of the world, the ultimate reality of a personal God has been assumed in this pluralistic model. It has not been relegated to a status secondary to the one Real *an sich*.

The last theological issue that is addressed concerns the notion of incarnation. Incarnation appears most prominently in two major religious traditions—Hinduism and Christianity. While the former entertains the notion that there are multiple incarnations of the deity, Christianity has asserted that there is only one incarnation. First, it must be noted that this pluralistic model need not include nor exclude an incarnational theology as part of its theistic possibility.[8] However, this model is incompatible with an exclusivistic or inclusivistic incarnational theology, such as articulated in many forms of Christianity.[9] Not all interpretations of incarnation are decidedly antipluralistic.[10] One example is worth citing—namely, Panikkar's. In the following, he states the Christian expectation regarding Christ and then proceeds to offer his understanding.

> Nobody is ultimately satisfied with partialities. A Christian, for instance, will say that Christ represents the totality or is the universal savior or the center of the universe, to utilize different metaphors, the interpretation of which does not enter now into the picture. We may well demythicize them. Nevertheless the Christian will not be satisfied with a partial view, that Christ is just one *avatāra* among many, and be content with it as the Christian's lot (or *karma*?). In short, Christians will have to say that in Christ they find the truth—and with qualifications, the whole truth.[11]

From the outset of this work, I have agreed with the notion that people are not generally satisfied with partialities. Religious traditions seek to know the truth, to experience the truth and to be transformed by and to the truth. Panikkar's explanation of how Christianity and other religions can know the truth provides one model for understanding the notion of incarnation that seems to avoid the problem of partiality and also seems strikingly like this holographic proposal, whether or not the latter includes an incarnational option. He says:

> We should, further, be aware that we see the *totum per partem*, the whole through a part. We will have to concede that the other, the non-Christian, for instance, may have a similar experience and that the non-Christian will have to say that the Christian takes the *pars pro toto*, for from the outside one only sees the *pars*, not the *totum*—the window, not the panorama. How to combine these apparently contradictory statements? We will have to say that the other is right in discovering that we take the *pars pro toto* (because the outsider sees the window), but that we are also right in seeing the *totum per partem* (because we see the panorama). It is a *totum* for us, but *per partem*, limited to our vision through the one window. We see the *totum*, but not *totaliter* one may say (because we do not see through other windows). We see all that we can see. The other may see equally the *totum* through another window, and thus describe it differently, but both see the *totum*, although

> not *in toto*, but *per partem. Rota in rotae (trochos en trocho)* said Christian mystics on Ezechiel 1:16.[12]

Panikkar's passage is reminiscent of Richard of St. Victor's description of divinity—the Fifth and Sixth Contemplations, the Unity and Trinity of God—in which he describes the relationship between part and whole (chapter 5, note 59). Richard told us that "the part is not less than the whole, nor the whole is more universal than its parts; indeed, where the part is not lessening the whole, and the whole is not made up of parts."[13] It is also remarkably consistent with the relationship between part and whole in holography and in the model that we have been developing here. Whether Panikkar's description, Richard's insight and their relation to holography can serve as a model for Christians (and Hindus) to understand the notion of incarnation in a pluralistic manner, I will leave to Christians (and Hindus) since this model stands with or without the notion of incarnation.

I conclude this section by reflecting upon Panikkar's statement and its relation to this project. Each religious tradition, in its inclusivistic and exclusivistic nature, sees the *totum per partem*, but believes that it is seeing the whole in itself and by itself. Our ordinary experience tells us that we cannot experience the whole through only a part. Therefore, if we have experienced the whole, we assume that we have not experienced this through one part. On the other hand, the model that we are developing here sees that a part can reveal the whole. (Recall that each piece of the hologram reveals the whole image, but it does this as if one is looking through a window.) Furthermore, as I have postulated in the previous chapter, *one part can reveal the nature of all Being, emptiness and so forth*, but in this holographic model, *it does not reveal all the natures of Reality*. Each religious tradition following a specific path may discover an ultimate reality that is coextensive with all other ultimate realities, but it does not reveal all ultimate realities. This has been the basic thesis of this work.

## THE ISSUE OF SOTERIOLOGICAL EXCLUSIVITY

The final question that needs to be addressed concerns the mutually exclusive nature of each of the soteriological conclusions. In this model, ontologically, Being is emptiness and emptiness is Being. They are not other than each other. Furthermore, ontologically, individuality is emptiness and emptiness is individuality. They are not other than each other and neither is other than the nondual Being. If Being is emptiness and emptiness is Being and if Being and emptiness are the duality of the individual and the Other, then a final question arises. Can one realize more than one ultimate reality as ultimate, not just as penultimate? (Certainly, different traditions claim to have experienced one ultimate reality as ultimate and another as penultimate.)

It may seem logical to assume that because one can know each ultimate reality, one can also experience each ultimate reality as soteriologically final. However, I would like to ponder whether these ultimate realities must remain soteriologically distinct and mutually exclusive. The following scenarios illuminate this issue. If a theist who has realized her ultimate dependence on the Divine Other subsequently tries to realize a nondualistic ultimate reality as ultimate and not as penultimate, then would the theist be forced to overcome her feeling of utter dependence on the Divine Other? In order to realize this second, nondualistic ultimate reality, it would seem as if the theist must realize that her utter dependence can be eclipsed by shifting her awareness to the nonduality of Being or to the emptiness of all reality. In so doing, how could one still be a theist? Likewise, how could a nondualist who had realized that there is no self and no Other subsequently realize the ultimate significance of the I–Thou relation? How could one recognize his utter dependence upon the Other and still be a nondualist? Such a recognition would seem to demand that a nondualist affirm the ultimate significance of duality and the ultimate significance of the Divine Other. This would imply that the nondualist would have to become a theist.

In light of the preceding questions and the model that has been presented, I conclude with the following. It seems that each ultimate reality can be realized independently of the other ultimate realities and each remains soteriologically distinct. This would imply that the final state of different individuals could be different. Having followed different paths and having achieved different ultimate goals, different individuals can end up in different places—there are different paths to different summits.

I do not know if any of the preceding is true. I have no idea that there really is any form of liberation or salvation—no idea that there is any form of nonduality or any Divine Other. All of the claims made by the different religious traditions about different ultimate realities may be completely false. For all I know and in light of my previous research, these different claims regarding ultimate realities may reflect different experiences of a holographic brain perceiving itself in different ways.[14] For all I know, the ontological referent of these epistemological claims may find us limited to our neurological networks.

My goal has not been to make pronouncements of truth. Rather, my goal has been to entertain how we can look at old information in a new way. It is my hope that individuals will begin to look at the relationship between religious traditions in a different light—one that does not imply that my being right demands that you are wrong. It is also my hope that this model, whether entertained in itself, will allow us to raise new questions that can move the study of comparative religions forward.

## NOTES

1. Creation is another issue that can surface in a comparative study of religion. Specifically, it can be asked whether there was an absolute beginning by God to the creation of all existence as proposed in some forms of Western theology. Or, is the notion of a creation out of nothing (*ex nihilo*) to be rejected in favor of the beginninglessness of existence? Like the two previous problems, the debate about the nature of creation is independent of the soteriological issues raised in this work.

2. Certainly, the mechanism for such a process would be unclear. However, the mechanism for how human morality is judged is unclear. How does God know every action and intention?

3. I have addressed this problem from the perspective of God's love and grace. I have not addressed the issues surrounding the notion of God's power. The latter may be understood in a number of ways from an all-powerful, all-controlling deity to a God of persuasion. These different perspectives on God's power would certainly impact this model in different ways.

4. In holography, we have seen how one implicate domain can enfold multiple explicate domains and how multiple explicate domains can be unfolded from a single implicate domain. Imagining how two or more explicate, physical objects can be unfolded simultaneously and possibly in the same place would be very difficult. However, this model may allow us to imagine how there can be physical objects such as we normally experience enfolded in and unfolded from an implicate domain that also enfolds and unfolds other types of explicate entities—call them virtual entities, spiritual entities, mental entities and so on. It should also be noted that in the theistic tradition we have been examining, notably Christianity, it maintains that God and souls are not physical objects; they are spiritual objects. The precise nature of such entities is debated and often understated in the different traditions. Therefore, I do not begin to suggest any more than the idea that this model would allow us to imagine that different kinds of explicate entities—physical and nonphysical—could be unfolded from the one implicate domain which is the Being and emptiness of the world.

5. Michael Stebbins, "Soul," in *The HarperCollins Encyclopedia of Catholicism*, Richard B. McBrien ed. (San Francisco: Harper San Francisco, 1995), 1210–1211. See also P. B. T. Bilaniuk, "Soul, Human: Theology," in *The New Catholic Encyclopedia*, Volume 13 (New York: McGraw-Hill, 1967), 462. "The definition of the soul's personal immortality (Denz 1440) leaves open the question whether it is naturally immortal because of its spiritual quality, or supernaturally because of a special gift of the God (however it is stated that Christ makes men participators in His immortality: Denz 413)." Furthermore, one can see the discussion of human immortality by Simon Tugwell, *Human Immortality and the Redemption of Death* (Springfield, Ill.: Templegate Publishers, 1991), 163. Here Tugwell says:

> Apart from its usefulness in interpreting and reinforcing belief in the resurrection, christian tradition is remarkably uninterested in claiming immortality for the soul by right, and the language of the Bible and the liturgy is, if anything, inimical to such a claim, treating immortality rather as something belonging only to God by right and then, by God's gift, to the risen Christ and those who are saved in him as a result of the resurrection. It is a hope proposed to the believer, not a property inherent in the human soul. The only formal appearance of immortality by right in christian doctrine is, as we have seen, in the ill-conceived Bull of Leo X, which was intended to settle a philosophical, not a doctrinal dispute.

None of these citations is intended to prove the notion that immortal souls are not immortal according to Christian doctrine. Rather, they are only intended as food for thought concerning the implications of this pluralistic proposal.

6. For a fuller discussion of Hick's treatment of this subject, see John Hick, *An Interpretation of Religion* (New Haven: Yale University Press, 1989), 269 ff. Here, Hick discusses two models within religious thought that can be used to articulate the relationship between the different Gods. Each of these models apparently has two versions. The first model he cites is that of the Trinity understood either in terms of a social conception of the Trinity or in the sense derived from the Latin *persona*. The second model refers to the Buddhist notion of the three bodies of the Buddha.

7. John Hick, "A Religious Understanding of Religion: A Model of the Relationship between Traditions," in *Inter-religious Models and Criteria*, J. Kellenberger ed. (New York: St. Martin's Press, 1993), 29.

8. On the holographic model, one may speculate that an incarnation would represent the embodiment of the divine reality in an explicate domain different from the explicate domain that is identified with the essence of the divine personality. Insofar as all explicate domains are distinct from each other, the manifestation of the divine nature into this explicate domain would constitute a crossing over of the divine nature from one explicate domain to another explicate domain (*avatāra*). In this model, this crossing over would be made possible by the notion that these different explicate domains share an implicate domain. Thus, this model allows us to imagine what an incarnation would mean and how an incarnation could take place between different explicate worlds. This understanding of the process of incarnation does not tell us if such event actually occurs, who an incarnation is or how many incarnations may occur.

9. Basically, Christianity has asserted that there is only one incarnation, Jesus Christ. Karl Rahner, for example, tells us that any other alleged incarnations such as those described in Hinduism are not to be mistaken for the true incarnation.

> Nor has belief in the Incarnation anything to do with ideas derived from oriental religions, for in all of these the "incarnation" is only a transient sign of the deity within the realm of that which has no real being, a sign which perishes, and therefore can always be repeated, whereas in the Word made flesh the created world, though always a creature finds its definitive and permanent validity. (Karl Rahner and Herbert Vorgrimler, "Jesus," in *Theological Dictionary*, Cornelius Ernst ed., Richard Strachar trans. [New York: Herder and Herder, 1965], 240)

The issue here is not to debate this interpretation of "oriental religions," but rather to note that (1) Rahner rejects the idea of incarnation in oriental religions, and (2) he affirms the notion that Jesus Christ is the only incarnation. He continues by adding that the events surrounding Jesus are the events "on which the final and ultimate salvation of the world depends" (Ibid., 241) and the grace of God and Jesus Christ is everywhere. This inclusivistic understanding of the incarnation and Christianity is not pluralistic. All may be saved, but they are saved only by Jesus Christ whether they know it or not. Here we have the notion of the anonymous Christian. Such a notion of salvation and incarnation cannot be harmonized with the model that is being presented here. As stated in the introduction, this model can accept as true that which a tradition declares to be true; however, this model for soteriological pluralism cannot accept as false that which a tradition declares to be false.

10. For example, see John Hick and Paul Knitter eds., *The Myth of Christian Uniqueness* (Maryknoll: Orbis Books, 1987).

11. Raimundo Panikkar, "The Invisible Harmony: A Universal Theory of Religion or a Cosmic Confidence in Reality," in *Toward a Universal Theology of Religion*, Leonard Swidler ed. (Maryknoll: Orbis Books, 1987), 140.

12. Raimundo Panikkar, "The Invisible Harmony," 140.

13. Richard of St. Victor, *Mystical Ark*, Book 4:4, 263–264.

14. See the works of Karl H. Pribram, and by this author, *Hermeneutics, Holography and Indian Idealism* (Delhi: Motilal Banarsidass, 1987).

# Select Bibliography


Abe, Masao. *Buddhism and Interfaith Dialogue*. Edited by Steven Heine. Houndmille: Macmillan Press Ltd., 1995.

Anacker, Stephen. *Seven Works of Vasubandhu: The Buddhist Psychological Doctor*. Delhi: Motilal Banarsidass, 1984.

Anderson, Robert M., Jr. "A Holographic Model of Transpersonal Consciousness." *Journal of Transpersonal Psychology* 9 (1977): 119–128.

Apczynski, John V. "John Hick's Theocentrism: Revolutionary or Implicitly Exclusivistic?" *Modern Theology* 8 (1992): 39–52.

Austin, William H. "Explanatory Pluralism." *Journal of the American Academy of Religion* 66 (1998): 13–37.

Barbour, Ian. *Myths, Models and Paradigms: A Comparative Study in Science and Religion*. New York: Harper and Row Publishers, 1974.

———. *Religion in an Age of Science: The Gifford Lectures 1989–1991*, Volume I. San Francisco: Harper and Row Publishers, 1990.

Basham, A. L. *The Wonder That Was India*. Calcutta: Fontana Books, 1971.

Berner, Jeff. *The Holography Book*. New York: Avon Books, 1980.

Bhattacharyya, Krishnachandra. *Studies in Philosophy*, Volume I. Edited by Gopinath Bhattacharyya. Calcutta: Progressive Publishers, 1956.

———. *Studies in Philosophy*, Volume II. Edited by Gopinath Bhattacharyya. Calcutta: Progressive Publishers, 1958.

Bilaniuk, P. B. T. "Soul, Human: Theology." Pp. 462–464 in *The New Catholic Encyclopedia*, Volume 13. New York: McGraw-Hill, 1967.

Black, Max. *Models and Metaphors: Studies in Language and Philosophy*. Ithaca, N.Y.: Cornell University Press, 1962.

Bohm, David. "The Enfolding-Unfolding Universe: A Conversation with David Bohm," conducted by Renee Weber. *RE-VISION* 1 (1978): 24–51.

———. "Fragmentation and Wholeness in Religion and Science." *Zygon* 20 (1985): 125–133.

———. "Hidden Variables and the Implicate Order." *Zygon* 20 (1985): 111–117.

———. "The Implicate Order: A New Approach to the Nature of Reality." Pp. 12–37 in *Religious Pluralism*, edited by Leroy S. Rouner. Notre Dame: University of Notre Dame Press, 1984.

———. "Quantum Theory as an Indication of a New Order in Physics: Part A." *Foundation of Physics* 1 (1971): 359–381.

———. "Quantum Theory as an Indication of a New Order in Physics: Part B." *Foundation of Physics* 3 (1973): 139–168.

———. "Response to Schindler's Critique of My *Wholeness and the Implicate Order*." *International Philosophical Quarterly* 22 (1982): 329–339.

———. *Wholeness and the Implicate Order*. London: Routledge and Kegan Paul, 1980.

Bohm, David, and B. J. Hiley. *The Undivided Universe: An Ontological Interpretation of Quantum Theory*. London: Routledge, 1993.

Bohm, David, and Sean Kelly. "Dialogue on Science, Society and the Generative Order." *Zygon* 25 (1990): 449–467.

Bohm, David, and F. David Peat. *Science, Order, and Creativity*. Toronto: Bantam Books, 1987.

Borg, Marcus J. *The God We Never Knew*. New York: Harper San Francisco, 1998.

Carmen, John Braisted. *The Theology of Rāmānuja*. New Haven: Yale University Press, 1974.

Chase, Steven. *Angelic Wisdom: The Cherubim and the Grace of Contemplation in Richard of St. Victor*. Notre Dame: University of Notre Dame Press, 1995.

Cobb, John. *Beyond Dialogue*. Philadelphia: Fortress Press, 1982.

———. "Beyond 'Pluralism.'" Pp. 81–95 in *Christian Uniqueness Reconsidered*, edited by Gavin D'Costa. Maryknoll: Orbis Books, 1990.

———. "Bohm's Contribution to Faith in Our Time." Pp. 38–50 in *Religious Pluralism*, edited by Leroy S. Rouner. Notre Dame: University of Notre Dame Press, 1984.

———. "Bohm and Time." Pp. 154–166 in *Physics and the Ultimate Significance of Time*, edited by David Griffin. New York: State University of New York Press, 1986.

———. "The Meaning of Pluralism for Christian Self-Understanding." Pp. 161–179 in *Religious Pluralism*, edited by Leroy S. Rouner. Notre Dame: University of Notre Dame Press, 1984.

———. "Toward a Christocentric Catholic Theology." Pp. 86–100 in *Toward a Universal Theology of Religion*, edited by Leonard Swidler. Maryknoll: Orbis Books, 1987.

Cole, Colin A. *Asparsa Yoga: A Study of Gaudapada's Mandukya Karika*. Delhi: Motilal Banarsidass, 1982.

Comans, Michael. *The Method of Early Advaita Vedānta: A Study of Gauḍapāda, Śaṅkara, Sureśvara and Padmapāda*. Delhi: Motilal Banarsidass, 2000.

Conio, Caterina. *The Philosophy of the Mandukya-Karika*. Varanasi: Bharatiya Vidya Prakashan, 1971.

Cousins, Ewert. "Bonaventure's Mysticism of Language." Pp. 236–257 in *Mysticism and Language*, edited by Steven T. Katz. New York: Oxford University Press, 1992.

———. "A Theology of Interpersonal Relations." *Thought* 45 (1970): 65–66.

Dalai Lama. *Ethics for the New Millennium*. New York: Riverhead Books, 1999.

Dasgupta, Surendranth. *History of Indian Philosophy*, Volume II. Cambridge: Cambridge University Press, 1976.

D'Costa, Gavin. "Christ, the Trinity, and Religious Pluralism." Pp. 16–29 in *Christian Uniqueness Reconsidered*, edited by Gavin D'Costa. Maryknoll: Orbis Books, 1990.

———. "The Impossibility of a Pluralist View of Religion." *Religious Studies* 32 (1996): 223–232.

Dean, Thomas. "Universal Theology and Dialogical Dialogue." Pp. 162–174 in *Toward a Universal Theology of Religion*, edited by Leonard Swidler. Maryknoll: Orbis Books, 1987.

Deferrari, Roy J., trans. *The Sources of Catholic Dogma*. From the Thirtieth Edition of Henry Denzinger's *Enchiridion Symbolorum*. St. Louis: B. Herder Book Co., 1957.

Eck, Diana. *Encountering God: A Spiritual Journey from Bozeman to Banaras*. Boston: Beacon Press, 1993.

Forman, Robert K. C. "Paramartha and Modern Constructivists on Mysticism: Epistemological Monomorphism versus Duomorphism." *Philosophy East and West* 39 (1989): 393–418.

———, ed. *The Problem of Pure Consciousness*. New York: Oxford University Press, 1990.

Fort, Andrew O., and Patricia Mumme, eds. *Living Liberation in Hindu Thought*. New York: State University of New York Press, 1996.

Frauwallner, E. "On the Date of the Buddhist Master of the Law Vasubandhu." *Serie Orientale Roma* III, 1951.

Frescura, F. A. M., and B. J. Hiley. "The Implicate Order, Algebras, and the Spinor." *Foundations of Physics* 10 (1980): 7–31.

Gauḍapāda. *The Āgamaśāstra of Gauḍapāda*. Edited and translated by Vidhushekhara Bhattacharyya. Calcutta: University of Calcutta, 1943.

———. *Māṇḍūkyopaniṣad, Gauḍapādīya Kārikā, Śaṅkarabhāṣya*. Gorakhapur, Uttar Pradesh: Gita Press, Samvat 2026.

Gazzaniga, Michael S. "Review of the Split Brain." Pp. 89–96 in *The Human Brain*, edited by M. C. Wittrock et al. Englewood Cliffs: Prentice Hall, 1977.

———. "The Split Brain Revisited." *Scientific American* 279 (July 1998): 51–55.

Gimello, Robert. "Mysticism in Its Contexts." Pp. 61–88 in *Mysticism and Religious Traditions*, edited by Steven T. Katz. Oxford: Oxford University Press, 1983.

———. "Mysticism and Meditation." Pp. 170–199 in *Mysticism and Philosophical Analysis*, edited by Steven T. Katz. New York: Oxford University Press, 1978.

Griffin, David Ray. "Bohm and Whitehead on Wholeness, Freedom, Causality, and Time." Pp. 127–153 in *Physics and the Ultimate Significance of Time*, edited by David Griffin. New York: State University of New York Press, 1986.

———. *Physics and the Ultimate Significance of Time: Bohm, Prigogine, and Process Philosophy*. Albany: State University of New York Press, 1986.

———. *Parapsychology, Philosophy and Spirituality: A Postmodern Exploration*. Albany: State University of New York Press, 1997.

Griffiths, Paul J. *An Apology for Apologetics*. Maryknoll: Orbis Press, 1991.

———. *On Being Mindless: Buddhist Meditation and the Mind-Body Problem*. LaSalle, Ill.: Open Court, 1986.

———. "The Uniqueness of Christian Doctrine Defended." Pp. 157–173 in *Chris-*

*tian Uniqueness Reconsidered*, edited by Gavin D'Costa. Maryknoll: Orbis Books, 1990.

———, ed. *Christianity through Non-Christian Eyes*. Maryknoll: Orbis Books, 1990.

Halbfass, Wilhelm. *Philology and Confrontation: Paul Hacker on Traditional and Modern Vedānta*. Albany: State University of New York, 1995.

Harbage, Alfred, ed. *William Shakespeare, The Complete Works*. New York: Viking Press, 1969.

Hayes, Richard P. "Gotama Buddha and Religious Pluralism." *Journal of Religious Pluralism* 1 (1991): 65–96.

Heim, S. Mark. *Salvations: Truth and Difference in Religion*. Maryknoll: Orbis Books, 1995.

Heschel, Abraham. *Quest for God: Studies in Prayer and Symbolism*. New York: Crossroads, 1982.

Hesse, Mary. "Models and Analogy in Science." Pp. 354–359 in *The Encyclopedia of Philosophy*, Vol. 5, edited by Paul Edwards. New York: Macmillan and Free Press, 1967.

Hick, John. *God Has Many Names*. Philadelphia: Westminister Press: 1982.

———. *An Interpretation of Religion*. New Haven: Yale University Press, 1989.

———. "The Non-absoluteness of Christianity." Pp. 16–36 in *The Myth of Christian Uniqueness*, edited by John Hick and Paul F. Knitter. Maryknoll: Orbis Press, 1987.

———. "Religious Pluralism and Absolute Claims." Pp. 193–213 in *Religious Pluralism*, edited by Leroy S. Rouner. Notre Dame: University of Notre Dame Press, 1984.

———. "A Religious Understanding of Religion: A Model of the Relationship between Traditions." Pp. 21–36 in *Inter-religious Models and Criteria*, edited by J. Kellenberger. New York: St. Martin's Press, 1993.

Hollenback, Jess Byron. *Mysticism: Experience, Response and Empowerment*. University Park, Pa.: Pennsylvania State University Press, 1996.

"Holography." *Encyclopedia Britannica*. CD-ROM 98.

Idel, Moshe, and Bernard McGinn, eds. *Mystical Union in Judaism, Christianity, and Islam: An Ecumenical Dialogue*. New York: Continuum, 1996.

Ingalls, Daniel H. H. "Samkara's Arguments against the Buddhists." *Philosophy East and West* 3 (1954): 291–306.

———. "The Study of Samkaracarya." *Annuals of the Bhandarkar Oriental Research Institute* 33 (1952): 1–14.

Iovine, John. *Homemade Holograms: The Complete Guide to Inexpensive Do-It-Yourself Holography*. Blue Ridge Summit, Pa.: TAB Books, 1990.

Isayeva, Natalia. *From Early Vedanta to Kashmir Shaivism: Gaudapada, Bhartrhari and Abhinavagupta*. Albany: State University of New York Press, 1995.

———. *Shankara and Indian Philosophy*. Albany: State University of New York Press, 1993.

Jaini, P. S. "On the Theory of Two Vasubandhu's." *Bulletin of the School of Oriental and African Studies* 21 (1958): 48–53.

John Paul II. *Crossing the Threshold of Hope*. Edited by Vittorio Messori. New York: Alfred A. Knopf, 1994.

Joshi, L. M. "Gauḍapāda's Rapproachment between Buddhism and Vedānta." *Journal of Akhila Bharatiya Sanskrit Parishad* 1 (1969): 11–22.

———. *Studies in Buddhistic Culture of India during the Seventh and Eighth Centuries A.D.* Delhi: Motilal Banarsidass, 1987.

Kaplan, Stephen. "An Appraisal of a Psychological Approach to Meditation." *Zygon* 13 (1978): 83–101.

———. "Culture, Genre and the Māṇḍūkya Kārikā: Philosophical Inconsistency, Historical Uncertainty, or Textual Discontinuity." *Asian Philosophy* 6 (1996): 129–145.

———. *Hermeneutics, Holography and Indian Idealism.* Delhi: Motilal Banarsidass, 1987.

———. "A Holographic Alternative to a Traditional Yogācāra Simile: An Analysis of Vasubandhu's Trisvabhāva Doctrine," *Eastern Buddhist* 23 (1990): 56–78.

———. "A Holographic Analysis of Religious Diversity: A Case Study of Hinduism and Christianity." *Journal of Religious Pluralism* 2 (1993): 29–59.

———. "Three Levels of Evil in Advaita Vedānta and a Holographic Analogy." Pp. 116–129 in *Evil and the Response of World Religion,* edited by William Cenkner. St. Paul, Minn.: Paragon House, 1997.

———. "The Yogācāra Roots of Advaita Idealism? Noting a Similarity between Vasubandhu and Gauḍapāda." *Journal of Indian Philosophy* 20 (1992): 191–218.

Kapstein, Mathew. "Mereological Considerations in Vasubandhu's 'Proof of Idealism.'" *Idealistic Studies* 18 (1988): 32–54.

Kasper, Joseph E., and Steven A. Feller. *The Complete Book of Holograms: How They Work and How to Make Them.* New York: John Wiley and Sons, 1987.

Katz, Steven T. "The 'Conservative' Character of Mystical Experience." Pp. 3–60 in *Mysticism and Religious Traditions,* edited by Steven T. Katz. New York: Oxford University Press, 1983.

———. "Language, Epistemology, and Mysticism." Pp. 22–74 in *Mysticism and Philosophical Analysis,* edited by Steven T. Katz. New York: Oxford University Press, 1978.

———, ed. *Mysticism and Language.* New York: Oxford University Press, 1992.

King, Richard. *Early Advaita Vedānta and Buddhism: The Mahāyāna Context of the Gaudapādīya-karika.* Albany: State University of New York Press, 1995.

———. "Śūnyatā and Ajāti: Absolutism and the Philosophies of Nāgārjuna and Gauḍapāda." *Journal of Indian Philosophy* 17 (1989): 385–405.

King, Sallie B. "Two Epistemological Models for the Interpretation of Mysticism." *Journal of the American Academy of Religion* 56 (1988): 257–279.

Kliever, Lonnie D. "Moral Education in a Pluralistic World." *Journal of the American Academy of Religion* LX (1992): 117– 134.

Knitter, Paul. *No Other Name?* Maryknoll: Orbis Books, 1990.

———. "Toward a Liberation Theology of Religions." Pp. 178–200 in *The Myth of Christian Uniqueness,* edited by John Hick and Paul F. Knitter. Maryknoll: Orbis Press, 1987.

Kung, Hans. "What Is True Religion? Toward an Ecumenical Christology." Pp. 231–250 in *Toward a Universal Theology of Religion,* edited by Leonard Swidler. Maryknoll: Orbis Books, 1987.

LaFargue, Michael. "Radically Pluralist, Thoroughly Critical: A New Theory of Religions." *Journal of the American Academy of Religion* 40 (1992): 693–716.

Larson, Gerald. "Contra Pluralism." *Soundings* 73 (1990): 303–326.

Larson, Gerald James, and Ram Shankar Bhattacharya, eds. *The Encyclopedia of Indian Philosophies: Sāṁkhya: A Dualist Tradition in Indian Philosophy*. Princeton: Princeton University Press, 1987.

Lehmann, D., G. W. Beeler and D. H. Fender. "EEG Responses during the Observation of Stabilized and Normal Retinal Images." *Electroencephalography and Clinical Neurophysiology* 22 (1967): 136–142.

Lott, Eric. *Vedantic Approaches to God*. New York: Barnes and Noble Books, 1980.

Mahadevan, T. M. P. *Gaudapada: A Study in Early Advaita*. Madras: University of Madras, 1952.

Mayeda, Sengaku. "On the Author of the Māṇḍūkyopaniṣad and the Gauḍapāda-bhāṣya." *Adyar Library Bulletin* 31–32 (1967–1968): 73–94.

McFague, Sallie. *Metaphorical Theology: Models of God in Religious Language*. Philadelphia: Fortress Press, 1982.

McGinn, Bernard, John Meyendorff and Jean Leclercq. *Christian Spirituality: Origins to the Twelfth Century*. New York: Crossroads, 1987.

Miller, Barbara, trans. *The Bhagavad Gita*. Toronto: Bantam Books, 1986.

Min, Anselm Kyongsuk. "Dialectical Pluralism and Solidarity of Others: Towards a New Paradigm." *Journal of the American Academy of Religion* 65 (1997): 587–604.

Moore, Peter. "Mystical Experience, Mystical Doctrine, Mystical Technique." Pp. 101–131 in *Mysticism and Philosophical Analysis*, edited by Steven T. Katz. New York: Oxford University Press, 1978.

Murti, T. R. V. *The Central Philosophy of Buddhism*. London: George Allen and Unwin, 1968.

Nagao, Gadjin. "The Buddhist World-View As Elucidated in the Three-Nature Theory and Similes." *Eastern Buddhist* 16 (1983): 1–18.

———. "What Remains in Śūnyatā: A Yogācāra Interpretation of Emptiness." Pp. 66–82 in *Mahāyāna Buddhist Meditation: Theory and Practice*, edited by Minoru Kiyota. Honolulu: University of Hawaii Press, 1978.

Nakamura, Hajime. "Buddhism." Pp. 247–257 in *Dictionary of the History of Ideas Volume I*, edited by Philip P. Wiener. New York: Charles Scribner's Son, 1973.

Narranjo, Claude, and Robert Ornstein. *On the Psychology of Meditation*. New York: Viking Press, 1974.

"Notes on Holography." Berkeley: Lawrence Hall of Science, 1978 (reprint).

Ogden, Schubert M. *Is There Only One True Religion or Are There Many?* Dallas: Southern Methodist University Press, 1992.

Olivelle, Patrick, trans. *Upaniṣads*. Oxford: Oxford University Press, 1996.

Otto, Rudolf. *Mysticism East and West: A Comparative Analysis of the Nature of Mysticism*. Translated by Bertha L. Bracey and Richenda C. Payne. New York: Macmillan, 1970.

Panikkar, Raimon. "The Defiance of Pluralism." *Soundings* 79 (1996): 169–191.

———. "The Invisible Harmony: A Universal Theory of Religion or a Cosmic Confidence in Reality." Pp. 118–153 in *Toward a Universal Theology of Religion*, edited by Leonard Swidler. Maryknoll: Orbis Books, 1987.

———. "The Jordan, the Tiber, and the Ganges." Pp. 89–116 in *The Myth of Christian Uniqueness*, edited by John Hick and Paul F. Knitter. Maryknoll: Orbis Press, 1987.

———. "The Metaphysical Challenge." Pp. 97–115 in *Religious Pluralism*, edited by Leroy S. Rouner. Notre Dame: University of Notre Dame Press, 1984.

———. "The Pluralism of Truth." *World Faiths Insight* 26 (1990): 7– 16.

Penner, Hans H. "The Mystical Illusion." Pp. 89–116 in *Mysticism and Religious Traditions*, edited by Steven T. Katz. Oxford: Oxford University Press, 1983.

Pepper, Stephen C. *World Hypothesis*. Berkeley: University of California Press, 1972.

Peters, Ted. "David Bohm, Postmodernism, and the Divine." *Zygon* 20 (1985): 193–217.

Potter, Karl H. *Encyclopedia of Indian Philosophies: Advaita Vedānta up to Śaṁkara and His Pupils*, Volume III. Delhi: Motilal Banarsidass, 1981.

———. *Presuppositions of Indian Philosophy*. Englewood Cliffs: Prentice Hall, 1962.

———. "Was Gauḍapāda an Idealist?" Pp. 183–199, in *Sanskrit and Indian Studies*, edited by M. Nagatoni, B. K. Matilal, J. M. Masson and E. Dimmock. Dordrecht: D. Reidel Publishing Co., 1979.

Pribram, Karl H. *Languages of the Brain: Experimental Paradoxes and Principles in Neuropsychology*. Pacific Grove, Calif.: Brooks/Cole Publishing Co., 1977.

———. "Mind, It Does Matter." Pp. 97–111 in *Philosophical Dimensions of the Neuro-Medical Sciences*, edited by Stuart F. Spicker and H. Tristram Engelhardt. Boston: D. Reidel Publishing Co., 1976.

Pritchard, Roy M. "Stabilized Images on the Retina." *Scientific American* 204 (June 1961): 72–78.

Proudfoot, Wayne. *Religious Experience*. Berkeley: University of California Press, 1985.

Rahner, Karl, and Herbert Vorgrimler. "Jesus Christ." Pp. 236–242 in *Theological Dictionary*, edited by Cornelius Ernst, translated by Richard Strachar. New York: Herder and Herder, 1965.

Rahula, Walpola. "Vijñaptimātratā Philosophy in the Yogācarā System and Some Wrong Notions." *Maha Bodhi* 80 (1972): 324–330.

Rāmānuja. *Vedāntasāra of Bhagavad Rāmānuja*. Edited by Pandit V. Krishnamachary with English translation by Sri M. B. Narasimha Ayyangar. Madras: Adyar Library, 1953.

Richard of Saint Victor. *Selected Writings on Contemplation*. Translated with an introduction and notes by Clare Kirchberger. London: Faber and Faber, 1957.

———. *The Twelve Patriarchs, the Mystical Ark, the Book of the Trinity*. Translated and introduction by Grover A. Zinn. New York: Paulist Press, 1979.

Ross, Philip E. "The Hologram Remembers." *Forbes* 154 (September 26, 1994): http://proquest.umi.com.

Russell, Robert John. "The Physics of David Bohm and Its Relevance to Philosophy and Theology." *Zygon* 20 (1985): 135–157.

Śaṅkara. *Brahma-Sūtra-Bhāṣya of Srī Śaṅkarācārya*. Translated by Swami Gambhirananda. Calcutta: Advaita Ashrama, 1965.

———. *The Bṛhadāraṇyaka Upaniṣad with the Commentary of Śaṅkarācārya*. Translated by Swami Madhavananda. Calcutta: Advaita Ashrama, 1965.

———. *A Thousand Teachings: The Upadeśasāhasrī of Śaṅkara*. Translated with introduction and notes by Sengaku Mayeda. Japan: University of Tokyo Press, 1979.

Sarvajñātman. *Saṁkṣepaśārīraka*. Translated and edited by N. Veezhinathan. Madras: Centre for the Advanced Study in Philosophy, 1972.

Schindler, David L., ed. *Beyond Mechanism: The Universe in Recent Physics and Catholic Thought*. Lanham, Md.: University Press of America, 1986.

Schmithausen, Lambert. "Sautrāntika-Voraussetzungen in Viṃśatikā and Triṃsikā." *Wiener Zeitschrift für die kunde Süd und Ostasiens und Archiv für indische Philosophie* 11 (1967): 109–136.

Schumacher, John A. "Prolegomena to Any Future Inquiry: A Paradigm of Undivided Wholeness." *International Philosophical Quarterly* 21 (1981): 439–457.

Sharpe, Kevin J. *David Bohm's World: New Physics and New Religion*. Lewisburg: Bucknell University Press, 1993.

———. "Holomovement, Metaphysics and Theology." *Zygon* 28 (1993): 47– 60.

———. "Relating the Physics and Religion of David Bohm." *Zygon* 25 (1990): 105–122.

Short, Larry. "Mysticism, Meditation and the Non-linguistic." *Journal of the American Academy of Religion* 63 (1995): 659– 675.

Smart, Ninian. "Models for Understanding the Relations between Religions." Pp. 58–67 in *Inter-religious Models and Criteria*, edited by J. Kellenberger. New York: St. Martin's Press, 1993.

———. "The Purification of Consciousness and the Negative Path." Pp. 117–130 in *Mysticism and Religious Traditions*, edited by Steven T. Katz. Oxford: Oxford University Press, 1983.

———. "Understanding Religious Experience." Pp. 10–21 in *Mysticism and Philosophical Analysis*, edited by Steven T. Katz. New York: Oxford University Press, 1978.

Smith, Howard M. *Principles of Holography*. New York: Wiley-Interscience, 1969.

Smith, J. Z. *Divine Drudgery: On the Comparison of Early Christianities and the Religions of Late Antiquity*. Chicago: University of Chicago Press, 1990.

Soskice, Janet Martin. *Metaphor and Religious Language*. Oxford: Claredon Press, 1987.

Stace, W. T. *Mysticism and Philosophy*. London: Macmillan, 1960.

———. *Teaching of the Mystics*. New York: Mentor Books, 1960.

Stambler, Irwin. *Revolution in Light: Lasers and Holography*. New York: Doubleday and Co., 1972.

Stebbins, Michael. "Soul." Pp. 1210–1211 in *The HarperCollins Encyclopedia of Catholicism*, edited by Richard B. McBrien. San Francisco: Harper San Francisco, 1995.

Surin, Kenneth. "A Certain Politics of Speech: Religious Pluralism in the Age of McDonald's Hamburger." *Modern Theology* 7 (1990): 67–100.

Swidler, Leonard, ed. *Toward a Universal Theology of Religion*. Maryknoll: Orbis Books, 1987.

Swinburne, Richard. *The Christian God*. Oxford: Clarendon Press, 1994.

Talbot, Michael. *Beyond the Quantum*. Toronto: Bantam Books, 1988.

Thomas, Owen C. "Religious Plurality and Contemporary Philosophy: A Critical Survey." *Harvard Theological Review* 87 (1994): 197–213.

Thurman, Robert A. "Transcendence and the Sacred in the Mahāyāna Middle Way." Pp. 100–114 in *Transcendence and the Sacred*, edited by Alan M. Olson and Leroy S. Rouner. Notre Dame: University of Notre Dame Press, 1981.

Tola, Fernando, and Dragonetti, Carmen. "The Trisvabhāvakārikā of Vasubandhu." *Journal of Indian Philosophy* 11 (1983): 225–266.

Toṭakācārya. *Extracting the Essence of the Śruti: The Śrutisārasamuddharaṇam of Toṭakācārya*. Translated with commentary by Michael Commans. Delhi: Motilal Banarsidass, 1996.

Tracy, David. *Plurality and Ambiguity: Hermeneutics, Religion and Hope*. San Francisco: Harper and Row, 1989.

Tugwell, Simon. *Human Immortality and the Redemption of Death*. Springfield, Ill.: Templegate Publishers, 1991.

Van Buitenen, J. A. B. *Rāmānuja on the Bhagavadgītā: A Condensed Rendering of His Gītābhāṣya with Copious Notes and an Introduction*. Delhi: Motilal Banarsidass, 1974.

Vetter, Tilmann. "*Die Gauḍapādīya-Kārikās: Zur Enstehung und zur Bedeutung von (A)dvaita.*" *Wiener Zeitschrift für die Kunder Süd und Ostasiens* 22 (1978): 95–113.

Wade, Jenny. *Changes of Mind: A Holonomic Theory of the Evolution of Consciousness*. Albany: State University of New York Press, 1996.

Wayman, Alex. "Vasubandhu—Teacher Extraordinary." *Studia Missionalia* 37 (1988): 245–281.

———. "Yogācāra Idealism." *Philosophy East and West* 15 (1965): 65–73.

Westlake, Philip R. "The Possibilities of Neural Holographic Processes within the Brain." *Kybernetik* 7 (1970): 129–153.

Whaling, Frank. "Sankara and Buddhism." *Journal of Indian Philosophy* 7 (1979): 1–42.

Willis, Janice Dean. *On Knowing Reality*. New York: Columbia University Press, 1979.

Yadav, Bibhuti S. "Anthropomorphism and Cosmic Confidence." Pp. 175–191 in *Toward a Universal Theology of Religion*, edited by Leonard Swidler. Maryknoll: Orbis Books, 1987.

———. "Vaishnavism on Hans Kung: A Hindu Theology of Religious Pluralism." *Religion and Society* 27 (1980): 31–44.

Zaehner, R. C. *Mysticism: Sacred and Profane*. London: Oxford University Press, 1973.

# Index

# About the Author

**Stephen Kaplan** is professor of Indian and Comparative Religions at Manhattan College in the Bronx. In addition to *Hermeneutics, Holography and Indian Idealism,* he has published in a number of journals and contributed to several edited volumes. Kaplan has also been involved in the reform movement of the New York City public school system. He helped establish P.S. 51 (The Bronx New School) as an independent k-5 school with its own building. He is also a founding member of the Jonas Bronck Academy, a public, magnet middle school located on the Manhattan College campus. Currently, he is working to develop new sites to help relieve public school overcrowding in the northwest Bronx.